William Gibson

# McFarland Literary Companions

By Mary Ellen Snodgrass

1. *August Wilson* (2004)
2. *Barbara Kingsolver* (2004)
3. *Amy Tan* (2004)
4. *Walter Dean Myers* (2006)
5. *Kaye Gibbons* (2007)
6. *Jamaica Kincaid* (2008)
8. *Peter Carey* (2010)
10. *Leslie Marmon Silko* (2011)

By Phyllis T. Dircks

7. *Edward Albee* (2010)

By Erik Hage

9. *Cormac McCarthy* (2010)

By Rocky Wood

11. *Stephen King* (2011)

By Tom Henthorne

12. *William Gibson* (2011)

# William Gibson

## A Literary Companion

TOM HENTHORNE

McFarland Literary Companions, 12

McFarland & Company, Inc., Publishers
*Jefferson, North Carolina, and London*

LIBRARY OF CONGRESS CATALOGUING-IN-PUBLICATION DATA

Henthorne, Tom.
William Gibson : a literary companion / Tom Henthorne.
p.   cm. — (McFarland literary companions ; 12)
Includes bibliographical references and index.

ISBN 978-0-7864-6151-6
(softcover : 50# alkaline paper) ∞

1. Gibson, William, 1948 – — Handbooks, manuals, etc.   2. Science
fiction, American — History and criticism.   I. Title.
PS3557.I2264Z75   2011        813'.54 — dc22        2011021161

British Library cataloguing data are available

On the cover: William Gibson (photograph by Michael O'Shea);
background image © 2011 Shutterstock

Manufactured in the United States of America

*McFarland & Company, Inc., Publishers
Box 611, Jefferson, North Carolina 28640
www.mcfarlandpub.com*

# Acknowledgments

I should first thank my brother, Bill, who gave me his copy of *Neuromancer* on the way to a Giants game and then took it from me when I wouldn't stop reading it once we got there. And I should thank my family — my sisters, Nancy and Susan; my children, Juliet, Zane, and Paul; and my partner, Patricia Way — for everything they do to make projects like this possible.

Special thanks go to Gwen Limbach for reading as much she could of this; Sid Ray and Jonathan Silverman for looking over parts of this on short notice; and Lindsey Lee and Kristen di Gennaro for their help with the timeline. The Pace librarians and staff also deserve special thanks for their help, as do Pace administrators like Nira Herrmann, Adelia Williams-Lubitz, and Joe Franco for making it possible to do research at a teaching institution.

Thanks also go to Sarah Blackwood, Joey Blush, Carol Dollison, Ivano di Gennaro, Martha Driver, Amy Foerster, Stephanie Hsu, Karla Jay, Agie Markiewicz, Tony Murphy, Richard Nardi, Bill Offutt, Nancy Reagin, Lee Transue, Holly Scalera, Tomm Scalera, Catherine Zimmer, and the many other students, friends and colleagues who help in all sorts of ways.

Finally, I have to thank Starbucks and Borders for providing free Wi-Fi and clean bathrooms, both of which proved essential to the writing of this book. And Wikipedia and Google, who are always there for me.

# Table of Contents

"I am, by trade, a science-fiction writer. That is, the fiction I've written so far has arrived at the point of consumption via a marketing mechanism called 'science fiction.'"
— William Gibson (1989)

"All fiction is speculative. So is all history."
— William Gibson (2010)

# *Preface*

*William Gibson: A Literary Companion* is designed both for general readers and for scholars interested in Gibson and his work. In addition to providing a literary and cultural context for works ranging from Gibson's very first short story, "Fragments of a Hologram Rose" (1977), to his recent, best-selling novel, *Zero History* (2010), the *Companion* offers commentary on Gibson's subjects, themes, and approaches. It also surveys existing scholarship on Gibson's work in a way that should be accessible to non-specialists and provides complete references to facilitate further study.

The volume begins with a detailed chronology of Gibson's life, information being drawn from an autobiographical sketch Gibson posted on his blog, more than forty of the interviews he has given over the last 25 years, publications about him, and even statements he posted on his Twitter account. As readers new to Gibson will discover, his story is, in part, the story of the counterculture and of the information age — stories that are themselves inextricably linked, as John Markoff and Fred Turner have recently demonstrated. The chronology is followed by A-to-Z entries on Gibson's works, characters, themes, interests, approaches, and influences. These entries, which are comprised largely of commentary and analysis, have been carefully cross-referenced so that readers can quickly find information they need. Most entries also include suggestions for further reading.

The final section of the book — the back matter, so to speak — includes a glossary containing terms such as "MacGuffin," "razorgirl," and "*zaibatsu*" that readers might not immediately be familiar with; a timeline of technological developments that occurred during Gibson's lifetime so that readers can quickly contextualize the technologies featured in his work; research and study topics designed for both students and teachers; and an extensive bibliography of primary and secondary sources.

There is no substitute, of course, for reading Gibson's works themselves and the secondary materials on them. It is my hope that introducing readers to novels and short stories that they may have not read yet and to some of the scholarly thought on them will generate further interest. As readers who pursue the suggested readings will discover, a lot of excellent work has already been done on Gibson's novels and short stories. More remains to be done, however, not only because Gibson is still writing but also because his ideas are still important — more important than ever, it seems, given the way in which new technologies are impacting our lives.

# Introduction

William Gibson is a science fiction writer. There is no denying that; even he identifies himself as such. Although his most recent novels are set in the present rather than the future, they can still be found in the Science Fiction and Fantasy sections of bookstores—at least once they are moved from the best sellers' displays. In part this is because Gibson initially became known as a science fiction writer, his first novel, *Neuromancer*, selling over seven million copies and winning both the Hugo and Nebula awards: as Gibson learned very early, once one is established as a science fiction writer, it is difficult to be recognized as anything else (Gilmore Interview). More importantly, though, Gibson's work still reads like science fiction, largely because he uses what he terms the science fiction "toolkit" to explore a present that turned out to be "richer, stranger, more multiplex, than any imaginary 21st century could ever have been" (William Gibson's blog 5/31/2010). In other words, he writes about the present as if it were the future.

Having said that, there is also no denying that Gibson is also a literary artist, employing the sorts of narrative strategies and stylistic devices associated with novelists like William S. Burroughs, Thomas Pynchon, and Don DeLillo. Indeed, Gibson's literariness has been recognized from the very start. Gerald Jonas of the *New York Times*, for example, describes *Neuromancer* as being "freshly imagined, compellingly detailed and chilling in its implications," adding that "[t]he 'cyberspace' conceit allows him to dramatize computer hacking in nontechnical language." It is more than just his prose style and stylistic innovations that make Gibson's work literary: he also approaches his subjects in a literary way, employing what Dave Itzkoff identifies as "modernist realism": whether writing about an imagined future, the present, or the recent past, Gibson represents reality as it is experienced by his characters rather than in purportedly objective terms. As a result, even though his works are a part of a popular genre, they nonetheless present themselves as serious fiction, addressing not just the human condition but the very nature of existence.

Gibson's self-conscious literariness originally hurt him, at least among those science fiction readers who read primarily for content, many of whom were unwilling to work through challenging texts. Gibson was very much aware of this, observing, "'Genre' SF readers say that *Neuromancer* and *Count Zero* are impossibly dense, literally impossible to read" (McCaffery Interview). The very same literariness brought him recognition among literary critics and scholars, however, his work being widely discussed in academic books and journals, particularly after prominent theorist Fredric Jameson indicated in *Postmodernism, or, the Logic of Late Capitalism* (1991) that "representational innovations ... mark his [Gibson's] work as an exceptional literary realization within a predominately visual or aural postmodern production" (38). Much of the academic debate that followed centered on whether Gibson could properly be regarded as postmodern writer or not. Critics like Claire Sponsler argue that that despite postmodern settings, Gibson's novels are essentially humanist, his protagonists being "invested with a heroic and romantic power that ultimately undermines the resolutely unromantic surface world he has set up" (639): consequently, according to her, there is a tension in his work, one that makes them failures at least as postmodern texts since they are ultimately resolved with the characters asserting agency, the narratives thus "falling back into realist or romantic paradigms" (643). Others contend that Gibson's work is radically postmodern, Lewis Call, for example, arguing that in his representation of virtual communities in *The Bridge Trilogy*, Gibson represents a form of "postmodernism anarchism" that offers a viable means of resistance to the social order (101). Jameson himself continues to regard Gibson as being of central importance, observing that works like *Pattern Recognition* (2003) are "sending back more reliable information about the contemporary world than an exhausted realism (or an exhausted modernism either)" (Jameson 2005, 384).

Finally, there is no denying that William Gibson is a culturally significant figure, his work having had a discernable effect upon not only the ways in which technology is both developed and utilized. That he introduced the term "cyberspace" to the English language is widely known, the *Oxford English Dictionary* officially recognizing this fact in 1997. Gibson did more than just supply a term, however: as Sabine Heuser demonstrates, his representation of cyberspace has had "a far-reaching and lasting effect well beyond Gibson's specific usage, since it has infiltrated other domains of discourse and passed into common English speech" (100). He also was among the first to explore the implications of virtual communities, reality television, nanotechnology, the digital divide, locative art, and ubiquitous computing.

Recognizing just how "visionary" Gibson's work is, *Time* named *Neuromancer* as one of the 100 most important novels since the magazine was founded, Lev Grossman noting that science fiction has become "a crucial tool by which an age shaped by and obsessed with technology can understand itself." Since then Gibson has gone on to become a bestselling novelist and highly-regarded commentator on technology and society. Gibson does more than just explain technology and its impacts upon us: his work helps us explore technology for ourselves, to imagine its possibilities and consequences—in short, to think it through critically. As Scarlett Thomas suggests, Gibson is particularly important *because* he is a science writer: "[I]n a world where fiction is becoming indistinguishable from reality, as the philosopher [Jean] Baudrillard suggested, the flow of 'truth' goes both ways. It's just as likely that fiction will come true as it is that the truth will turn out to have been fiction all along." Accordingly, who better than Gibson, whose fictions about cyberspace, virtual communities, and new media were in many ways realized, to help us apprehend what our world is becoming as new technologies continually change not only the way we live but the way we are? Gibson's stories, as wild as they may seem, are our stories, making them worthy of further study.

# Chronology of Gibson's Life and Works

## 1948–1955: Early Childhood

William Ford Gibson III was born to Elizabeth Otey Williams and William Ford Gibson, Jr., on March 17, 1948, in Conway, South Carolina, a town near Myrtle Beach, where his parents regularly vacationed. His mother was a homemaker and his father a manager for a large construction firm.

Gibson himself seems uncertain about the particulars of his early life, indicating in an interview that he thinks his family was living in Tennessee near the Oak Ridge National Laboratory when he was born but is not sure (Owens Interview). He does remember, however, the purchase of their first television set in the early 1950s, an indication of the family's relative affluence. He also recalls learning to read using his mother's bound volumes of Walt Kelly's *Pogo*, a popular and sometimes overtly political comic strip set in a Georgia swamp that is today remembered for the line, "We have met the enemy and he is us." In addition, he remembers a favorite children's book, Willy Ley's *The Conquest of Space* (1949), noting on his blog that as a child he believed "passionately in space travel."

The family moved frequently because of his father's work assignments to housing projects in various parts of the South before finally settling in Norfolk, Virginia, where Gibson began elementary school. Although Gibson has said little about either himself or his family during this period, he does occasionally refer to his father's indirect involvement with the Manhattan Project, his father having helped install plumbing in Oak Ridge, Tennessee, where Uranium-235 was being collected.

Not surprisingly, given his age at the time, his recollections are general rather than specific: "I have this memory of being on the edge of this strange, big deal.... My mother liked to tell the story of how my father was called into an office and given the names of three guys to keep an eye on. And he realized that he was on somebody else's list. For me, that story was like an early introduction to Kafka" (Sullivan Interview). Although he was born after the war, his father's wartime work and the secrecy surrounding it became part of Gibson's "family mythology" and may have influenced Gibson later when he began writing about technology, espionage, and security measures (Owens Interview).

## 1956–1962: Late Childhood and Early Adolescence

Gibson's family life was disrupted when his father choked to death in a restaurant while on a business trip. In interviews Gibson reports his age at the time as being either six or eight, but *Agrippa (A Book of the Dead)*, a poem that references his father, indicates that he owned a 1957 De Soto Firedome, suggesting that Gibson was at least eight. Gibson's mother, who was about fifty when her husband died, returned to Wytheville, Virginia, the small, mostly white town where she had grown up. There she remained a homemaker, living in her mother's house and never remarrying. Gibson describes his mother in this period as being "chronically anxious and depressive" and his grandmother as a "very, very old lady" who referred to the Civil War as the "Northern Invasion" (Murray Interview). He adds that, between his mother and grandmother, it was like being "raised by Edwardians." The racial attitudes of his grandmother also seemed to trouble him, indicating in an interview that she would "correct him" if he said "'Colored lady'" because she thought the phrase "was an oxymoron" (Barker Interview).

The attitudes of Gibson's grandmother and many of the other townspeople might not be surprising, given that Wytheville is located in the Blue Ridge highlands of southwest Virginia. Gibson describes it as "serious, serious Appalachia," adding that when he lived there in the 1950s and early 1960s it was the "old, old, old, backward, weird, isolated kind of South" reminiscent of an early Cormac McCarthy novel (Murray Interview). In an autobiographical sketch he published in his blog, he indicates that moving there was like being "abruptly exiled ... to what seemed like the past," something that led him to find escape in science fiction ("Since 1948"). In "Time Machine Cuba," Gibson recalls finding the Classics Illustrated version of *The Time Machine* on a wire rack in a local store and making "Wells's Victorian future nightmare ... a favorite fantasyland." Ironically, many of the original readers of *Neuromancer* and the other Sprawl stories had a similar experience, regarding Gibson's dystopian future as somehow empowering. By the time he was thirteen, the world of Morlocks and Eloi was just "part of a personal and growing collection of alternate universes" to which Gibson had access.

He also found *National Geographic* magazine, back issues of which filled a hallway bookcase. Gibson reports taking "a five-inch stack" to bed with him "from ages six to sixteen," speculating that doing so "probably had some profound, unimaginable effect on me because I had this sense of all these different places, and it was almost entirely visual. I doubt that I ever read much more than the captions on the photographs" ("Since 1948"). In addition to shaping Gibson's visual sensibilities, the magazine's photography may well have contributed the sense of liberal humanism that is evident in his early work, the images emphasizing a common humanity even as they present difference (Lutz and Collins).

Like many other youths of that time, Gibson had an interest in science and technology as well, having not only a chemistry set but also a Heath electronic kits, though even then he seemed to be interested as much in relationship between technology and culture as he was in technology itself. For example, he recalls wondering at about age twelve what would happen if a circuit were made according to *loa* symbols found in Robert Tallant's *Voodoo in New Orleans* rather than the circuit diagrams provided in his Heathkits (Blume Interview; Gibson, "Since 1948"). In addition to reflecting a creative bent of mind, the bizarre thought experiment suggests that Gibson was trying to find a way of understanding racial and cultural relationships. In *Count Zero*, his second novel, he returns to this idea, albeit in different form, populating cyberspace with *loa*.

Neither athletically nor academically inclined, Gibson seems to have been a detached child, describing himself as "exactly the sort of introverted, hyper-bookish boy you'll find in the biographies of most American science fiction writers, obsessively filling shelves with paperbacks and digest-sized magazines, dreaming of one day becoming a writer myself" ("Since 1948"). As he notes in an interview, science fiction not only helped him come to realize that he "wasn't totally isolated in perceiving the world as being monstrous and crazy" but also "was the only source of subversive information" available to him until he discovered writers like William S. Burroughs and the Beats (McCaffery Interview 276). According to him, at age thirteen he "surreptitiously purchased an anthology of Beat writing — sensing, correctly, that my mother wouldn't approve" ("God's Little Toys"). He reports: "I had read this stuff, or tried to, with no idea at all of what it might mean, and felt compelled — compelled to what, I didn't know. The effect, over the next few years, was to make me, at least in terms of my Virginia home, Patient Zero of what would later be called the counterculture" ("Since 1948"). Burroughs's work in particular seemed to have an impact on Gibson, especially *Naked Lunch*, even though he had access only to excerpts, not finding a complete copy until traveling in Europe many years later. Burroughs's literary technique also fascinated him; Gibson reports in "God's Little Toys" that when he read Burroughs's essay on his "cut-up method ... the hairs on my neck stood up, so palpable was the excitement," adding, "Burroughs was interrogating the universe with scissors and a paste pot...." Upon becoming a writer, Gibson experimented with the technique himself in works such as "The Gernsback Continuum," "Academy Leader," and *The Difference Engine*.

## 1963–1966: Adolescence

In 1963 Gibson left Wytheville, where he was attending George Wythe High School, for the Southern Arizona School for Boys in Tuscon. Gibson and his mother seemed to agree on this decision, though Gibson would have preferred to attend school in Southern California; his mother apparently hoped that boarding school would help Gibson focus on his education and that Arizona would not only be cheaper than California but better for his allergies. In any case, boarding school offered Gibson an escape from southwest Virginia, which was less accommodating to his interest in the then developing counterculture than the Southwest. Living closely with other adolescents also forced him to become more sociable, and Gibson began to make friends. He remained an indifferent student, however, resenting the highly structured demands of the school (Sale Interview). His interest in Burroughs and the Beats continued, though he did stop reading science fiction and thought little about becoming a writer. All told, Gibson has little to say in his interviews and autobiographical sketches about the three years he spent in Arizona, save that "puberty had arrived" and he had little thought of any literary future (Poole Interview).

During Gibson's senior year at the Southern Arizona School, his mother died suddenly of a stroke. After the funeral, he returned to school briefly but did not graduate, explaining in one interview, "They saw me reading Kerouac and suspected me of smoking pot ... I took it as a golden opportunity to split" (Poole Interview). After a brief return to Wytheville, he began to travel, visiting California and Europe among other places. After undergoing a physical and psychological examination by his local draft board in southwestern Virginia and being told to return for an interview in three months, Gibson reported in an interview that he "got on a bus, went to Toronto and stayed" (Poole Interview). Gibson later revealed that his decision was social as much as political: He "wanted to be somewhere where there would be girls and soft drugs and music" (Graham Interview). Indeed, in a 2008 interview he admits to taking "credit for draft evasion" early in his career when he "shouldn't have," noting that he was never actually drafted and so "never had to make the call" (Newitz Interview). He adds: "I don't know what I would have done if I'd really been drafted. I wasn't a tightly wrapped package at that time. If somebody had drafted me I might have wept and gone."

## 1967–1972: Experiencing the Counterculture

Gibson spent the so-called "Summer of Love" in the Yorkville neighborhood of Toronto that he later described as "the local Haight equivalent" (blog 5/01/2003). He can actually be seen in a short documentary, *Yorkville: Hippie Haven*, that was broadcast on September 4, 1967; Gibson was paid $500 by the Canadian Broadcasting Company to serve as an on-camera guide to the hippie scene. In the first part of the film, the strikingly tall and thin nineteen-year-old Gibson is shown traversing part of the neighborhood while eating a popsicle; in a voice-over, he explains the hippie concept of love. Bespectacled, clean-shaven, and wearing newish-looking clothes, Gibson was hardly the stereotypical hippie, though his characteristically slow style of speech and use of abstract terms may have made him sound stoned to some viewers. He appears again toward the end of the film, this time walking with his arm around a young woman: here he talks about hippie attitudes toward sex, explaining that it "doesn't have any particular importance attached to it," that "it's really not differentiated from eating or sleeping or breathing."

Gibson was later to assert on his blog that nothing he says in the film is "even remotely genuine," something that seems to be confirmed by the fact that he apparently represented himself to the CBC as "a real hippie" who had "wandered from Vancouver to San Francisco" at the beginning of "the movement" (blog 5/01/2003). Although Gibson's account of the hippie movement may not be credible because Gibson was no hippie, the film demonstrates that even then he could tell a convincing story. Ironically, Gibson used the money he was paid for the appearance to get his "ass out of Yorkville," which he had by that time become "fed-up with" (blog 5/01/2003). In a 2007 interview, he indicated that he spent a total of a year and a half in Vancouver before returning to the United States for two years (Linnemann Interview). Although Gibson has said little about what he did during this period, he does mention participating in protests in Washington, D.C., attending part of Woodstock, and being in Northern California in 1969 when four people were killed at a Rolling Stones concert, an event that to many people marks the end of the 1960s, at least in spirit.

Returning to Toronto, Gibson shared a house with an artist, Gibson reporting that he had vague hopes of becoming a painter or doing something else creative (Zuckerman). There he met Deborah Jean Thompson, and the two began a relationship, founded in part on their similar interests in literature. The two traveled to Europe, using money from Gibson's mother's estate. Returning to Canada so that Thompson could continue her studies, the couple married in Toronto in June 1972 (McCaffery Interview 283). Soon afterward they moved to Vancouver, where Thompson finished her B.A. at the University of British Columbia (UBC) and then began the Master's program in linguistics. In a 1991 *People* magazine interview, Gibson, who remains married to Thompson, commented, "Only when I got together with Deb did I get a life" (Zuckerman).

## 1973–1980: Marriage and Education

Gibson soon determined that pursuing a B.A. in English literature would be a better way of supporting himself than washing dishes, working in a boat factory, or picking through thrift stores for items he could sell to specialty retailers, all of which he did at some point, since financial aid was readily available. Although not academically oriented or particularly sympathetic to the highly theoretical approaches to literature that were prevalent at the time, Gibson did well enough in his studies to seriously consider entering the Master's program in English; in particular, he considered focusing on fascist elements in the science fiction of writers like Robert Heinlein. Though he never pursued the topic, he reports that it got him "thinking seriously about what SF did, what it was, which traditions had shaped it and which ones it had rejected. Form/content issues" (McCaffery Interview 278). Some of his thinking here appears to be reflected in "The Gernsback Continuum" (1981), a short story that is critical of the ideological content of Golden Age science fiction.

At UBC he took a science fiction course with Susan Wood that was particularly important to his development as a writer since he was allowed to submit a short story in lieu of a paper. Although Gibson recalls receiving only a B+ on it, "Fragments of a Hologram Rose" was accepted for publication in *UnEarth*, a short-lived science fiction magazine that featured the work of new writers, appearing in the summer 1977 issue. Wood's class—and the $23 he received from *Unearth*—helped rekindle Gibson's childhood interest not only in science fiction but also in becoming a writer. He still lacked confidence, however, and did not submit any more stories for publication for years (Van Belkom Interview). He did, however, establish contact with another young writer, Bruce Sterling, whose first novel, *Involution Ocean*, had just been published. Although the two would not meet in person for a number of years, they quickly became friends, sharing similarly critical attitudes toward the science fiction establishment. The two also shared an interest in the then-nascent punk movement and in the cut-up technique pioneered by William Burroughs, which Sterling utilized extensively in his novel.

Gibson completed his studies at the University of British Columbia in 1977, the same year his first child, Graeme, was born, and afterward he became largely a stay-at-home dad, though he did work as a teaching assistant in film studies at the university for several years. He also began attending science fiction conventions and writing occasional reviews, including one on John Shirley's *Dracula in Love* (1979) for *Science Fiction Review*. The relationship he afterward established with Shirley proved to be critical, not only because Shirley, like Sterling, shared Gibson's interest in punk but also because he encouraged Gibson to submit his stories to *Omni*, one of the most lucrative and important venues for science fiction stories in the late 1970s and early 1980s. The two of them also collaborated on a short story, "The Belonging Kind," that appeared in *Shadow*, a horror anthology, in 1981.

## 1981–1983: Early Career

With the publication of "Johnny Mnemonic" in *Omni* in May 1981, Gibson began to establish himself professionally, not only because the story appeared in a high-profile magazine but because it was nominated for a Nebula Award. The story, which he recalls as being only the second he ever wrote, also provided him with a source of income that he quickly came to rely upon. Gibson remarked, "By the time I'd sold two or three stories, I was earning enough money that I couldn't actually afford to stop" (Poole Interview). Another story, "Hinterlands," also appeared in *Omni* in 1981, and more importantly, perhaps, "The Gernsback Continuum" was solicited by Terry Carr for his popular anthology, *Universe*. As Laura Lambert notes, the highly influential Carr "quickly became one of Gibson's unflagging supporters," soon commissioning a novel from Gibson for his Ace Science Fiction Specials (110). In October Gibson submitted a brief outline for a novel entitled *Jacked In*, which he soon renamed *Neuromancer*. Gibson also began circulating what is arguably his most celebrated short story, "Burning Chrome," in 1981, sending the manuscript to Sterling, who presented it at the Turkey City Writer's Workshop; soon afterwards Gibson presented the story himself at a science fiction convention in Denver. Its publication in *Omni* in July 1982 marks the first time the word "cyberspace" appeared in print, according to the *Oxford English Dictionary*.

In 1982 Gibson, Shirley, Sterling, and Lewis Shiner launched what later came to be known as the cyberpunk movement at a science fiction panel in Amarillo, Texas when the four of them appeared together on a panel titled, "Behind the Mirrorshades: A Look at Punk SF." That same year, Gibson began drafting *Neuromancer*, a novel that has since been identified as "the archetypal cyberpunk work" (Person). Gibson later reported feeling unready to write the book Carr had commissioned: "I said 'Yes' almost without thinking, but then I was stuck with a project I wasn't sure I was ready for. In fact I was *terrified* once I actually sat down and started to think about what it meant. I didn't think I could fill up so many pages; I didn't even know how many pages the manuscript of a novel was 'supposed' to have" (McCaffery Interview 268). He adds that is was "Panic. Blind animal panic" that got the book going. His need to get a manuscript together quickly for Carr forced him to utilize what had "worked for [him] before," putting the Molly Millions character from "Johnny Mnemonic" into a situation drawn from "Burning Chrome."

Describing himself at the time as "a guy you might buy a drink for but not loan money to," Gibson wrote *Neuromancer* attending to his young son, while Thompson, who was soon pregnant again, continued her work as an English as a Second Language (ESL) instructor at UBC (Adams Interview). "[A]lways sleep-deprived, always crazy," he continued working on the novel into 1983, exceeding Carr's deadline by six months. In another interview he reports that while writing the book he had the conviction that he "was going to be permanently shamed when it appeared" (McCaffery Interview 268). He adds: "And even when I finished it I had no perspective on what I'd done. I still don't, for that matter. I always feel like one of the guys inside those incredible dragons you see snaking through the crowds in Chinatown. Sure, the dragon is very brightly colored, but from the inside you know the whole thing is pretty flimsy — just a bunch of old newspapers and papier-mâché and balsa struts." Toward the latter part of 1983, Gibson and Thompson's second child, Claire was born, completing their family. Although Gibson was to continue being a stay-at-home parent for some time, professional demands increasingly infringed upon his family time.

## *1984–1988:* Neuromancer *and* The Sprawl Trilogy

Despite Gibson's misgivings about *Neuromancer*, the novel appeared in July 1984 to great acclaim, winning the Nebula and Philip K. Dick Awards for 1984 and the Hugo and Ditmar Awards for 1985. The novel's success brought Gibson instant celebrity, at least within the science fiction world, and gave cyberpunk new legitimacy as a movement. Although it was not the first work to feature virtual domains, computer networks, or hackers—John Brunner's *The Shockwave Rider* (1975) and Vernor Vinge's novella, "True Names" (1981) precede it, for example—it was the first to become a best seller and win major awards, establishing the subgenre as a viable alternative to the hard science fiction that was then dominant. Although Gibson was soon to disavow the cyberpunk label as a "marketing strategy," one that "trivializes" what he was doing artistically, he used his newfound prominence to promote the work of other cyberpunk writers and contributed to Bruce Sterling's *Mirrorshades: The Cyberpunk Anthology* (1986) and Larry McCaffery's *Storming the Reality Studio: A Casebook of Cyberpunk and Postmodern Fiction* (1991). "New Rose Hotel," another cyberpunk story set in what came to be known as the Sprawl universe, also appeared in July 1984 in *Omni*.

Gibson published only one story in 1985, "The Winter Market," which was commissioned by *Vancouver* magazine. Although rarely discussed by critics, it is not only an outstanding story, earning a Nebula nomination for best novelette, but an important one in that it anticipates Gibson's later preoccupation with celebrity and new media. The following year Gibson collected "The Winter Market," along with most of his other previously published short fiction, in the *Burning Chrome* collection, which was enthusiastically received by fans and critics.

In 1986 Gibson also published, *Count Zero*, the second volume of what became *The Sprawl Trilogy*. Although it received significantly less attention than *Neuromancer*, it was nonetheless a popular success and nominated for both the Hugo and Nebula awards. As Istvan Csicsery-Ronay observes, *Count Zero* can be regarded as an effort to unwrite *Neuromancer*, "to correct the blockbuster first novel's slick nihilism" by being more humanistic (63). Certainly the novel is less flashy than its predecessor, and Gibson invests much more in developing characters and relationships. The novel also focuses on the social and ideological functions of art, Gibson thereby introducing a subject that continued to be a concern in much of his future work.

Following *Count Zero* Gibson was under contract with Arbor House to write a novel entitled *The Log of Mustang Sally*, which was supposed to be a space opera, albeit one with postmodern elements. Gibson indicates in his blog that he "shamelessly ducked out" of the contract following a dispute over the cover art for *Count Zero*, and the novel was never written. Instead he wrote *Mona Lisa Overdrive* (1988), the final volume of *The Sprawl Trilogy*, a novel that introduces some of the slickness of *Neuromancer* into the story of Bobby Newmark and Angelina Mitchell that he began in *Count Zero*. The novel, unlike his previous two, was published as a Quality Paperback by Bantam and included in their Book Club, exposing Gibson to a broader market. The novel sold well and, like *Count Zero*, garnered both Hugo and Nebula nominations.

Gibson, who was spending an increasing amount of time in Hollywood making largely unrealized plans for his work to be adapted for film, completed his first screenplay in 1988, a script for *Aliens 3* based on a treatment by Walter Hill and David Giler, the producers of the first two films. The film was never produced, however, in part because when he wrote it Sigourney Weaver had not committed to participating in the project and therefore Gibson did not create a part for her character, Ellen Ripley. Gibson's version also had a Cold War theme that became dated with the dissolution of the Soviet Union. Gibson continued writing for Hollywood for the next decade or so, reporting that he had completed "eight or ten screenplays to contract over the years" (Van Belkom Interview). He adds: "I think that being a novelist and being paid for it is just about the best job I could have, and being a Hollywood screenwriter and being paid for it is easily the worst job I've had."

### 1989–1992: *Professional Interlude*

Even as he was completing *Mona Lisa Overdrive* and the screenplay for *Aliens 3*, Gibson was collaborating with Sterling on *The Difference Engine*, a counterfactual novel that imagines how history would have been different if Charles Babbage's computers had been put into production during the steam age. Though not the first "steampunk" novel, it is the best known and arguably the finest, at least in literary terms. It is also noteworthy because Gibson and Sterling employ cut-up techniques pioneered by William Burroughs, Gibson describing it as "an enormous collage of little pieces of forgotten Victorian textual material which we lifted from Victorian journalism, from Victorian pulp literature.... Then we worked it, we sort of air-brushed it with the word-processor, we bent it slightly, and brought out eerie blue notes that the original writers could not have. It's sort of like Jimi Hendrix playing 'The Star-Spangled Banner'" (Fischlin Interview). Though a challenging read, the novel sold well and was positively received, being nominated for a Nebula Award and several other prizes.

In 1990 Gibson also completed a story titled "Skinner's Room" that was commissioned by the San Francisco Museum of Modern Art for its "Visionary San Francisco" exhibition. The story, which was republished in slightly different form by *Omni* the following year, imagined that the Bay Bridge that links San Francisco to Oakland is taken over by the homeless, who squat there, making it their own. Although little more than a sketch, "Skinner's Room" provided a basis for Gibson's next major project, the series of novels that came to be known as *The Bridge Trilogy*.

Gibson's other major work of this period is *Agrippa (A Book of the Dead)*, a long, autobiographical poem based upon an Eastman Kodak photo album containing photographs of Gibson's father and his father's immediate family, dated 24 years before Gibson was born. In describing the photos, Gibson conveys a sense of not only his father, whom he lost at a young age, but himself and his own upbringing in Wytheville. Although the text itself is striking, what makes the poem most memorable is the medium in which it was published. Gibson collaborated with painter Dennis Ashbaugh and publisher Kevin Begos, Jr., to create a work of art that self-destructs after it is read so that it only exists in the reader's mind, just as memories do. Their artistic intent was undercut almost immediately as the text of the poem was quickly uploaded onto the net and thereby widely available in concrete form. Ultimately, Gibson posted a definitive version on his blog so as to preserve "the original line-breaks, etc."

### 1993–2000: The Bridge Trilogy *and Other Projects*

Gibson, who had became increasingly familiar with both Los Angeles and the film industry in the late 1980s, sets *Virtual Light* (1993), the first volume of what became *The Bridge Trilogy*, in a near-future world in which Southern California has been divided from Northern California. The novel is markedly different from his earlier work in that it is overtly satirical, targeting, among other things, reality television, American litigiousness, and televangelism. Although commercially successful — it was the first of Gibson's novels to make the *New York Times* best seller list — readers who expected either another tale of cyberspace or a high-tech *noir* adventure story were disappointed. Critics, too, were generally less enthusiastic about the novel than they were about his earlier work, which they considered more ground-breaking.

Like *Virtual Light*, which focuses on television, virtual reality, and fashion, Gibson's work in this period reflected his increasing interest in various forms of media. For example, he made a cameo appearance in ABC's *Wild Palms* mini-series, wrote song lyrics for Deborah Harry ("Dog Star Girl," on the *Debravation* album), published a travel piece on Singapore for *Wired* magazine ("Disneyland with the Death Penalty"), provided a voice-over for the song "Floating Away" on NOT YMO's *Technodon* album, and collaborated with the band U2 on its *Zoo TV* tour. In addition, Gibson made a foray into public policy in 1993, giving a speech to the National Academy of Sciences in Washington, D.C., about technology and education. Speaking after Bruce Sterling, he made "three modest proposals": (1) that public school teachers be given free professional access to long-distance services; (2) that public school teachers be given free access to software; and (3) that these privileges not be extended to teachers in private schools. It is the last proposal, of course, that is most radical since it challenges the trend towards the privatization of education that became popular in the Reagan era, leading to a further erosion of the middle class.

Gibson also worked on the screenplay for *Johnny Mnemonic*, which went into production in 1994. Gibson seems to have enjoyed the filmmaking process, working closely with both the director, Robert Longo, and the cast, which included Keanu Reeves, Takeshi Kitano, Dina Meyer, and Dolph Lundgren, all of whom were relatively unknown at the time. After *Speed* (1994), a film starring Reeves set on a speeding bus, became a box office hit, however, Gibson and Longo lost creative control over *Johnny Mnemonic* when Tri-Star Pictures tried to exploit Reeves's newfound celebrity. Gibson reports: "All of a sudden the studio that had been leaving us blissfully alone descended upon us like white on rice and all of a sudden we were being made to include things. One of the questions that came up was, 'Can you include a bus in it?!'" (Telegraph Interview). Gibson was very much disappointed in the final result, indicating that he published the screenplay afterwards only to "demonstrate the difference between what I wrote, and what we shot, and what they [TriStar] released" (blog 5/01/2000).

Not surprisingly perhaps, given his experiences in Hollywood and in the record industry, *Idoru* (1996), Gibson's next novel, focuses on celebrity, the "idoru" the book is named for being an entirely artificial pop entity. The book also features a half–Irish, half–Chinese rock superstar named Rez, a character based at least in part on U2's Bono. Although the book sold well, critical reviews were mixed, and it was the first of Gibson's novels to fail to be nominated for either a Hugo or Nebula Award. Following *Idoru*, Gibson took a vacation of sorts: "...I just woke up one day and I thought, 'Well, who am I? What am I doing here? What's my life like? I'll check that out today and see what's going on.' And then I got to the next day and I thought, 'That was fun.' ... So I just kept doing that, and I did it for about a year and half" (DuPont Interview). Returning to work in 1997, he wrote some short reviews and essays, including the Introduction to *The Art of the X-Files*. He also co-authored an episode for the *X-Files* with Tom Maddox that featured an artificial intelligence that tries to become autonomous ("Kill Switch").

In 1999, Gibson finally completed *The Bridge Trilogy* with *All Tomorrow's Parties*, arguably his most sophisticated novel up to that time. Named for an early Velvet Underground song, the story introduces the concept of paradigm shifts, or "nodal changes," that were to figure in much of Gibson's work thereafter. The novel is of particular note because it marked a change in the way critics received Gibson's work, *The Guardian*'s Stephen Poole, for example, writing that the novel completes Gibson's "development from science-fiction hotshot to wry sociologist of the future" (Poole 1999). Poole's observation seems to be confirmed by the fact that for all of its critical success, *All Tomorrow's Parties* failed to be nominated for any major science fiction awards and placed only fifteenth in *Locus* magazine's annual reader's poll for best science fiction novel.

Following the release of *All Tomorrow's Parties*, Gibson and Maddox co-authored another episode of *The X-Files* ("First-Person Shooter" 2000). He also wrote an Introduction for *The Art of the Matrix* and an article on Steely Dan's comeback album, *Two Against Nature*, as well as some other short pieces. In addition, he was featured in *No Maps or These Territories* (2000), a full-length documentary made by Mark Neale in which he discusses issues ranging from his childhood to nanotechnology. U2's Bono and the Edge also appear in the film, the former reading from *Neuromancer*. Gibson's friends and fellow science fiction writers Bruce Sterling and Jack Womack also make appearances.

## *2001 to the Present:* The Bigend Trilogy

Gibson had already begun his next novel, *Pattern Recognition*, when the September 11th attacks occurred. To Gibson, the destruction of the World Trade Center was a "nodal point" in history, an event that changes everything. Accordingly, he returned to the manuscript, which was then about 100 pages, and reconceived it in terms of the terrorist attacks (Leonard Interview). The resulting novel tells two stories at once, stories that at first appear to be related only thematically but interconnect in other ways as well. Although the protagonist, Cayce Pollard, is ultimately able to come to terms with the death of her father, who disappeared near the World Trade Center on 9/11, she, like everyone else, has been changed by the event in a fundamental way. As Lisa Zeidner notes in her review, despite having a "James Bond-ish edge," *Pattern Recognition* "manages to be, in the fullest traditional sense, a novel of consciousness—less science fiction than Henry James." The novel became Gibson's first mainstream best seller since *Virtual Light*, peaking at #4 on the *New York Times* best seller list for hardcover fiction, and has received more attention from academics than any of his works since *Neuromancer*.

Around this time Gibson seems to have finally accepted the role of being a public intellectual, writing articles on technology and culture for periodicals ranging from a lengthy review of a U2 concert for *Wired* to a piece on living in an information society for the *New York Times*. He also began a blog in 2003, where he posted an autobiographical sketch, the texts of various articles and speeches, and a lengthy interview with Amazon.com. Gibson also posts on a variety of subjects, such as watching *Mysterious Dr. Satan* on television in the early 1950s and what he thinks of people who post on the message boards of his own blog. Although there are months-long lapses in his postings at times, the blog is nonetheless expansive, the postings for January of 2003 alone totaling about 13,000 words. In the run-up to the 2004 U.S. elections, the blog temporarily became more political; Gibson explained that he was making "an abrupt lurch into the political.... Because the United States currently has, as Jack Womack so succinctly puts it, a president who makes Richard Nixon look like Abraham Lincoln" (blog 10/13/2004). He follows this up with a quote from Miguel de Unamuno: "At times, to be silent is to lie."

Although the blog became less overtly political following the election, Gibson's next novel, *Spook Country* (2007), was more politically engaged than his previous ones, targeting FOX news, military contractors like Blackwater, and the neo-conservative agenda in general, the MacGuffin of the novel being a shipping container of U.S. currency meant for Iraq that has been mismanaged. The novel was a commercial and critical success, reaching #6 on the *New York Times* best seller list and being listed as a book of "particular interest" in the Editor's Choice section of the *Sunday Book Review*. In his review of the novel, Dave Itzkoff remarks that *Spook Country* "moves farther from science-fiction speculation and immerses itself fully in modernist realism." He adds: "More than a post–9/11 novel, it is arguably the first example of the post-post–9/11 novel, whose characters are tired of being pushed around by forces larger than they are — bureaucracy, history and, always, technology — and are at long last ready to start pushing back."

In addition to doing the usual interviews in support of the novel's release, he blogged about *Spook Country* frequently, beginning in October 2006 and gave a reading from it on *Second Life* in August 2007; his avatar stepped from a shipping container lowered from a ceiling, reading from the novel, and then took questions from those assembled (Parsons). Gibson, who had once described *Second Life* as "a cross between being in some suburban shopping mall on the outskirts of Edmonton in the middle of winter and the worst day you ever spent in high school," emphasizes that in his own depictions of virtual worlds in *The Bridge Trilogy*, the focus is on the "interstitial," on the ways in which people resist the sort of corporatization of cyberspace *Second Life* itself represents (Amazon Interview).

In 2008 his blog again became decidedly political as U.S. Election Day approached: "Are you planning to vote for Obama? Let me advise you to do what it takes, Tuesday, to do that. Don't be a part of that part of the electorate that, for whatever reason, intends to vote, but doesn't. Whichever way this election goes, you will not want to journey into your personal future, the future of the United States, or the future of the world, without having cast your vote in this election. If I know anything about the future, I know that" (blog 11/07/2008). The evening before Obama's inauguration, he wrote: "Tomorrow (it's not yet midnight, here) will be one of most significant days in the history of the United States. And I, to my own amazement, have had no idea of the relief my heart would feel" (blog 1/19/2009). Gibson was relieved and maybe a little surprised that Obama was not only elected but also able to take power without interference from the far Right.

In 2009 Gibson became a regular user of Twitter, employing the username "GreatDismal," apparently in reference to a swamp he lived near as a child. He reports initially just experimenting with it "for a laugh," fully expecting "to make fun of it later" (Canavan Interview). To his surprise, he found it to be a very pleasing way of having people "around in a virtual way." Gibson, who has long used magazines as means of not only entertaining himself but keeping current, finds that Twitter has "astonishing power as an aggregator of novelty": "It does in a few hours what one hundred professionally produced magazines could scarcely do in a month, skimming the world's weirdest, most wonderful things and depositing them on your desktop to be snacked on." Not surprisingly, as he began using Twitter more, he blogged less, often going months between postings. In addition to answering questions and making comments, Gibson made queries himself as he researched *Zero History*, asking London followers, for example, about the color of coffee cup lids at Caffe Nero (Memetic Engineer).

The year 2010 saw the publication of Gibson's first short story in more than a decade. "Dougal Discarnate," which appeared in *Darwin's Bastards*, is one of just two stories in which Gibson himself appears as a character, the other being "Hippie Hat Brain Parasite" (1983). In both stories Gibson seems to distance himself from the drug culture that was very much a part of his earlier life; "Dougal Discarnate" is the more interesting of the two, at least from a biographical standpoint, since it includes much more about Gibson and his relatively tame life in Canada following his marriage in 1972. He also published "Google's Earth," an op-ed piece in the *New York Times* that suggests that Google has become a form of artificial intelligence, even if it is not generally recognized as such. He adds that cyberspace has "everted," effectively turning "itself inside out," as it were, "[m]aking Google a central and evolving structural unit not only of the architecture of cyberspace but of the world." The article also addresses the fact that we have put ourselves in a position where a for-profit corporation has "to be trusted never to link one's sober adulthood to one's wild youth," cheap storage and efficient processing now ensuring that information about us will never just go away.

    *Zero History*, of course, is Gibson's most important publication of 2010, the novel peaking at #9 on the *New York Times* best seller list and receiving generally positive reviews. Like the previous volumes of *The Bigend Trilogy*, *Zero History* is set in the near past, the world still recovering from the economic crisis that began in 2008. Although the novel includes characters from both *Pattern Recognition* and *Spook Country*, it is different in kind from the others and is, arguably, Gibson's darkest work to date.

• *References and further reading*

Dalton, Stephen. "Cyber Class: The Neuroromance Between U2 and William Gibson." *Achtung Stations (Part Two)*. Uncut Magazine, 26 Oct. 2004. Web.
Gibson, William. "Alfred Bester, SF and Me." *Frontier Crossing: A Souvenir of the 45th World Science Fiction Convention*. Ed. Robert Jackson. Brighton, U.K., Conspiracy '87: 1987. Print.
_____. Foreword. *Multimedia: From Wagner to Virtual Reality*. Ed. Randall Packer. New York: Norton, 2001. Print.
_____. "God's Little Toys." Wired.com, *Wired* 13.7 (2005). Web.
_____. "My Obsession." Wired.com, *Wired* 7.1 (1999). Web.
_____. "Since 1948." *Source Code*. 6 Nov. 2002. Web.
_____. "Time Machine Cuba." *Infinite Matrix*. 8 Aug. 2004 Web.
_____. "U2's City of Blinding Lights." Wired.com, *Wired* 13.8 (2005). Web.
Lambert, Laura, et al. *Internet: A Historical Encyclopedia*. Santa Barbara, CA: MTM Publishing, 2005. Print.
McCaffery, Larry. *Storming the Reality Studio: A Casebook of Cyberpunk and Postmodern Science Fiction*. Ed. Larry McCaffery. Durham: Duke University Press, 1991. 366–73. Print.
Olsen, Lance. *William Gibson*. Mercer, WA: Starmount House, 1992. Print.
Sterling, Bruce. Preface. *Mirrorshades: The Cyberpunk Anthology*. New York: Arbor House, 1986. Print.
Suvin, Darko. "On Gibson and Cyberpunk SF." *Foundation: The Review of Science Fiction* 46 (1989): 40–51. Print.
Zuckerman, Edward. "William Gibson: Teen Geek Makes Good, Redefines Sci-Fi." People.com, *People*, 10 June 1991. Web.

# William Gibson: A Literary Companion

## "Academy Leader"

Although introduced as an essay in *Multimedia: From Wagner to Virtual Reality*, "Academy Leader" (1991) is arguably as much a work of fiction as non-fiction since its text is largely drawn from works such as William Burroughs's *Naked Lunch* and *Nova Express*. The piece also draws passages from a number of Gibson's own works, including "Darwin," "Skinner's Room," and "Rocket Radio," the last being an article he wrote for *Rolling Stone*. As Gibson indicates in the Foreword he wrote for *Multimedia*, "Academy Leader" explores the tension between fiction and non-fiction — and between artists and engineers, or what he refers to as "artboys" and "geeks" — by using the cut-up technique pioneered by Burroughs to create a verbal collage that can simultaneously be read as a story and as an essay. Composed of other texts itself, "Academy Leader" also highlights the fact that all texts are products of other texts, that writing is largely a matter of selection and arrangement of what already exists. In addition, Gibson suggests that meanings ultimately rest with the person interpreting the text since the writer relinquishes control when the words are issued. Finally, "Academy Leader" reveals the creative power of cut-up by depicting how Gibson used the technique to create the word "cyberspace."

The title of the piece appears to be taken from the first line of a story Gibson never published, a line Gibson reports working on for years: "Seated each afternoon in the darkened screening room, Halliday came to recognize the targeted numerals of the Academy leader as sigils preceding the dream state of film" (blog 4/07/2010). The term "Academy leader" here refers to the countdown leader that is used in film labs to coordinate the film with its soundtrack and by projectionists as a reminder to turn on the lamp when a film is being shown. Presumably most readers would fail to recognize the technical film reference and instead create a meaning for themselves based on their understandings of the words and their context; for example, to some readers "Academy Leader" might mean "top student" while to others it might seem like the title of a science fiction story. The fact that a fixed meaning cannot be determined demonstrates both the plasticity of language and the play inherent in it as it is used to communicate thoughts and ideas; although words may be intended to express a particular idea, once they are issued, the writer has no control over them, and it is the reader who determines the meaning, a formulation very similar to Gibson's pronouncement in "Burning Chrome" that "the street finds its own uses for things." Significantly, these words appear *verbatim* in "Academy Leader" as well. The text's most interesting point, however, concerns the creative potential of cut-up, a point Gibson demonstrates by indicating that his own neologism, "cyberspace," was a product of the technique: "Assembled word *cyberspace* from small and readily available components of language. Neologic spasm: the primal act of pop poetics. Preceded any concept whatever. Slick and hollow — awaiting received meaning" (249). Although a novel combination, neither the word "cyber" nor "space" was new, and, as Gibson suggests, the culture at large imposed a meaning upon it as it entered usage, in effect creating cyberspace.

   *See also* Cut Up; Uncollected Stories

- *References and further reading*

Gibson, William. "Academy Leader." *Cyberspace: First Steps*. Ed. Michael Benedikt. Cambridge: MIT Press, 1991. Print.
_____. "Burning Chrome." *Burning Chrome*. New York: Ace, 1986. Print.
_____. Foreword. *Multimedia: From Wagner to Virtual Reality*. Ed. Randall Packer. New York: Norton, 2001. Print.


## Agrippa (A Book of the Dead)

   *Agrippa (A Book of the Dead)* is a remarkable work, not only because it is Gibson's only published poem to date but also because it initially appeared in an ephemeral form, effectively erasing itself as it was read. Originally a part of a limited edition artist's book, *Agrippa* is the product of a larger collaboration between Gibson, visual artist Dennis Ashbaugh, and publisher Kevin Begos, Jr. A "deluxe" edition of the book was run at 95 copies, priced at $1,500 apiece, and a "small," simpler edition was set at 350 copies at $450 apiece. The latter run was not completed, however, and it is not known how many copies were released. The book was simultaneously launched at several venues on December 9, 1992; Begos provided commentary and comedian/illusionist Penn Jillette read Gibson's poem aloud. An unauthorized transcription of Jillette's performance was posted to various newsgroups on the Internet within hours, making the text widely available. Ten years later, Gibson posted the full text on his website so that a definitive version would be freely available.

   As Peter Schwenger observes, the deluxe edition *Agrippa* presents itself as a "Black box recovered from some unspecified disaster," the contents of which are damaged but not destroyed (617). The wrought metal box is marked only by a small label on the upper-right-hand modeled upon that of a Kodak "Agrippa" photo album that was issued in 1920. The book contained therein is wrapped in a shroud, its title burned onto the cover and many of its pages singed around the edges. The first 62 pages of the book are filled with either DNA from a gene of a fruitfly or abstract etchings by Ashbaugh. The pages that follow are glued together to form a solid block, into which a cavity has been carved. Therein lies a black floppy disk containing Gibson's poem. When run on a Macintosh computer, the 305-line poem scrolls by at a set speed, erasing itself as it goes: it can be neither paused nor rewound so that after one viewing, it exists only in the viewer's memory. Ashblaugh's etchings also self-destruct, fading as they are exposed to light. According to the original press release, the "book-as-object" is intended to raise "unique questions about Art, Time, Memory, Possession — and the Politics of Information Control" ("Online Archive").

Gibson's poem raises questions similar to those that the book itself does, albeit in a much more personalized, reflective way. It opens with a description of the "time-burned" Agrippa photo album that had belonged to Gibson's father and proceeds to describe some of the photographs therein, photographs taken long before Gibson was born. The speaker supplies the original captions to the photos, some of which are partially lost, and brief descriptions of the photos themselves. As the speaker suggests, the images convey information but not knowledge because they and the persons and object represented within them are removed from their original time and place by the camera's shutter, which, when it closes, forever divides "that from this." In the sections that follow, the speaker goes on to suggest that our world is filled with mechanisms that, like cameras, not only mediate our experiences but remake them, alienating us from our very selves. Whether in the form of a gun or a traffic light, technology informs our every act, the camera's shutter swinging "across the very sky." The poem ends with the speaker thinking about the bus station in the town where he grew up as he walks through central Tokyo in the rain; recalling that the station has since been demolished and now exists only in memory, he realizes that he is "in the mechanism" himself.

Although the poem centers on a photo album that had belonged to Gibson's father and even describes a photograph of him, the poem is more about his absence than his presence: the speaker suggests that the information conveyed by the photograph does not amount to real knowledge of him — an image is just an image. On another level, the speaker addresses absence in general, the suggestion being that mediation always involves loss, and in an information society, the loss is everywhere, manifesting itself in alienation.

*Agrippa* was reviewed widely, not only as a literary work but also as an artistic event, with stories appearing in publications ranging from *The Village Voice* to *Omni*. Academics took an interest in the work as well, addressing it in numerous scholarly articles and monographs. In 2005 Alan Liu established an online archive on the book at the University of California, Santa Barbara that includes not only primary and secondary documents pertaining to the text but also images of both editions, a clip of the book's original transmission in 1992, and simulations of the poem as it appears to viewers. Although the text of Gibson's poem is commented upon less frequently than the unusual, ephemeral medium in which it appears, *Agrippa* is considered a seminal event in the development of electronic literature, one that helped establish the concept that the development of new media calls for the development of new art forms.

• *References and further reading*

Jonas, Gerald. "The Disappearing $2,000 Book." New York Times.com, *New York Times*, 29 Aug. 1993. Web.
Lindberg, Kathryne V. "Prosthetic Mnemonics and Prophylactic Politics: William Gibson among the Subjectivity Mechanisms." *Boundary* 23.2 (1996): 47–83. Print.
"Online Archive of Agrippa (A Book of the Dead)." University of California, Santa Barbara. Web.
Schwenger, Peter. "*Agrippa*, or, The Apocalyptic Book." *Flame Wars: The Discourse of Cyberculture.* Ed. Mark Dery. Durham: Duke University Press, 1994. 61–70. Print.

## All Tomorrow's Parties

Even though *All Tomorrow's Parties* (1999) is set in the same near-future world as the rest of *The Bridge Trilogy* and includes many of the same characters, it departs from the earlier volumes both conceptually and stylistically. In a sense, it is a millennial novel since it is addresses the anxieties and disruptions that looming changes can sometimes bring.

As William Linne puts it, the novel serves as "a meditation on the alienation that pervades our lives as we face the death of a century," adding that "Gibson evokes images of a society winding down, in love with its past and unsure of its future." The novel, which is, in fact, set in the early twenty-first century, does not address the turning of the millennium itself, but a "nodal point in history" that central character Colin Laney senses is about to occur, a point where everything changes, the last one happening just before the First World War with the development of the atomic theory and the beginning of modernism (5). The novel's action centers on public relations billionaire Cody Harwood's efforts to shape the coming change to his own advantage, and Colin Laney's efforts to prevent him from doing so. The fact that Gibson is vague about the exact nature of the coming paradigmatic shift that will result from the popularization of nanofax assemblers— that is, fax machines that can duplicate solid objects—leads Ty Burr to call the novel an "empty house" and Frank Houston to comment that "Gibson has trouble making his endings as vivid and precise as all the details leading up to them." As Graham Murphy observes, however, in refusing to be reductive or offer easy closure, Gibson avoids "insulting" the reader (85). According to Gibson, the novel does not depict "what lies on the other side" of a technological 'singularity'" because "what lies on the other side of a black hole" is "unknowable" (Du Pont Interview).

Like all of Gibson's work, *All Tomorrow's Parties* is more about people than technology. As Gibson indicates, he is less "concerned with technological "toys" than with how the technologies behind them "impact the social animal in ways that the developers ... never thought of" (Johnston Interview). Gibson focuses in particular on the ways technologies impact different social classes, the haves and the have-nots. Accordingly, neither Fontaine, the owner of a pawn shop, nor Berry Rydell, an unemployed security guard, apprehends the significance of the approaching paradigm shift — a shift that is deeply important to the rich and powerful Cody Harwood; indeed, Rydell does not even recognize the change when it occurs, observing that the "end of the world thing, everything changing, it looked like it hadn't happened" (330). The shift means little to street people like Boomzilla and Silencio, either, even though the latter plays a critical role in preventing Harwood from manipulating the shift to his advantage and "hack[ing] reality" (255). Although the introduction of nanotechnology into the everyday world will certainly impact them, as members of an underclass they have no say in how it might be used or any comprehension of its social implications. This becomes most evident at the end of the novel when Boomzilla sees that a duplicate of Rei Toei has emerged from the nanofax of every Lucky Dragon convenience store and walked out the door into the street (326). Contemplating the strangeness of a "butt-naked girl" emerging from a fax machine only briefly, he is primarily concerned with his next meal (326). Upon learning that the store is out of "Muff-Lettes," he tells an employee to "fax" him one "from fucking Paris" (327). To him, nodal point and technological singularities mean nothing: a nanofax machine is just another way to get breakfast.

Unlike the members of lower classes, denizens of the Walled City, a virtual community of hackers, *otaku*, and technophiles, take a very active interest in technological change and its social implications. Rather than try to shape the coming change to their advantage, however, they act in order to prevent it from being manipulated by others. As an "otherwhere of outlaw iconoclasts" that formed in response to both the regulation and privatization of the net (200), which had once been a place "where you could do what you wanted" (*Idoru* 292), the Walled City resists Harwood's effort to restrict the coming change so that his "place" in the coming world is "equivalent" to his place in the existing world (304). Aligning themselves with Laney, they oppose Harwood because the future he tries to enact is one in which new technologies are controlled by corporate interests. Just as in *Idoru*, the Republic of Desire acts to preserve interstices by thwarting plans to develop a "seamless" San Francisco with nanotechnology, the Walled City tries to prevent Harwood from developing a seamless world.

Of course, Harwood represents more than just corporate interests. By describing Harwood as "a twenty-first-century synthesis of Bill Gates and Woody Allen" (198), Gibson suggests Harwood is a corporate interest in-and-of himself, a self-obsessed megalomaniac willing to risk the well-being of everyone else in order to enhance his personal power (198). By identifying him with Bill Gates, in particular, someone he describes in an interview as having a "kind of Citizen Kane mega looniness," Gibson seems to target people whose corporations act as extensions of themselves (Blair Interview). Like Hubertus Bigend in Gibson's more recent novels, Harwood's idiosyncrasies and whims affect billions not only as they are expressed through his organization but as they cascade throughout the culture.

In terms of style, *All Tomorrow's Parties* represents a departure from *Idoru*, which alternates between two narrative lines, each chapter ending with a hook. *All Tomorrow's Parties* is much more complex, at least structurally, as it is comprises multiple storylines, some of which merge into others and some of which remain largely independent. As Cory Doctorow notes, the novels also differ in the way that "scene changes are announced by turning points in the character's internal monologue, rather than in plot." Not surprisingly, readers accustomed to Gibson's earlier style found the novel's structure disconcerting, William Linne, for example, complaining that many of the novel's characters "do not move the plot along so much as muck it up."

*All Tomorrow's Parties* also seems to be more self-consciously literary than Gibson's earlier works, as evidenced by its opening paragraphs, which use an extended river metaphor to convey the subway commute in Tokyo. By beginning the novel in a poetic register, Gibson marks the book as being something other than genre fiction. The novel is also more literary in structure, presenting not only multiple points of view but temporal dislocations. According to Fred Warren, Gibson's use of such devices opens the narrative up to the reader on a number of levels: "Time and reality are malleable and, ultimately, illusory in Gibson's world, and the narrative reflects this sense of fluid existence-always moving, always changing, a river that is never experienced the same way twice. We see the impending event, and its fallout, through the eyes of most of the main characters, individually and in chorus, as they're drawn inexorably into the nodal point, the focus of change." As Warren suggests, Gibson structures the text so that readers experience what the characters do, at least on some level. Finally, the book is markedly different from those that precede it in seriousness of tone. Although the novel is amusing and even at times silly, he never uses humor to undercut its seriousness, eschewing the easy jokes that permeate *Virtual Light*, the first book in the *Trilogy*.

## POST-STRUCTURALISM

*All Tomorrow's Parties* differs from Gibson's earlier work in the way it addresses philosophical issues directly, engaging with post-structuralism on its own terms only to ultimately reject it — or at least the tenet central to post-structuralism that since things cannot be known, individuals cannot know how to act. As Naomi Weisstein observes, such a philosophy ultimately leads to paralysis since "once knowledge is reduced to insurmount-able personal subjectivity, there is no place to go; we are in a swamp of self-referential passivity." Gibson addresses this issue primarily through Laney, who senses that there is an "underlying absence" in the core of his being, that he exists only in context with other things (84). Rather than allowing himself to be paralyzed by the sense that he is, in him-self, nothing, Laney enters into a "new mode of being," one that demands present action since events not only have a shape but also can be shaped (201). As he realizes, he may only be a "microscopic cog" in the larger sense of things, but he is "centrally" positioned and therefore it is incumbent upon him to act (85).

Superficially at least, Laney's realization that he must act in the now resembles the attitude of Taoist assassin Konrad, who endeavors to always "remain in the moment" (242). Whereas Konrad employs the Tao as a means of detaching himself from a painful past, one that haunts him despite his efforts to dismiss it, Laney's realization leads to increased involvement, Laney not only accepting moral responsibility for past actions but also acting morally in the present. In this he resembles Rydell, whose drive to behave morally make him virtually unemployable. As Laney himself observes, since the future is "inherently plural," there is a place for the "will" and individual action can make a differ-ence (128).

## KONRAD, "DO EASY," AND EXISTENTIALISM

Konrad emerges as one of the novel's most fascinating characters, almost stealing "the book away" as Michael Dirda notes, in part because his ongoing personal struggle to live in the moment gives him a complexity that characters other than Laney and Rei Toei seem to lack. Drawing from William Burroughs's "The Discipline of DE ["Do Easy]," which itself seems to be based loosely, at least, on the Tao, Gibson presents Konrad as an expert assassin who stands apart from others because he puts his Do Easy into practice in his work. Like Wyatt Earp, whom Burroughs quotes as saying, "It's not the first shot that counts. It's the first shot that hits," Konrad is able to focus entirely on the task at hand, giving him almost superhuman powers (391). At the same time, however, he has difficulty in detaching himself from the past and, for all of his efforts to act with "unthinking cer-tainty," he appears to think deeply and reacts emotionally. For example, after being reminded of a woman he had loved had who had drowned long ago, he goes to the Bridge to find "someone to kill" (119). At the end of the novel Konrad again loses his sense of detachment, deciding that he has "been too long in the pay" of those seeking to control the world, and turning on Harwood, makes him his next victim (331). The message that Gibson presents through Konrad is essentially the same one that he presents through Laney and Rydell, giving the novel an existential flavor: it is our actions that ultimately define us rather than our attitudes since the former reflect the moral choices we have actually made.

*See also The Bridge Trilogy*; Counterculture; *Idoru*; Japan; Laney, Colin; Toei, Rei; *Virtual Light*

• *References and further reading*

Berressem, Hanjo. "'Of Metal Ducks, Embodied Idorus, and Autopoietic Bridges': Tales of an Intelligent Materialism in the Age of Artificial Life." *The Holodeck in the Garden: Science and Technology in Contemporary American Fiction.* Ed. Peter Freese and Charles B. Harris. London: Dalkey, 2004. 72–99. Print.

Burroughs, William. "The Discipline of DE." *Word Virus: The William Burroughs Reader.* New York: Grove Press, 1998. Print.

Gibson, William. *All Tomorrow's Parties*. New York: Berkley, 2003.
_____. *Idoru*. New York: Berkley, 1997.
_____. *Virtual Light*. New York: Bantam Spectra, 1994.
Leaver, Tama. "Interstitial Spaces and Multiple Histories in William Gibson's *Virtual Light, Idoru*, and *All Tomorrow's Parties*." *Limina: A Journal of Historical and Cultural Studies* 9 (2003). Web.
Murphy, Graham. "Post/Humanity and the Interstitial: A Glorification of Possibility in Gibson's Bridge Sequence." *Science Fiction Studies* 30 (2003): 72–90. Print.
Proietti, Salvatore. "Out of Bounds: The Walled City, the Virtual Frontier, and Recent U.S. Science Fiction." *America Today: Highways and Labyrinths*. Ed. Gigliola Nocera. Siracusa, It.: Grafià, 2003. 247–54. Print.
Warren, Fred. "Book Review: *All Tomorrow's Parties*." Frederation, n.d. Web.

## Art

Although generally regarded as a writer primarily concerned with the impact new technologies have on the individual and society, Gibson frequently addresses the effects technology has on art, considering not only existing media but imagining new forms such as simstim and locative art. Indeed, art emerges as an important subject in much of his work as Gibson explores its social and ideological functions, suggesting that it does not simply convey meanings but rather affords us opportunities to make meanings for ourselves. To Gibson, art is essentially a collaborative process in which the consumer is as important as the creator, creating for her or himself the meaning that is needed.

Many of Gibson's early works address simstim — that is, "simulation stimulation," a form of virtual reality in which the neural activity of a simstim artists is recorded so that it can experienced by others. In his representations of this new media, Gibson makes it clear that simstim is an artistic medium, with performers such as Angelina Mitchell modulating their experiences so that they will be experienced in a particular way. In contrast to what Gibson terms "meat puppets," people who are passive while their bodies are being exploited by others in what amounts to a hi-tech version of prostitution, simstim artists are active, orchestrating their output to achieve certain effects. In "The Winter Market," for example, Lise is able to shape her experiences so as to affirm what so many people already have come to feel in a society that is increasingly comprised of have-nots as the middle class disappears— that there are "[n]o dreams, no hope" (134).

Even though Gibson addresses art only obliquely in *Neuromancer*, his second novel, *Count Zero*, is a *kunstlerroman* of sorts, not only because it represents the process through which Angelina Mitchell becomes a simstim artist but also because it tells the story of Bobby Newmark, a young man who escapes the stultifying Jersey suburbs to master the art of cyberspace. Ironically, the most interesting artist in the novel is the artificial intelligence who makes Cornell Boxes out of ephemera of the Tessier-Ashpool family since the AI employs the Burroughs's "cut-up" technique. *Mona Lisa Overdrive*, the final volume of *The Sprawl Trilogy* can also be regarded as an art novel: in addition to continuing the story of Mitchell and Newmark's development, it presents Slick Henry's efforts to address trauma through the creation of kinetic sculptures. The novel could even be read as a *kunstlerroman* in that it tells the story of Mona Lisa, a young woman who goes from being a prostitute to a simstim star: freed from her pimp and others who would exploit her by Molly Millions (aka Sally Shears), she moves from passive to active, gaining a measure of control over her own life. As for many of Gibson's artists, the experience of moving from the passive to the active is essential to her later work: having been a meat puppet — which can be read as a metaphor for the human condition in Gibson's imagined future — enables her to communicate effectively with those still locked into passive roles through her art.

Although *The Bridge Trilogy* focuses primarily on the celebrity of popular artists such as Rez, a rock superstar modeled in part on U2's Bono, and Rei Toei, a computer-generated popstar who becomes sentient, Gibson continues to explore the impact new technologies have on art and artistic media. Toei presents a particularly interesting case since in *Idoru*, at least, she exists only digitally, a "desiring machine" of sorts, constituting an "architecture of articulated longing" (191). Being digital rather than corporeal, she is initially presented as having the potential, at least, to be everything to everyone. In order to accomplish this, however, she must continually acquire information about the desires of others, giving her an essential dynamism that eventually leads to sentience on her part. As such she represents a new artistic medium, one that is not only interactive but infinitely plastic.

*The Bigend Trilogy* addresses art through a variety of media, including film, locative art, and fashion. *Pattern Recognition* is set in the period immediately following the 9/11 attacks, a period that Gibson identifies as a rupture in history, one in which new meanings must be created. The novel explores meaning-making processes through "the footage," snippets of film anonymously being posted on the Web that become objects of obsessive interest to those, like the novel's protagonist Cayce Pollard, who are trying to make sense of the post–9/11 world. As the novel's title suggests, the ability to not only discern patterns but create them is Gibson's primary focus; the creator of the footage integrates this tendency into her work to involve "footageheads" in the meaning-making process—in effect, viewers, including Pollard, are able to make the footage mean what they need it to. *Spook Country* can also be read as an art novel because of its engagement with locative art; that is, works of art that are integrated into real-world environments, encouraging localized social interactions. Again Gibson seems to be most interested in the ways new technologies create new media. GPS technology in this case makes possible new forms of localized art, an example being a virtual recreation of River Phoenix's death in the exact spot where he died. *Zero History*, in turn, focuses primarily on fashion as an art, addressing the idea of remix, the novel's MacGuffin being a line of clothing designed by Pollard, who remains sensitive to things that are overly derivative. Employing the cut-up method just as the maker of the footage does, Pollard's clothing line combines existing materials in ways that are suggestive but still open to alternative meanings, allowing for customers to participate in the meaning-making process.

In addition to representing the effects of new technologies on artistic forms in his novels, Gibson experimented with technology himself in *Agrippa (A Book of the Dead)*, a lengthy poem he wrote in conjunction with visual artist Dennis Ashbaugh, who designed and illustrated the book containing it. Gibson's poems, which is named for a Kodak photo album his father had kept long before he was born, addresses memory and loss. The poem itself was loaded onto a Macintosh-compatible floppy disc that was designed to scroll through the contents once, effectively erasing itself line-by-line as it was displayed. By having the poem erase itself as it was being presented, Gibson was able to, in effect, create a text that exists only in memory since it cannot not be reread, thereby using new media in novel way.

*See also Agrippa*; *Count Zero*; Music; *Pattern Recognition*; "The Winter Market

• *References and further reading*

Gibson, William. *Count Zero*. New York: Ace 1987. Print.
_____. *Idoru*. New York: Berkley, 1997. Print.

\_\_\_\_\_. *Mona Lisa Overdrive*. New York: Bantam Spectra, 1997. Print.

\_\_\_\_\_. *Pattern Recognition*. New York: Berkley, 2005. Print.

\_\_\_\_\_. *Spook Country*. New York: Berkley, 2009. Print.

\_\_\_\_\_. "The Winter Market." *Burning Chrome*. New York: Ace, 1986. Print.

\_\_\_\_\_. *Zero History*. New York: Putnam, 2010. Print.

Link, Alex. "Global War, Global Capital, and the Work of Art in William Gibson's *Pattern Recognition*." *Contemporary Literature* 49.2 (2008): 209–31. Print.

Rapatzikou, Tatiani G. *Gothic Motifs in the Fiction of William Gibson*. Amsterdam: Rodopi, 2004. Print.

## Bigend, Hubertus

Hubertus Bigend is one of Gibson's more interesting, original characters, if only because he figures largely in *The Bigend Trilogy* even though relatively little of the narrative focuses on him. In a sense, he is emerges from the text as a *what* more than a *who*, a being who can only approximate humanness. In this regard he resembles Wintermute in *Neuromancer*, an artificial intelligence who presents himself to Henry Case in human form but is never quite convincing as such. Like Wintermute, Bigend is frightening because he is not quite knowable, being something entirely new: a villain-figure that is not quite a villain because human categories do not apply to him.

In *Pattern Recognition*, Bigend is very much the sort of two-dimensional character one might expect to find in a postmodern novel, the name "Bigend" itself highlighting the character's artificiality. *Pattern Recognition* is hardly a postmodern novel, however: Bigend and other flat characters such as Billy Prion and Boone Chu serve as a point of contrast for more fully-rounded characters such as Cayce Pollard and the Volkova sisters. This is not to suggest, though, that Bigend is a minor character or that he does not play an important role in the novel: he not only sets the novel's plot in motion by hiring Pollard but also articulates important ideas, such as the notion that the world is changing so quickly now that there is no time to imagine a future any more. In the end, though, Bigend is more a caricature than anything else, a Tom Cruise lookalike with a permit that allows him to park his Hummer anywhere and an inability to imagine "that others wouldn't want to do whatever it is he wants them to" (70). Though he is entirely self-absorbed, showing little concern for how his actions might adversely affect others, he appears innocuous enough, in part because, as the owner of the Blue Ant marketing agency, he is interested primarily in advertising and promotion.

Bigend plays a similar role in *Spook Country*, initiating the action by hiring Hollis Henry to locate Bobby Chombo, the engineer behind certain works of art that employ GPS technology. In this novel Bigend's interests extend far beyond marketing, for, unbeknownst to Henry, he hopes to locate a shipping container that holds currency intended by the U.S. government for use in Iraq through Chombo, who is tracking the container for an unknown third party. Ironically, although Bigend appears less frequently in this novel than in the previous one, his presence seems greater, largely because his ambitions have grown and because he directs the actions Henry's actions even more closely than he did Pollard's. Ultimately, Henry is unable to resist his will, effectively delivering Chombo to him, though she does manage to keep him from learning the fate of the container. The novel ends with Henry commissioning an artwork of her own, a gigantic Mongolian Death Worm, which to her symbolizes "any major fear" that she cannot "quite get a handle on," entwining itself around the top of Blue Ant headquarters (453).

It is in *Zero History*, however, that Bigend fully emerges as something other than human, something that cannot quite be narrated. On the surface he is just another of

Gibson's Faust figures, in this case a rich and powerful man who can "afford to satisfy" his "curiosity," as he explains to Milgrim (67). As it turns out, however, his curiosity is anything but idle: with the assistance of Chombo, whom he virtually holds prisoner, he hopes to determine "order flow"—that is, attain advance knowledge of all market activity, knowledge that will allow him to control entire economies. What makes Bigend so remarkable is not that he ultimately obtains such knowledge but that he remains the same flat, two-dimensional character that he was in *Pattern Recognition* and *Spook Country*. In effect, flatness—as represented by Bigend—triumphs in *Zero History*, the world becoming the sort of two-dimensional, postmodern dystopia imagined by Baudrillard and others. In this world Bigend, who was never the subject in any of the volume of the *Trilogy*, emerges as its *only* subject, the world now belonging to him. In representing Bigend's success, Gibson effectively reverses the outcome of *The Bridge Trilogy*, in which Cody Harwood, a two-dimensional Faust figure who seeks control of the future, is defeated by Colin Laney, the sort of humanist hero one might find in a Dickens novel.

See also *The Bigend Trilogy*; Counterculture; Dystopia; Henry, Hollis; Milgrim; *Pattern Recognition*; Pollard, Cayce; *Spook Country*; *Zero History*

• *References and further reading*
Gibson, William. *Pattern Recognition*. New York: Berkley, 2005. Print.
_____. *Spook Country*. New York: Berkley, 2009. Print.
_____. *Zero History*. New York: Putnam, 2010. Print.
Youngquist, Paul. *Cyberfiction: After the Future*. New York: Palgrave Macmillan, 2010. Print.

## The Bigend Trilogy

*The Bigend Trilogy*, which is sometimes referred to as "The Blue Ant Trilogy," is named for Hubertus Bigend, the owner and chief executive officer of the Blue Ant agency, a media corporation that works in advertising, trend forecasting, and brand transmission. The *Trilogy* marks a departure from Gibson's earlier work in that Gibson represents the world as it is now rather than refracting it through an imaginary future. He indicates that began writing about the present because it is increasingly becoming indistinguishable from the future, the two collapsing as it were. As Bigend himself explains in *Pattern Recognition* (2003), "Fully imagined cultural futures where the luxury of another day, one in which 'now' was of some greater duration. For us, of course, things can change so abruptly, so violently, so profoundly, that futures like our grandparents' have insufficient 'now' to stand on. We have no future because our present it too volatile (58–9).

Although each volume of the *Trilogy* addresses an important historical event, the novels are less concerned with the events themselves than with their immediate aftermaths, the protagonists of each volume being forced to negotiate the entirely new worlds they find themselves in. *Pattern Recognition* centers on Cayce Pollard, a young woman who lost her father in New York in the September 11th attacks and must come to terms both with his death and with the implications of living in a world where change is not only unexplained but inexplicable. Ultimately the novel suggests that human beings not only discern patterns in events but impose patterns upon them, making meaning as much as discovering it. *Spook Country* (2007), in turn, is set in the midst of the so-called "War on Terror." Like Pollard, the protagonist of this novel, Hollis Henry, must negotiate a world that has been fundamentally changed, in this case by war being declared on a state of mind rather than a physical enemy. In *Zero History* (2010), which also features Henry as a protagonist, the world changes again, this time because the global economic crisis has allowed those already in power to consolidate control. What Henry learns in this novel that is that the world has become a place where resistance can be no more than a gesture, a world in which we have "Orwell's boot in [our] face *forever*," as Voytek Biroshak, a Polish-born Russian who came to Great Britain to escape totalitarianism, observes (289).

In terms of style, the volumes of the *Trilogy* rank among Gibson's most experimental. In *Pattern Recognition*, Gibson employs dramatic irony in a unique way, incorporating identifiable patterns into his narrative that his characters do not discern. Although some of these patterns are trivial or idiosyncratic, others are of great significance as Paul Youngquist suggests: "Militarism, for instance, saturates the fads that Cayce and Bigend pursue, but neither recognizes it in any terms other than style.... For all their market savvy, Gibson's characters remain oblivious to the militarization of everyday life that has followed 9/11 with its encroachments on civil liberties and international mobility" (195). Gibson thus attempts to engage readers on a cognitive level: they participate in the meaning-making process by identifying the very patterns that the characters miss. In *Spook Country* patterns themselves are not so important as the ways in which the protagonist engages with them: Hollis Henry is, in essence, a modernist character in a postmodern novel, a person seeking definitive answers in a world surfeit with information. Even though in the end she finds the information she seeks—that is, the location of the shipping container filled with U.S. currency—she cannot know its significance, beyond the fact that it is part of a shell game of sorts in which meaning is endlessly deferred. *Zero History* is arguably the most radical of the three novels and the most chilling since it ends with past, present, and future effectively being collapsed together as Bigend acquires the means to determine the "order flow" of the world's markets and thus gains control over them. The end result of the Information Age, Gibson seems to suggest, will be a world in which the control of information leads to the control of everything.

*See also* Bigend, Hubertus; Henry, Hollis; Milgrim; Pollard, Cayce; *Pattern Recognition*; *Spook Country*; *Zero History*

• *References and further reading*
Gibson, William. *Pattern Recognition*. New York: Berkley, 2005. Print.
_____. *Spook Country*. New York: Berkley, 2009. Print.
_____. *Zero History*. New York: Putnam, 2010. Print.
Youngquist, Paul. *Cyberfiction: After the Future*. New York: Palgrave Macmillan, 2010. Print.

## The Bridge Trilogy

Set just after the millennium, *The Bridge Trilogy* is comprised of *Virtual Light* (1993), *Idoru* (1996), and *All Tomorrow's Parties* (1999). Named for the Bay Bridge that connects Oakland to San Francisco, the Trilogy differs from Gibson's earlier work in both style and content. Although sometimes classified as "cyberpunk," the novels lack the *noir* elements often associated with that subgenre and are not so preoccupied with what Gibson referred to as "the street" in his earlier work. Rather, the novels are light in tone, particularly *Virtual Light*, and even though serious events occur, their *gravitas* is usually undercut with humor and/or satire.

In the near future Gibson imagines, California has been split into two sections, both San Francisco and Tokyo have been heavily damaged by earthquakes, and Japan has become the dominant power both technologically and economically. In contrast to Tokyo, which has been largely remade using nanotechnology following its quake, becoming a twenty-first century city, San Francisco has simply been repaired, as evidenced by the gigantic splint on the spire of TransAmerican Pyramid. More significantly, perhaps, the Bay Bridge, which was permanently closed to traffic in the aftermath of a quake, has been taken over by squatters, who have built added a superstructure, one that employs "every imaginable technique and material": the "result" is something "amorphous, startling organic," something possessing "a queer medieval energy" (69). In effect, those who have become dispossessed, disenfranchised, and dislocated by twenty-first century society have located an interstice in its physical infrastructure, making it their own. In the novels that comprise *The Bridge Trilogy*, the Bridge is not just a refuge for those who have been displaced but a possible point of resistance to the new social order, which is controlled almost entirely by corporations.

Although both the first and third novels of the *Trilogy* focus largely on the Bridge, it is represented differently in each. In *Virtual Light*, the Bridge functions as a heterotopia of sorts, that is, as a space outside the dominant culture, one free of surveillance and control. In *All Tomorrow's Parties*, however, a novel set several years later, the Bridge has become a tourist attraction, complete with a Lucky Dragon convenience story being located on near the western approach. Although the Bridge is nearly destroyed at the end of the novel by explosives placed by agents of Cody Harwood, the Bridge community works together to save themselves and their home, and though damaged, the Bridge still stands, suggesting just how resilient popular resistance movements can be.

In terms of style, the novels that comprise *The Bridge Trilogy* are arguably Gibson's most Pynchonesque, largely because of the way the characters are drawn and because the novels maintains a light, satirical tone even when the most serious of issues are being addressed. For example, both Berry Rydell and Colin Laney lose their livelihoods because of ridiculous-seeming legal threats, Rydell being sued by the girlfriend of a man who was holding both her and her children at gunpoint and Laney liable to a similar action because he tried to prevent a suicide: in both cases their lives are changed irrevocably. The novels also frequently target Christian Evangelism, reality television, celebrity culture, and the commercialization of public spaces like Golden Gate Park.

*The Bridge Trilogy* marks the beginning of Gibson's transition from being a science fiction writer to mainstream writer, *Virtual Light* being the first of his novels to make the *New York Times* best seller list. Although the novels include science fiction elements such as nanotechnology and virtual reality entertainment systems, they are set in the near rather than distant future and address contemporary social issues in a satirical manner rather than a fantastical one, aligning them more with the work of writers like Pynchon and Don DeLillo than David Brin and Kim Stanley Robinson. With this in mind it is not surprising perhaps the Idoru was the first of Gibson's novels to be nominated for neither a Hugo nor a Nebula award.

*See also All Tomorrow's Parties*; Counterculture; Hackers; *Idoru*; Japan; Laney, Colin; Toei, Rei; *Virtual Light*

• *References and further reading*

Berressem, Hanjo. "'Of Metal Ducks, Embodied Idorus, and Autopoietic Bridges': Tales of an Intelligent Materialism in the Age of Artificial Life." *The Holodeck in the Garden: Science and Technology in Contemporary American Fiction.* Ed. Peter Freese and Charles B. Harris. London: Dalkey, 2004. 72–99. Print.

Call, Lewis. "Anarchy in the Matrix: Postmodern Anarchism in the Novels of William Gibson and Bruce Sterling." *Anarchist Studie*s 7.2 (1999): 99–117. Print.

Chun-li, Hui. *The Re/Shaping of the Posthuman, Cyberspace, and the Histories in William Gibson's Bridge Series*. Saarbrücken: VDM. 2009. Print.

Farnell, Ross. "Posthuman Topologies: William Gibson's "Architexture" in *Virtual Light* and *Idoru*." *Science Fiction Studies* 26.3 (1998): 459–60. Print.

Gibson, William. *All Tomorrow's Parties*. New York: Berkley, 2003. Print.

_____. *Idoru*. New York: Berkley, 1997. Print.

_____. *Virtual Light*. New York: Bantam Spectra, 1994. Print.

Murphy, Graham. "Post/Humanity and the Interstitial: A Glorification of Possibility in Gibson's Bridge Sequence." *Science Fiction Studies* 30 (2003): 72–90. Print.

## "Burning Chrome" (Story)

The title story of a collection of Gibson's earliest short works, "Burning Chrome" was originally published in *Omni* in 1982 and nominated for a Nebula award for best novelette. Although today it is remembered primarily as the first published text to employ the world "cyberspace," the story is frequently taught in colleges and universities, not only as a dry run for *Neuromancer*, Gibson's much acclaimed first novel, but as a seminal text in its own right. Narrated by Automatic Jack, a hardware specialist who partners with console cowboy Bobby Quine to "burn" Chrome — that is, to infiltrate the database of a local crime figure who calls herself "Chrome" and steal her assets — the story combines "high tech" and "low life" in a manner characteristic of the cyberpunk subgenre (Ketterer).

In addition to offering a vivid account of Quine's run on Chrome's database, the story tells of a love triangle involving Quine, Jack, and an aspiring simstim artist named Rikki Wildside. Quine, who according to Jack, treats women as if they "were counters in a game" uses Wildside, a young woman who "definitely had the goods," to motivate himself to take risks, she being a symbol of everything he wanted and couldn't have, everything he'd had but couldn't keep" (174, 176). Jack, too, hopes to possess Wildside, in part because of an ongoing rivalry he has with Quine. The fact that the two men treat Wildside as an object does not make her one, of course: in the end she leaves them to pursue her own interests. Although Quine proves incapable of understanding the reasons for Wildside's departure, Jack ultimately recognizes agency is more important than material comfort and accepts her decision.

Despite being one of Gibson's first stories, "Burning Chrome" is sophisticated structurally, interweaving two storylines in order to develop the story's main themes. The first storyline, which focuses on the "burning" of Chrome, reveals the essential misogyny of Quine and Jack, both of whom identify Chrome with the database they raid. As Lance Olsen notes, their run on Chrome amounts to a "metaphorical" rape, the two of them taking particular pleasure in asserting power over Chrome on both a real and virtual level (55). Gibson connects this storyline with the one centering on Wildside by having Jack fantasize about Wildside while "burning" Chrome: as he and Quine penetrate the "walls of ice" that protect her database, Jack blots Chrome's "pretty childlike" face "out with a picture of Rikki," imagining the latter in "an old shirt of Bobby's frayed khaki cotton drawn across her breasts" (169). The Chrome and Wildside storylines intersect again when Jack learns that Wildside has been working as a prostitute in Chrome's brothel in order to earn the money necessary to begin a career in simstim. In the end Jack realizes that Wildside and Chrome are not so different from people like himself and Quine, that their condition is, in a sense, the human condition, the world having become a place where most people have to pull some sort of hustle in order to survive.

*See also* Cyberspace; Gender; Hackers; *Neuromancer*

• *References and further reading*
Gibson, William. "Burning Chrome." *Burning Chrome.* New York: Ace, 1986. Print.

## *Burning Chrome* (Collection)

A collection of most of his short fiction through 1986, *Burning Chrome* demonstrates Gibson's range as a writer, including as it does straight-forward, first-person narratives such as "Johnny Mnemonic" (1981) and "New Rose Hotel" (1984), more complex, experimental narratives such as "Hinterlands" (1981) and "The Winter Market" (1985), hard science fiction like "Burning Chrome" (1982), and soft science fiction like "The Gernsback Continuum." It also contains Gibson's first published story, "Fragments of a Hologram Rose" (1977). In addition, the volume includes three collaborative stories: "The Belonging Kind" (1981) with John Shirley, "Red Star, Winter Orbit" (1983) with Bruce Sterling, and "Dogfight" (1985) with Michael Stanwick.

As Bruce Sterling indicates in his preface — which itself is notable as an abbreviated cyberpunk manifesto — Gibson's early work offers "an instantly recognizable portrait of the modern predicament" — a predicament resulting from the advent of "Big Science" (x–xi). From his very first story, Gibson is much more concerned with the ways in which technology affects people than he is with technology itself. Even "Burning Chrome" and "The Winter Market," the most technologically oriented of the stories, focus on issues such as alienation and class division that result from corporate domination of cyberspace and the new media.

*Burning Chrome* is more than just a sum of its parts. The stories seem to be arranged so as to suggest an overall theme in a manner reminiscent of concept albums such as The Velvet Underground's *White Light/White Heat* or even *Sgt. Pepper's Lonely Hearts Club Band.* The opening story, "Johnny Mnemonic," establishes a tone which is somehow hopeful in a world gone wrong, a tone that gives way to despair or hopelessness in stories like "Hinterlands" and "The Winter Market," only to be re-established in "Red Star, Winter Orbit" and, finally, "Burning Chrome," the last story in the collection. Although, taken as a whole, the stories suggest that technology is leading to a society that increasingly interpellates people as subjects, they also allow for resistance as individuals adapt technology to their own needs, an attitude that is reflected in Gibson's celebrated statement, "the street finds its own uses for things" ("Burning Chrome" 186). Gibson's imagined worlds may be dark and even dystopic, but they are not abject since there is at least hope for real change.

*See also* "Burning Chrome"; "Fragments of a Hologram Rose"; "The Gernsback Continuum"; "Hinterlands"; "Johnny Mnemonic"; "New Rose Hotel"; "The Winter Market"

• *References and further reading*
Gibson, William. *Burning Chrome.* New York: Ace, 1986. Print.

## Count Zero

Set approximately seven years after *Neuromancer*, *Count Zero* (1986) is a sequel only in the sense that it is set in same future world and follows up on the unification of two artificial intelligences, Wintermute and Neuromancer, that occurs at the end of Gibson's first novel. Henry Case, the protagonist of *Neuromancer*, is mentioned only incidentally by Finn, as are Molly Millions and Armitage, and Finn himself is a minor character, appearing at length in just one chapter (124). The novel also structured differently, providing three narrative perspectives rather than one, those of Turner, Marly Krushkova, and Bobby Newmark. Gradually, the three strands are drawn together as the mysteries surrounding a fourth primary character, Angelina Mitchell, are solved.

The Turner strand seems to be closely patterned on the pre-war detective novels like those of Dashiell Hammett in the sense that it focuses on a tough, street-hardened agent who feels compelled to redress a betrayal. Hired to help scientist Christopher Mitchell defect from Maas Biolabs to Hosaka Corporation, Turner is betrayed by his contact, Conroy, who sabotages the mission in an effort to deliver Mitchell to Josef Virek, a Faust-like character who hopes to use experimental biochips designed by Christopher to make an evolutionary jump so he can exist independently within the matrix (139). Turner, who escapes with Christopher's daughter, Angelina, rather than with Christopher, soon learns that Angelina is able to enter the matrix directly because of biochips grafted into her brain. Acting as her protector, he is unwittingly drawn into the larger story, which involves Angelina's relationship with the *loa*-like beings that inhabit cyberspace. The Turner strand ends just in the manner of *noir* detective novels. Like Hammett's Sam Spade, Turner adheres strictly to a professional code of conduct even as he becomes increasingly invested in his work on a personal level. At the end of the novel the personal and the professional merge as Turner discovers that the man who betrayed him is also the man who brought about the death of his brother; Turner avenges both by passing along information that brings about Conroy's death

If the Turner strand allows Gibson to work elements of from detective fiction into the novel, the Marly Krushkhova strand allows him to work within the thriller genre. Krushkhova, a Parisian art dealer whose professional standing is ruined because she sells a forged Joseph Cornell "box," is hired by Josef Virek to discover the source of a series of similar artworks that have recently been mysteriously appearing. An ingénue reminiscent of a character in a 1930s thriller, Krushkhova traces the boxes to the abandoned orbiting station that once housed the Tessier-Ashpool computer cores but does not inform Virek of her discovery. Arriving there just ahead of Virek's agents who have been secretly tracking her, she discovers that the boxes are being made by the Artificial Intelligence belonging to 3Jane, the only surviving member of the Tessier-Ashpool family: the AI uses a remote construction unit to turn the personal effects of the family into art, the Cornell boxes being comparable to coffins. Ultimately, she learns a basic truth, one that brings all of the novel's disparate parts together: the AI that makes the boxes is also responsible for the design of the biochips in Angelina's head, the biochips that Virek believes could make him immortal. A "technological naïf," to borrow Istvan Csicsery-Ronay's term, she is most interested in the artistic implications of the boxes, sharing what she learns with no one. In the end she uses the money she earned while in Virek's employ to start a new art dealership and restore her professional credibility (73).

According to Csicsery-Ronay, the Krushkhova narrative "protrudes out" of the novel "as if it were a separate story" (73). While this is largely true, the choices that she makes do have consequences outside of the strand that centers on her, most particularly her refusal to admit Virek's agents to the Tessier-Ashpool computer cores. This delay, it seems, prevents Virek from coding his "personality" into the AI's "fabric," something that would have allowed him to transcend death (227). As in the pre-war thrillers of writers like Eric Ambler and Graham Greene, thrillers that featured ordinary people caught up in extraordinary events, Krushkhova's decision results more from a general sense of what right and wrong than from any specialized knowledge of what needs to be done at a particular time. Knowing only that "nothing he [Virek] wants can be good," she resists his will, completely unaware of how her actions might help others succeed in ultimately defeating him.

The novel's third strand, the one that gives the book its title, is more literary than the other two, at least in traditional generic terms since it functions as a *bildungsroman*—a "formation" novel—if not an *erziehungsroman*—an "education" novel, as Lance Olsen argues (104). At the beginning of the book, Bobby Newmark is, as his name suggests, a "new mark" in the sense that his childlike expectations of easy success as a "console cowboy" make him vulnerable to dangers the more experienced and skilled might avoid. "Hotdogging" in cyberspace from his mother's living room, he is almost killed by a security program he encounters as he experiments with black market software. Saved in cyberspace by Angelina, who does not identify herself to him, he is almost killed that same night on the streets when the software is stolen from him. He returns to consciousness in the power of a Vodou organization that is interested not only in the software but in ascertaining just what it was that saved Newmark from the security program. The organization takes Newmark to Jammer's, a nightclub located in the Sprawl, where he is put in the care of Jackie, a priestess of Danbala. Newmark, who was only beginning to realize "how precious little he knew about how anything worked" before his adventures began, learns even more about his own ignorance as he is exposed not only to the *loa*—sentient beings that exist only in cyberspace—but to the world as it exists outside of his suburban Barrytown, New Jersey, home (39).

The Turner and Newmark strands draw together when Turner and Angelina also appear at Jammer's, Angelina having been guided there by the *loa*. Newmark, who has been instructed in how to navigate the Web by Jackie, enters the matrix and encounters Jaylene Slide, who, like Turner, hopes to discover who sabotaged the Christopher Mitchell defection so that she can avenge it for the sake of her partner, Ramirez, who was killed (210). When, at Turner's urging, Newmark reveals to Slide that it was Conroy who betrayed the mission, Slide immediately kills Conroy, effectively ending the physical threats Newmark and his companions face. Newmark is also instrumental in ending virtual threats, since in entering the matrix at time when Virek's "systems are overextended," he creates a breach which Baron Samedi, Lord of the Graveyards, is able to exploit, manifesting himself through Newmark and destroying Virek. Following these actions, Turner, who, by helping to bring about Conroy's end has fulfilled the demands of the detective genre, affirms that Newmark has become the fully-fledged adult one would expect at the end of a *bildungsroman*, addressing him by his professional name, "Count," inducing a "surge of pride" in him (241). The novel ends with Newmark deciding not to return home to Barrytown, instead going to the Projects with Angelina to learn more about the *loa* and the changes that are occurring in cyberspace.

The style of *Count Zero* also differs from that of *Neuromancer*, although perhaps not as sharply as its content and structure do. Whereas in his first novel, Gibson utilizes a variety of figures to convey the almost overwhelming sensual way in which Henry Case experiences cyberspace, in his second he employs descriptive terms, primarily through his characters, who frequently talk about cyberspace but rarely enter into it. When Newmark finally ventures into cyberspace for the first time since the near-death experience that marks the beginning of his narrative, it is represented as a "workaday" place to the extent that it is presented at all (210): Newmark's experiences are mostly limited to encounters in particularized domains constructed and controlled by others such as Virek and Slide, cyberspace apparently being developed as if it were physical real estate (Csicsery-Ronay 67).

It is not just in passages pertaining to cyberspace that Gibson relies upon descriptive language: the novel is replete with it. Ironically, only the artificial intelligence that makes the Cornell boxes uses figurative language in an extensive way, explaining to Krushkhova how it went from near omnipresence to near isolation and why it turns flotsam from the lives of its creators into art: "Once I was not. Once, for a brilliant time, time without duration, I was everywhere as well.... But the bright time broke. The mirror was flawed. Now I am the only one.... But I have my song, and you have heard it. I sing with these things that float around me [the Cornell boxes], fragments of the family that funded my birth. There are others [the *loa*], but they will not speak to me. Vain, the scattered fragments of myself, like children. Like men" (226–27). The AI's poetic register contrasts sharply with the prosaic one that otherwise dominates the novel, highlighting the sense of loss and alienation it feels and thereby providing the novel with an emotional center. In *Count Zero*, it seems, machines are more capable of emotion than humans.

Gibson also focuses more on characterization in *Count Zero* than he does in *Neuromancer*, filling in characters' back stories and developing more complex relationships between them. His development of Turner is perhaps most telling since at first Turner seems to be the type of simply-drawn character one might find in a 1930s detective novel. Literally blown apart and then reassembled at the beginning of the novel at Conroy's behest so he can lead the Mitchell defection mission, he is mentally unstable, having only a professional know-how to draw upon. Unlike Armitage in *Neuromancer*, who unravels as the novel proceeds, Turner gradually recovers himself, largely because he returns to his childhood home, reconnecting with his brother, and because he establishes a bond with Angelina, becoming increasingly paternal towards her. That he has ultimately been rehumanized becomes evident at the end of the novel when he leaves his profession, returning to the ranch he grew up on to start a family. He novel closes with Turner reflecting that he is no longer like the "dumb" squirrels who return to the same place "over and over and get shot" (246).

LITERARINESS

In *Count Zero*, Gibson is more self-consciously literary than he was in *Neuromancer*, commenting in a 1986 *Rolling Stone* interview that he was "going for something a little bit different" (Gilmore Interview 107). He accomplishes this by focusing more on characterization and by adopting "a more deliberate" pace, one that allows him to focus on human relationships rather than technology (Gilmore Interview 108). *Count Zero* is also more self-consciously literary in the sense that it appears to be patterned upon the work of Thomas Pynchon, most obviously in the way that subplots converge as a conspiracy is uncovered. The book is further reminiscent of *The Crying of Lot 49* in the way that the boxes the Tessier-Ashpool Artificial Intelligence makes serve as a MacGuffin, that is, as objects that drive the plot even though they are not ultimately essential to it in themselves. As if to acknowledge this debt, Gibson employs the names a company that features prominently in the book, "Maas Biolabs," after Pynchon's protagonist, Oedipa Maas.

Gibson is also more self-consciously literary than he was in *Neuromancer* in the way he uses collage as a technique to induce readers to participate in the meaning-making process. As Istvan Csicsery-Ronay observes, whereas in *Neuromancer* Gibson uses "hooks" to draw readers into the narrative, in *Count Zero* he uses collage to "prevent the narrative pieces from fitting together," resulting in an "anti-narrative" of sorts, one that forces the reader to create meaning in a manner similar to metaphor (71, 72). For example, the artistic significance of the Cornell boxes made by the AI is never overtly stated. Although the narrative informs us that Krushkhova understands the significance of the Cornell boxes, what their significance is remains unstated, leaving readers to determine for themselves what the assemblages mean. Similarly, the significance of the *loa* is never quite articulated, though presumably the reader, like the Newmark and the other characters, recognize that they are an essential part of a larger whole. As a result, *Count Zero* remains open-ended, at least thematically, leaving readers, as Csicsery-Ronay observes, " without a reference-system of meaning, a terminus: Virek is foiled, the voodoo spirits are victorious. But for what? Marly has an epiphany, but for what? The ecstasy of attainment vanishes like a dream" (83). Although Csicsery-Ronay regards the lack novel's thematic open-endedness as a failure on Gibson's part, one could just as easily argue that it is this very same open-endedness that makes the novel postmodern in the sense that it suggests that nothing can ever be fully known. In this regard, too, *Count Zero* resembles works like *The Crying of Lot 49*, where, in the end, Oedipa Maas is represented as being on the verge of learning the truth about the Tristero conspiracy but the truth itself is never conveyed.

GENDER AND AGENCY IN *COUNT ZERO*

The novel also addresses—and, to an extent, partakes in—the objectification of women. For example, it represents Angelina Mitchell as someone who is acted upon rather than acts, culminating in her becoming a simstim star at the end of the novel, that is, an actor whose very being is recorded, edited, and then made available for others to experience. She has virtually no agency in the novel, passing from her father's care to Turner's, and then to that of the Sense/Net corporation. Although much of the novel centers on her, she is essentially a static character, never fully emerging as a protagonist. Marly Krushkova, in contrast, demonstrates not only agency but initiative, resisting Josef Virek's efforts to control her and ultimately discovering the source of the mysteries centering on the Cornell boxes and Angelina. As Gibson himself indicates, unlike the other characters who are guided either directly or indirectly by the *loa*, Krushkhova "goes to the heart of it ... through her own intellectual capacity and her ability to understand art" (Wershler-Henry Interview). In this she anticipates Cayce Pollard, the protagonist of *Pattern Recognition*, the critical difference being that while the knowledge Krushkhova attains remains essentially private, Pollard's discoveries bring an almost absolute closure to *Pattern Recognition*, resolving it not only thematically but structurally.

*See also* Cyberspace; Gender; Hackers; Literary Influences; Mitchell, Angelina; *Mona Lisa Overdrive*; *Neuromancer*; Newmark, Bobby; *The Sprawl Trilogy*

• *References and further reading*

Bukatman, Scott. *Terminal Identity: The Virtual Subject in Postmodern Science Fiction*. Durham: Duke University Press, 1993. Print.

Cavallaro, Dani. *Cyberpunk and Cyberculture: Science Fiction and the Work of William Gibson*. Athlone Press, 2000. Print.

Childers, Joseph, et al. "White Men Can't ... (De)centering Authority and Jacking into Phallic Economies in William Gibson's *Count Zero*." *Science Fiction, Canonization, Marginalization, and the Academy*. Ed. Gary Westfahl and George Slusser. Westport, CT: Greenwood, 2002. Print.

Csicery-Ronay, Istvan. "Antimancer: Cybernetics and Art in Gibson's *Count Zero*." *Science Fiction Studies* 22 (1995): 63–86. Print.

Gibson, William. *Count Zero*. New York: Ace, 1987. Print.

_____. *Mona Lisa Overdrive*. New York: Spectra, 1997. Print.

_____. *Neuromancer*. New York: Ace, 1984. Print.

Olsen, Lance. *William Gibson*. Mercer, WA: Starmount House, 1992. Print.

Hammett, Dashiell. *The Maltese Falcon*. New York: Alfred A. Knopf, 1930. Print.

Rapatzikou, Tatiani G. *Gothic Motifs in the Fiction of William Gibson*. Amsterdam: Rodopi, 2004. Print.

Schroeder, Randy. "Neu-Criticizing William Gibson." *Extrapolation: A Journal of Science Fiction and Fantasy* 35.4 (1994): 330–341. Print.

Sponsler, Claire. "Cyberpunk and the Dilemmas of Postmodern Narrative: The Example of William Gibson." *Contemporary Literature* 33.4 (1992): 625–644. Print.

## Counterculture

As a teenager in the 1960s Gibson was very much affected by the counterculture even though he was not a political activist and did not identify as a hippie, as a member of the drug culture, or as part of the *avant-garde*. Indeed, Gibson, who was born in 1948 and therefore already nineteen during the 1967 "Summer of Love," seemed to be more attuned to the desperate existentialism of Beat culture than to the idealism and spirituality of the hippies. Certainly the Beats had more of an intellectual influence on him than the counterculture that emerged in the late 1960s, and Gibson lists William S. Burroughs, Jack Kerouac, and Alan Ginsberg as important early influences ("Since 1948"). Apparently the sensibilities he developed as an early teen while reading the Beats allowed him to retain a certain distance from the counterculture even as he participated in it.

Gibson reports first encountering the Beats through an anthology he "surreptitiously" purchased at age thirteen, knowing that his "mother wouldn't approve" ("God's Little Toys"). To Gibson, who was living in his grandmother's home in a small town in the Blue Ridge highlands of southwest Virginia, the Beats came to represent a viable alternative to the closed, insular world in which he was living (Barker Interview). As a result, when he was sent to boarding school in Arizona several years later, he was at attuned to the restlessness and discontent that marked the emerging counterculture, describing himself as "Patient Zero" ("Since 1948"). Following his mother's death during his senior year in high school, Gibson, who was reading Kerouac at the time, left school without graduating, returning to Wytheville briefly and then beginning his own life on the road. He spent the Summer of Love in the Yorkville neighborhood of Toronto, which was then a local equivalent of Haight-Ashbury.

Oddly enough, Gibson can be seen posing as a hippie in a documentary filmed at the time — *Yorkville: Hippie Haven*. Apparently, he lied to the producers, telling them he was from Vancouver, and then used the $500 he was paid to get "his ass out of Yorkville" (blog 5/01/2003). As this episode suggests, Gibson's attitude towards the 1960s counterculture was complicated if not paradoxical: he was "thoroughly fed up" with what he later called "the Children's Crusade" even though he was a participant in it. His attitude toward Woodstock, which he attended, suggests the same thing: "It was extraordinarily uncomfortable. I left early and thought, 'That was like a Civil War battle.' I was up all night, got no sleep, was covered in mud, and getting back to D.C., where I lived at the time, was this epic, horrible experience.... The next morning I saw these headlines: 'Woodstock, it was so beautiful!' 'We're so lucky to have been there!' I remember having this total disconnect moment. I'm sure there were people who went who had a pleasant time, but there were also people who bought the headline, because they really wanted to buy the headline" (Holman Interview). As the above statement indicates, Gibson was at once drawn to hippie culture and repelled by it, and he was certainly no idealist or revolutionary, commenting that he "sort of wandered through" the 1960s, "mainly thinking, wow that was a good breakfast or she's got a great ass" rather than about the historical events that were taking place. "You're not thinking, oh it's the morning of the moratorium" (Deuben Interview). Gibson continued his itinerant lifestyle into the early 1970s, working sporadically and drawing money from his mother's estate to travel in the United States and Europe. Finally in 1972 he married and settled in Vancouver so that his partner, Deborah Jean Thompson, could pursue her education. Gibson later commented, "Only when I got together with Deb did I get a life," his words offering implicit commentary on what the counterculture had become by the early 1970s (Zuckerman).

Not surprisingly perhaps given that most of his stories and novels are set in the future, Gibson's 1960s experiences rarely figure in his work in obvious ways, the exceptions being two relatively unknown short stories, "Hippie Hat Brain Paradise" and "Dougal Discarnate." Both stories address 1960s drug culture, focusing on the damaging effects of LSD. Although "Hippie Hat Brain Parasite" could easily be dismissed as non-serious, "Dougal Discarnate" is significant because Gibson explores his own changing attitudes toward the drug culture in an extended way. Set in the Vancouver neighborhood where Gibson himself lives, the story is at least semi-autobiographical, the narrator being a science fiction writer who, as he begins his career, befriends the *ka* of a person he knew ten years earlier, Dougal Discarnate, whose soul had become disembodied while on an acid trip. On one level the story serves as an indictment of drug culture and the damage it does to people like Dougal who lose touch with reality and never become productive members of society: on another level, however, the story conveys a sense of the loss Gibson feels about the life he left behind, a life where he simply existed without being compelled to produce.

Although Gibson's personal experiences of 1960s counterculture rarely surface in his work, much of his political thinking appears to have been shaped by it, most obviously in the way he conceives of the social and political function of countercultures as alternative spaces from which resistance can be effected. In *Neuromancer* and his other early novels and stories set in the Sprawl, what he terms "the street" functions as a counterculture of sorts, the street being the a lawless, largely-unsurveilled space outside of official culture where people had a larger measure of control over their lives. It is from within this space that characters like Henry Case, Molly Millions, and Bobby Newmark are able to operate, challenging a social order dominated by multinational corporations and the very rich. In *The Bridge Trilogy* the role of countercultures is even more pronounced, becoming a subject in its own right. In *Virtual Light* the San Francisco–Oakland Bay Bridge is presented as an "interstice," that is, as a space within the social structure that can serve as a site of resistance. Although just as gritty and dangerous as "the street" of his earlier works, the Bridge has a positive sense of community, as becomes evident in *All Tomorrow's Parties* when the thousands of squatters living on it come together as it is attacked by Cody Harwood's agents, Harwood having deemed the Bridge community, with its "queer medieval energy," to be a threat to the social order he hopes to dominate. *The Bridge Trilogy* also features virtual interstices—the Republic of Desire in *Virtual Light* and the Walled City in *Idoru* and *All Tomorrow's Parties*—points within the Net from which the dominant order can be resisted. At the end of the *Trilogy*, Harwood's efforts to shape the future around his own interests are thwarted when operatives from various interstices work together, countering his efforts on every level. Arguably the collective action taken by various communities in *The Bridge Trilogy* reflects what happened in the late 1960s and early '70s as diverse interest groups came together in opposition to the Vietnam War.

Gibson's optimism about the potential to resist domination through the formation of a counterculture persists through the first volume of *The Bigend Trilogy*, *Pattern Recognition*, where Cayce Pollard defies media-magnate Hubertus Bigend's will by allying with other "footageheads," that is, the virtual community that develops around mysterious film clips that are posted anonymously on the Net. By the second volume, however, *Spook Country*, his optimism appears to dissipate as the post–9/11 new world order establishes itself: Hollis Henry's efforts to resist Bigend's will are reduced to a gesture, Henry arranging for a holographic image of a giant Mongolian Death Worm to be projected atop Bigend's headquarters. The potential subversiveness of her action is undercut by the fact that the projection can only be seen by those who know it is there and have the proper equipment to detect it. In *Zero History*, a novel set in the present and arguably the darkest of all Gibson's work, even gestures of resistance have become impossible as interstices themselves disappear and people like Bigend obtain unprecedented power. As professional prankster Garreth Wilson concedes, the time for "Surrealist gestes" and other "tricks" are "over" (261).

As the dark ending of *Zero History* suggests, by 2010 the idealism of 1960s counterculture has finally dissipated completely, giving way to despair of a hopeless present, an attitude fueled at least in part by the worldwide economic crisis that began in 2008. Even the hope Gibson apparently found in the election of Barack Obama seems to be gone, Wilson suggesting that instead of real change, the new administration has instead brought "more free-floating ambiguity" (293). Although Gibson never fully invested in the hopeful idealism of 1960s counterculture, until *Zero History* he always allowed for the possibility of a better future, one in which people had control over their own lives.

*See also All Tomorrow's Parties*; Bigend, Hubertus; *The Bridge Trilogy*; Dislocation; "Dougal Discarnate; "Hippie Hat Brain Parasite"; Literary Influences; Music; *Neuromancer*; Politics; *Spook Country*; *Virtual Light*; *Zero History*

• *References and further reading*
Bredehoft, Thomas. "The Gibson Continuum: Cyberspace and Gibson's Mervyn Kihn Stories." *Science Fiction Studies* 22.2 (1995): 252–63. Print.
Farnell, Ross. "Posthuman Topologies: William Gibson's 'Architexture' in *Virtual Light* and *Idoru*." *Science Fiction Studies* 26.3 (1998): 459–460. Print.
Gibson, William. *All Tomorrow's Parties*. New York: Berkley, 2003. Print.
_____. Dougal Discarnate." *Darwin's Bastards*. Ed. Gartner Zsuzsi. Vancouver: Douglas & McIntyre, 2010. 231–40. Print.
_____. "God's Little Toys." Wired.com, *Wired* 13.7 (2005). Web.
_____. "Hippie Hat Brain Parasite." *Modern Stories* (Apr. 1983). Print.
_____. *Idoru*. New York: Berkley, 1997. Print.
_____. *Neuromancer*. New York: Ace, 1984. Print.
_____. *Pattern Recognition*. New York: Berkley, 2005. Print.
_____. "Since 1948." *Source Code*. 6 Nov. 2002. Web.
_____. *Spook Country*. New York: Berkley, 2009. Print.
_____. "U2's City of Blinding Lights." *Wired.com Wired*, 2005. Web.
_____. *Zero History*. New York: Putnam, 2010. Print.
Olsen, Lance. *William Gibson*. Mercer, WA: Starmount House, 1992. Print.

Sanders, Leonard Patrick. *Postmodern Orientalism: William Gibson, Cyberpunk and Japan*. Doctoral Thesis. Massey University, 2008. Print.

## Cut Up

The cut-up technique is a method for incorporating non-linear elements into a text. As William Burroughs explains in "The Cut Up Method" (1963), the new can be assembled from the old through juxtaposition. In what he calls "the fold in method," for example, one text is folded across another creating a composite, which can then be "edited, re-arranged, and deleted as in any other form of composition." Texts can literally be cut up and rearranged as well, of course; the goal is to achieve spontaneity through accident. Burroughs goes on to assert that "all writing is in fact cut ups. A collage of words read heard overheard," and that everyone from filmmakers to military strategists find ways to incorporate the random into their work.

Gibson first encountered what Burroughs termed the "cut-up method" in the early 1960s in a beat anthology that included excerpts from Burroughs's *Naked Lunch* (1959), a novel that pioneered the technique. According to Gibson, "I had stumbled, in my ceaseless quest for more and/or better science fiction, on a writer named Burroughs— not Edgar Rice but William S., and with him had come his colleagues Kerouac and Ginsberg. I had read this stuff, or tried to, with no idea at all of what it might mean, and felt compelled — compelled to what, I didn't know." ("Since 1948"). He adds, "The effect, over the next few years, was to make me, at least in terms of my Virginia home, Patient Zero of what would later be called the counterculture." Burroughs's work influenced more than just Gibson's outlooks and behaviors; he incorporated elements of Burroughs's technique in works ranging from "The Gernsback Continuum" (1981), which incorporates elements of Golden Age science fiction into itself, to *Spook Country* (2007), in which he tries to see "what happens" when he "puts things together" (Blume Interview). As Gibson indicates in an early interview with Larry McCaffery, for him writing itself is a matter of "stitching together all the junk that's floating around in my head" (277).

"Academy Leader," which first appeared in Michael Benedikt's seminal *Cyberspace: First Steps* (1991), represents Gibson's most extensive use of the cut-up technique. In this piece, which is sometimes classified as an essay and sometimes as a story, Gibson not only argues that contiguity is essential to creativity but demonstrates it. Drawing from his own works as well as those of William Burroughs, Gibson creates a new text, juxtaposing passages so as to induce readers to participate in the meaning-making process. The effect is startling: though fragmented, the text somehow coheres into a whole, presenting a comprehensible statement about bricolage even though the parts do not fit together seamlessly.

*The Difference Engine* (1992), a book Gibson co-authored with Bruce Sterling, also makes extensive use of the cut-up technique, incorporating a number of Victorian texts into the novel. In an interview with *Science Fiction Studies*, Gibson identifies their method as "literary sampling," adding that he and Sterling "applied word-processing technology to a traditional process of plagiarism and did something really new" (Fischlin Interview). Commenting on the editing process that followed, Sterling said, "You can get quite extraordinary effects from using a piece of Victorian text verbatim and then deliberately forgetting where you got it and rewriting it four or five times" (Fischlin Interview). The book was well-received critically and commercially successful as well, helping to establish steampunk as a viable subgenre of science fiction. In his review of the book for the *New York*

*Times*, Thomas Disch, for example, finds the book highly original, writing that their collaborative effort "is even better than their earlier and considerable solo efforts."

Gibson is not just a practitioner of the technique but an advocate for it, arguing in "God's Little Toys: Confessions of a Cut and Paste Artist" (2005) that cut up involves simply claiming what is already ours, words (as well as art, music, and culture) belonging to all of us. As he suggests, what was once an *avant garde* technique has become the norm, cut up or sampling has become part of the popular aesthetic. Anticipating arguments that Lawrence Lessig makes at length in *Remix: Making Art and Commerce Thrive in a Hybrid Economy* (2008), Gibson writes: "We seldom legislate new technologies into being. They emerge, and we plunge with them into whatever vortices of change they generate. We legislate after the fact, in a perpetual game of catch-up, as best we can, while our new technologies redefine us—as surely and perhaps as terribly as we've been redefined by broadcast television." In his view, "there is little doubt as to the direction things are going"—like information, art wants to be free.

When it comes to intellectual property that he might very well claim as his own, Gibson's conduct is consistent with his artistic principles. Although he jokes occasionally about being "the unpaid Bill" because so many of his words and ideas have been incorporated into other people's work, Gibson rarely criticizes others for doing so, and he is not litigious (Telegraph Interview). This is not to suggest, however, that Gibson does not occasionally express dismay about the ways in which his work has been crassly commercialized. In an interview with Giuseppe Salza, for example, he observes that Billy Idol, whose 1993 *Cyberpunk* album included a track called "Neuromancer," has turned cyberpunk "into something very silly" and even gone so far as to caricature Idol in *Pattern Recognition*. In general, he seems to have a sense of humor about such things. For example, in order to protest the efforts of Autodesk to trademark the word "cyberspace," a word Gibson himself coined, Gibson applied for a trademark on the name "Eric Gullichsen," the owner of the company (Barlow).

*See also* "Academy Leader"; *The Difference Engine*; "The Gernsback Continuum"; Literary Influences

• *References and further reading*
Burroughs, William. "The Cut Up Method." *The Moderns: An Anthology of New Writing*. Ed. Leroi Jones. New York: Corinth Books, 1963. Print.
Gibson, William. "Academy Leader." *Cyberspace: First Steps*. Ed. Michael Benedikt. Cambridge: MIT Press, 1991: 27–29. Print.
_____. Foreword. *Multimedia: From Wagner to Virtual Reality*. Ed. Randall Packerl. New York: Norton, 2001. Print.
_____, and Bruce Sterling. *The Difference Engine*. New York: Bantam-Spectra, 1991. Print.

# Cyberpunk

Named for a short story by Bruce Bethke that was written in 1980 but not published until 1983 in *Amazing Stories*, "cyberpunk" was a movement within science fiction that, even though short-lived, had an impact on both literary and popular culture that still exists today. According to Bethke, the term originally referred to "the juxtaposition of punk attitudes and high technology," punk attitudes including a certain hostility towards both tradition and authority and a DIY (Do It Yourself) ethic. Although cyberpunk did not coalesce as a movement until the early 1980s, it was anticipated by works like William Burroughs's *Nova Trilogy*, Thomas Pynchon's *Gravity's Rainbow*, and Anthony Burgess's *A*

*Clockwork Orange*, all of these works focusing on "high tech and low life," to borrow Bruce Sterling's formulation. In 1984, Gardner Dozois, the influential editor of *Asimov's Science Fiction* magazine and a prize-winning author himself, used the term "cyberpunk" to describe the "bizarre, hard-edged, hi-tech" work of writers like Gibson, Lewis Shiner, Pat Cadigan, and Bruce Sterling. The "Movement," as it was then called, centered on Sterling, whose fanzine *Cheap Truth* excoriated "hard" science fiction writers like David Brin and Kim Stanley Robinson for writing books "Mom and Dad" would have liked while promoting edgier works "with real ideas and real sex and real language in them." With *Neuromancer* (1984), cyberpunk gained sudden prominence, the novel sweeping science fiction's major awards. As David Brin recalls, the science fiction community became polarized as the "Old Farts" were arrayed against the "young whippersnappers," the latter especially benefitting from the media attention the conflict generated: "Brilliantly managed, and backed by some works of estimable value, it [cyberpunk] snared and reeled in countless new readers, while opening fresh opportunities in Hollywood and the visual arts" (68). Literary critics also become increasingly interested in cyberpunk, particularly after Fredric Jameson referred to it as "the supreme literary expression if not of postmodernism, then of late capitalism itself" (Jameson 1991, 491n.). Following Jameson's lead, Claire Sponsler, for example, declared cyberpunk to be "in many ways quintessentially postmodern, noting that it "typically presents a montage of surface images, cultural artifacts, an decentered subjects moving through a shattered, affectless landscape" (627).

Ironically, even though Gibson was (and still is) widely regarded as cyberpunk's leading writer, he began disowning it as early as 1986, commenting in an interview with Larry McCaffery that it was "mainly a marketing strategy — and one that I've come to feel trivializes what I do" (79). He adds: "I'm tired of the whole cyberpunk phenomenon. I mean, there's already *bad imitation cyberpunk*, so you know it can only go downhill from here" (79). For Gibson, part of the problem was that as he became a more accomplished writer, he came to regard the flat characterization that was supposedly so postmodern as a deficiency. When asked about the "vivid yet disorienting sense of place and stunning, cutting-edge technology" featured in *Neuromancer*, Gibson replied simply that he "didn't have the skill to make the characters convincing,'" and so he had to shift focus to other elements such as settings, technology, and plot (Grimwood Interview). Gibson was also apparently troubled by the fact that what had once been an artistic movement had become a pose or fashion statement, something epitomized for Gibson by Billy Idol, who, in 1993 released an album entitled *Cyberpunk*: in a 1994 interview Gibson noted that Idol had turned cyberpunk "into something very silly," and in *Pattern Recognition* he based a ridiculous character on Idol, sneer and all (Salza Interview). He was much more impressed with *The Matrix*, which he reported enjoying even though it was "totally cyberpunk," complete with "skin-tight alligator vinyl cat suits and stuff" (Linnemann Interview). To him, the film "completed the arc of cyberpunk," meaning that "any bigger, shinier, more cyberpunk-flavored piece of pop" would necessarily be "post-cyberpunk" or "neo-cyberpunk" since cyberpunk's moment has passed. In his blog he concedes that, in a sense, cyberpunk will never "be any more 'over' than punk, or the hardboiled detective story. These things are modalities of some kind, and become part of the cultural palette" (blog 9/01/003).

*See also* "Burning Chrome"; "Johnny Mnemonic"; Music; Neuromancer; "The New Rose Hotel"; The Sprawl Trilogy

- *References and further reading*

Brand, David. "The Business of Cyberpunk: Symbolic Economy and Ideology in William Gibson." *Virtual Realities and their Discontents.* Ed. Robert Markley. Baltimore: Johns Hopkins University Press, 1996. 79–106.

Brin, David. *Through Stranger Eyes: Reviews, Introductions, Tributes & Iconoclastic Essays.* Ann Arbor, MI: Nimble Books, 2008. Print.

Cavallaro, Dani. *Cyberpunk and Cyberculture: Science Fiction and the Work of William Gibson.* Athlone Press, 2000. Print.

Delany, Samuel R. "Is Cyberpunk a Good Thing or a Bad Thing?" *Mississippi Review* 16.2–3 (1988): 28–35. Print.

Easterbrook, Neil. "Alternate Presents: The Ambivalent Historicism of *Pattern Recognition*." *Science Fiction Studies* 33 (2006): 483–503. Print.

Gibson, William. "Burning Chrome." *Burning Chrome.* New York: Ace, 1986. Print.

_____. *Count Zero.* New York: Ace, 1987. Print.

_____. "Johnny Mnemonic." *Burning Chrome.* New York: Ace, 1986. Print.

_____. *Mona Lisa Overdrive.* New York: Bantam Spectra, 1989. Print.

_____. "The New Rose Hotel." *Burning Chrome.* New York: Ace 1986. Print.

_____. *Neuromancer.* New York: Ace, 1984. Print.

Jameson, Fredric. *Postmodernism, or, the Logic of Late Capitalism.* Durham: Duke University Press, 1991. Print.

Ketterer, David. "William Gibson, *Neuromancer*, and Cyberpunk." *Canadian Science Fiction and Fantasy.* Ed. David Ketterer. Bloomington: Indiana University Press, 1992. 140–46. Print.

Sponslor, Claire. "Cyberpunk and the Dilemmas of Postmodern Narrative: The Example of William Gibson." *Contemporary Literature.* 33.4 (1992): 625–644. Print.

Suvin, Darko. "On Gibson and Cyberpunk SF." *Foundation: The Review of Science Fiction* 46 (1989): 40–51. Print.

Wood, Brent. "William S. Burroughs and the Language of Cyberpunk." *Science Fiction Studies* 23 (1996): 11–26. Print.

## Cyberspace

According to the *Oxford English Dictionary*, the term "cyberspace" was introduced into the English language in "Burning Chrome," a short story by Gibson first published in *Omni* in 1982. In *Neuromancer* (1984), Gibson uses the term extensively to refer to the "nonspace" or "void" containing the "matrix," which is itself described as a "graphic representation of data abstracted from the banks of every computer in the human system" (51). Although Gibson generally differentiates between the two concepts, he sometimes uses them in conjunction, as in "cyberspace matrix," and sometimes uses them interchangeably (55). Gibson's representation of cyberspace is frequently credited with having influenced the ways in which virtual domains developed, and by the 1990s the term "cyberspace" had entered the popular lexicon, becoming widely "accepted as the colloquial equivalent for the Internet or World Wide Web, especially among the Internet community," as Sabine Heuser notes.

In "Burning Chrome" Gibson presents cyberspace as a virtual place that provides a setting for the story's action as Bobby Quine and Automatic Jack raid the database of a local crime figure named Chrome and access her financial accounts electronically. In *The Sprawl Trilogy*, however, the cyberspace matrix becomes a character itself, albeit an unorthodox one, attaining sentience when two artificial intelligences merge to become a super-being, a story that is related in *Neuromancer*. In *Count Zero* we learn that, upon becoming aware of another matrix based in the Alpha Centauri system, cyberspace fragments, and the novel goes on to relate how its parts, which presents themselves as *loa* drawn from the Vodou tradition, induce Christopher Mitchell to develop biochip technology that would allow people to enter into cyberspace directly. Christopher grafts these biochips into his daughter, Angelina, so that her mind can be used as a template of sorts, providing the structure that the cyberspace matrix needs in order to reconstitute itself. *Mona Lisa Overdrive* continues the story of cyberspace, relating how the super-being reunifies itself once Mitchell's personality is incorporated into the matrix; the *Trilogy* ends with the reconstituted super-being poised to contact the "other" matrix based in Alpha Centauri.

## REPRESENTING CYBERSPACE

In *The Sprawl Trilogy*, Gibson presents cyberspace in paradoxical terms: even though it is a "nonspace," one nonetheless enters it, "jacking in," and moves within it in various directions at various speeds. The seeming contradiction is resolved by the fact that cyberspace is not an actual place but a "consensual hallucination," a conventionalized way of perceiving virtual domains. The matrix, too, is described as a consensual hallucination, data being represented by shape, color, and motion. One can navigate the matrix by moving through it or can "punch" directly to a particular location by entering its coordinates.

Gibson frequently uses figurative language to depict cyberspace, describing it in terms of physical spaces, DNA, Vodou, and even sexual intercourse. In addition to conveying immediate information at various points throughout the story, such figures contribute to a rhetorical matrix that collectively gives the concept semantic structure, a process Sabine Heuser describes in detail in *Virtual Geographies: Cyberpunk at the Intersection of the Postmodern and Science Fiction*. As she demonstrates, Cyberspace is defined over the course of the novel in interrelated ways, making it possible for readers to process the novel's climactic scene — the "Straylight run" in which Henry Case and McCoy Pauley raid the Tessier-Ashpool system — as if it were construed in concrete terms, generating a sense of immediacy that makes the narrative more compelling.

## THE INFLUENCE OF GIBSONIAN CYBERSPACE

Gibson's representation of cyberspace appears to have been instrumental in the development of conceptual infrastructure for virtual domains, as evidenced by *Cyberspace: First Steps* (1991), a seminal collection of essays edited by Michael Benedikt in which many of the articles reference Gibson. Gibson himself reports that in the late 1980s and early '90s, researchers working on virtual reality would distribute copies of *Neuromancer* to explain to people what cyberspace is, saying, "Read this. It's sort of like this" (Murray Interview). This is not to suggest researchers used Gibson's representation of cyberspace as a blueprint of sorts. Gibson did, however, provide researchers with a means of imagining virtual domains and communicating their ideas about them to others. As influential as Gibson's representation of cyberspace was, it is important to note that Gibson himself was influenced by existing graphic interfaces, including those found in arcade games, and virtual reality technologies being developed in the early 1980s. Indeed, Gibson himself insists that he had only a "minor" influence on how virtual domains developed, adding, "What has emerged in the world today doesn't have very much to do with what I was thinking of in the '80s at all, except in some organic way" (Murray Interview).

One could also argue that in presenting virtual domains as "spaces" or "places," Gibson's work has been instrumental in the commercialization of cyberspace to the extent that it has been developed as private property or real estate. Certainly the popularization of the term "cyberspace" in the 1990s coincided, at least loosely, with the dot.com boom, a period that included the privatization of the Internet and an increasing corporate presence online. Ironically, as the dystopian atmosphere of *The Sprawl Trilogy* suggests, Gibson seems to be implicitly critical of commercialization of virtual domains, an attitude he confirms in interviews (Josefsson Interview).

In philosophical terms, cyberspace, like many imagined spaces, has a utopian function, providing a means of rethinking social relationships. According to Wendy Chun, cyberspace can be regarded as a heterotopia, what Michel Foucault describes as "an effectively enacted utopia in which the real sites, all the other real sites that can be found within a culture, are simultaneously represented, contested, and inverted." In Chun's terms, cyberspace "others" real space, problematizing it, as it were (52). In particular *The Sprawl Trilogy* addresses issues such as globalization, permanent underclasses, sexual exploitation, and the digital divide, through its representation of cyberspace. The novels also address more esoteric matters such as abjection, alienation, and dislocation.

Although Gibson introduced the term "cyberspace," he is not the first writer to address it as a concept in his fiction. In "The Machine Stops" (1909), for example, E.M. Forster writes of "an accelerated" age in which physical space has been "annihilated" in favor of virtual space as defined by the Machine running the entire world, and in *Gravity's Rainbow*, Thomas Pynchon describes a "Grid" that seems to anticipate Gibson's "matrix" in some ways (Stonehill). Virtual spaces have also been featured in speculative fiction that preceded "Burning Chrome," including John Brunner's *The Shockwave Rider* (1975) and Octavia Butler's *Patternmaster* series, which began in 1976. Gibson himself said that "there were all sorts of pre-cursors in science fiction to what I did with cyberspace and for some reason people just don't recognize them. I mean everything from [Harlan] Ellison's 'I have No Mouth and I Must Scream' to [Vernor] Vinge's 'True Names.' ... When I started doing those early cyberspace stories, I remember thinking, 'This is kind of cool, but it's just too obvious.' This simply isn't going to amaze people. This idea has been around in larval form in a lot of other stories" (Van Belkom Interview). In a more recent interview he again asserts that his representation of cyberspace is "not that original," indicating that it as "some kind of McLuhanesque post–Orwellian television universe" (Rapatzikou Interview).

    *See also* "Burning Chrome"; *Count Zero*; Hackers; *Mona Lisa Overdrive*; *Neuromancer*; *The Sprawl Trilogy*

• *References and further reading*

Bukatman, Scott. *Terminal Identity: The Virtual Subject in Postmodern Science Fiction*. Durham: Duke University Press, 1993. Print.
Chun, Wendy. *Control and Freedom: Power and Paranoia in the Age of Fiber Optics*. Cambridge: MIT Press, 2006. Print.
Gibson, William. "Burning Chrome." *Burning Chrome*. New York: Ace, 1986. Print.
_____. *Count Zero*. New York: Ace, 1987. Print.
_____. *Mona Lisa Overdrive*. New York: Bantam Spectra, 1989. Print.
_____. *Neuromancer*. New York: Ace, 1984. Print.
Gozzi, Raymond. "The Cyberspace Metaphor." *ETC.: A Review of General Semantics* 51 (1994): 218–223. Print.
Hayles, N. Katherine. "How Cyberspace Signifies: Taking Immortality Literally." *Immortal Engines: Life Extension and Immortality in Science Fiction and Fantasy*. Ed. George Slusser, Gary Westfahl, and Eric S. Rabkin. Athens: University of Georgia Press, 1996. 111–21. Print.
Heuser, Sabine. *Virtual Geographies: Cyberpunk at the Intersection of the Postmodern*. New York: Rodopi, 2003. Print.
Lyon, David. "Cyberspace: Beyond the Information Society?" *Living with Cyberspace: Technology and Society in the 21st Century*. Ed. John Armitage and Joanne Roberts. New York: Continuum, 2002. 21–33. Print.
Markley, Robert. "Boundaries: Mathematics, Alienation, and the Metaphysics of Cyberspace." *Virtual Real-

*ities and Their Discontents.* Ed. Robert Markley. Baltimore: Johns Hopkins University Press, 1996. 55–77. Print.

## "Darwin"

Appearing in *Spin* magazine in April, 1990, "Darwin" is one of Gibson's darkest works in the sense that it presents the near future as essentially hopeless, not just for the story's young protagonist, Kelsey, but for everyone. At just a thousand words, the story offers a surprisingly comprehensive picture of a world that is dying through the careful selection and presentation of detail. The entire story takes place in a hotel room in Los Angeles where Kelsey and her brother, Trev, await the return of their mother from work. While Trev immerses himself in their virtual reality entertainment system, Kelsey, who is almost nine, looks out the hotel window. A denizen of a world where not just experience but life itself is mediated through technology (she is a product of *in vitro* fertilization), she has an epiphany, recognizing the world she lives in for what it is for the first time. From the window she can see the homeless trying to shield themselves from the UV radiation, dead palm trees, the brown air, and the police helicopters circling the city. Suddenly frightened, she "wills her mother's return" from work, wishing they were in Darwin, Australia, the next place her mother is to be sent on assignment. Global warming is the issue most obviously raised by the story, though it also addresses the emergence of multinational corporations as a new form of government and the increasing gap between rich and poor.

An earlier, shorter version of the story appeared in *The Face* in March, 1990 as "Doing Television," the title alluding to a phrase the narrator uses frequently in the story in reference to virtual reality entertainment systems that involve "doing" rather than just "watching." As he does in many of his works, Gibson seems to be suggesting that virtual worlds become increasingly attractive to people as the real world becomes less so.

• *References and further reading*
Gibson, William. "Darwin." *Spin*, Apr. 1990. Print.
\_\_\_\_\_. "Doing Television." *The Face*, Mar. 1990. Print.

## The Difference Engine

Co-authored by William Gibson and his friend, Bruce Sterling, *The Difference Engine* (1990) is a counterfactual novel that imagines how the world might be different had the computer revolution occurred near the beginning of the Victorian era rather than in the late twentieth century. Although generally identified by literary critics as an alternate history, *The Difference Engine* differs from novels like *The Man in the High Castle* (1962) and *For Want of a Nail* (1973) in that it incorporates fictional elements into itself as well as historical ones, for example basing Sybil Gerard on the title character of Benjamin Disraeli's *Sybil, or the Two Nations* (1845). Set primarily in London in the 1850s, the novel explores the ways in which advances in information technology transform not only the lives of individuals but also social institutions and class relationships.

In the alternative world that Gibson and Sterling create, the mechanical computers or "engines" designed by Charles Babbage in the early nineteenth century are put into immediate production by the British government. As a result a technocracy led by Lord Byron emerges, and the British Empire becomes even more powerful than it was, preventing the United States from emerging as an economic or military rival by playing the Union, the Confederacy, and the Texas and California Republics against one another. France also develops computers and becomes more powerful, preventing Germany from emerging as a nation-state and acquiring control of Mexico. Although Great Britain and France are not quite totalitarian states, their governments maintain records of people's activities, tracking them by number. Both nations also form domestic intelligence agencies to collect further information on both residents and visitors, and on some occasions people are made to "disappear," their very existences being expunged from official records in a manner reminiscent of George Orwell's *1984*.

As in Disraeli's novel, Sybil Gerard is the daughter of a prominent working-class activist who becomes romantically involved with Charles Egremont, the younger brother of a lord. Whereas in *Sybil, or the Two Nations*, Gerard and Egremont eventually marry, symbolizing the potential reconciliation of rich and poor, in *The Difference Engine* Egremont has betrayed Gerard, fathering a child with her and then marrying another. Living as a prostitute in London, she meets Mick Radley, another character based on one from *Sybil*, and becomes an "adventuress" under his tutelage. Radley, a publicist for Sam Houston, the deposed president of the Republic of Texas, has come into possession of the Modus program, written by Lady Ada Lovelace, Lord Byron's daughter. Although the program, is, in fact, a proof of Godel's theorem — that is, a proof that "any formal system must be both *incomplete* and unable to establish its own consistency"— it is highly sought after by criminals who believe that it will give them an advantage in gambling (421). Gerard takes possession of both the Modus and a fortune in diamonds after Radley is murdered by a Texas Ranger who has been sent to London to kill Houston and recover the valuables he has stolen from the Texas treasury. Relocating to France she gives the Modus to a hacker (termed "clacker" in the novel), who creates a new government identify for her in exchange. Towards the end of the novel we learn that the hacker has run the Modus program on the Grand Napoleon, France's greatest computer, establishing the fact that the "transfinite" can be achieved from the finite but destroying the Napoleon in the process. Years later Gerard meets Lady Ada, who comes to France to deliver a lecture on how the success of the Modus program implies that a sufficiently powerful computer employing a "transcendent meta-system of calculatory mathematics" could achieve self-awareness, becoming, in effect, sentient (421). Although Gerard understands little of Lady Ada's lecture, she presents her with one of the stolen diamonds, apparently in tribute to her as an adventuress, that is, as a woman who defies Victorian norms, living on her own terms.

Another narrative narrative — or "iteration," as they are termed in the novel, iteration being a programming term —centers on Edward Mallory, a paleontologist, who is given a copy of the Modus for safe-keeping by Lady Ada after two people try to take it from her at a racetrack. Seemingly the sort of stalwart gentleman one might expect to be the protagonist in a Victorian novel, Mallory makes himself Lady Ada's "paladin," not only accepting her charge to keep the program but also defending her honor at every opportunity (216). He proves to be anything but a stereotypical Victorian hero, however, when he crosses London in the midst of a riot for "a drink" and then takes up with a prostitute, Hetty, his activities with her being described in the most explicit of terms (209). Following this encounter, which, as Gibson puts it, allows us to see Victorian society "with its clothes off," Mallory appears to be a different man, more the hero of a twentieth-century thriller than a gentleman scientist (Fischlin Interview). He uses both cunning and violence to cross London again, this time to confront Captain Swing, the man who not only attacked Lady Ada at the track but besmirched Mallory's family honor and instigated the riot. He helps capture Swing, a character based on novelist Wilkie Collins, and returns to the relatively sedate life of an honored scientist.

A third primary character, Laurence Oliphant, brings the stories of Sybil Gerard and Mallory together as he investigates the intrigue surrounding the Modus program on behalf of British intelligence. Oliphant, who is based on a real-life discovers the truth about Gerard and Charles Egremont, using the information to prevent the latter from succeeding Lord Byron as Prime Minister and transforming Great Britain into a totalitarian state. Oliphant, it seems, is motivated by guilt he feels for his earlier role in promoting a domestic intelligence agency that engages in "*unacknowledged* violence" against British subjects (380). Indeed, he is continually haunted by the notion of there being an "all seeing" Eye that not only surveils but also controls every facet of human existence (388). At the very end of the novel his fears are realized as the novel jumps forward to 1991 and London's great engine acquires self-awareness, becoming alive, just as Lady Ada has predicted it would (422).

## ITERATIONS AND PSEUDO-ITERATIONS

Perhaps the novel's most remarkable feature is the way its organization into "iterations" parallels the iteration process by which certain types of mathematical problems are solved. In such problems approximate solutions are derived by substituting into the original equation values drawn from earlier calculations; through the repeated use of algorithms, something digital computers are well suited to do because of their speed, a satisfactory solution can be zeroed in on, so to speak. According to Joseph Conte, the five iterations into which the novel is divided into can be understood as five iterations of the same problem, with the epilogue, titled "Modus: the Images Tables," representing "a final compiling of the program," one that leads to self-awareness (43). As Gibson puts it, the novel can be read as a computer performing a "self-iteration" as it "attempts to boot itself up" (Fischlin Interview). By structuring the novel in such a manner, Gibson and Sterling are, in a sense, able to put us as readers inside the program as it compiles: we zero in on the significance of what is happening in the narrative just as the Modus program does, arriving at an approximate solution of sorts. We also gain insight into how metamathematics works since while zeroing in on the narrative's meaning, we learn how zeroing in itself works.

The novel's structure can also be understood in literary terms as an example of what Gerard Genette might call the pseudo-iterative — that is, a singular event that is narrated repeatedly in different ways — thereby affording the reader a potentially richer understanding of that event. In the case of *The Difference Engine*, the event being narrated is the mathematical operation represented by the Modus program, which itself corresponds to the notoriously difficult proofs of Godel's incompleteness theorems. The novel's iterative structure provides the reader with a rich context for understanding what might initially be taken for an abstraction. Gibson and Sterling, of course, are not the first to use the pseudo-iterative to make the seemingly abstract tangible. William Faulkner, for example, employs the pseudo-iterative in *The Sound and the Fury* to express Southern angst by presenting a Southern family through various multiple points of view, and in *Dubliners* James Joyce uses a number of loosely-related stories to express what it is to be Irish under colonial rule.

SAMPLING, COLLAGE, AND PASTICHE

*The Difference Engine* is also marked by its use of what Gibson calls "literary sampling," describing the book as "an enormous collage of little pieces of forgotten Victorian textual material which we lifted from Victorian journalism, from Victorian pulp literature" (Fischlin Interview). He adds that he and Sterling then "bent it slightly," bringing out the "eerie blue notes" as Jimi Hendrix does in his version of "The Star-Spangled Banner." Although the novel is not a collage to the extent that Gibson and Sterling modify existing pieces rather than simply select and arrange them, it certainly employs the general concept, giving the novel an "intimate texture," to borrow Gibson's phrase. Nowhere is this more evident than in the Hettie sequence, that is, in the extended encounter that Mallory has with a prostitute. According to Gibson, this section of the book is drawn largely from *My Secret Life*, a 4,000 page work published anonymously in the late–nineteenth century that details the author's sexual encounters in explicit detail. By drawing directly from a Victorian-era text, Gibson and Sterling are able to convincingly depict a scene that challenges existing stereotypes about Victorian prudery. Gibson and Sterling also fold in texts such as a statement Laurence Oliphant made in a sound recording and whole passages from Mary Braddon's *Lady Audley's Secret* (1862). Indeed, Gibson reports, "Virtually all of the interior descriptions, the descriptions of furnishings, are simply descriptive sections lifted from Victorian literature" (Fischlin Interview).

STEAMPUNK

In many regards, *The Difference Engine* can be considered the quintessential steampunk novel, steampunk being a subgenre of science fiction that typically set in alternative versions of the Victorian age. Whereas most science fiction is set in a possible future, steampunk is generally set in a non-existent past and thus, almost by definition, functions as an alternate history or counterfactual. Although the subgenre is often marked by a fascination with the combination of low- and high-technology, such as the steam-powered automobiles and computers like those featured in *The Difference Engine*, like most literary forms it offers commentary, if only implicitly, upon the times in which it was written. K.W. Jeter's *Morlock Night* (1979), for example, one of the sub-genre's founding texts, aligns itself with the conservative ideology of its day even though it is set in London in 1892. In the case of *The Difference Engine*, Gibson and Sterling seem to be offering commentary on the dangers that technology presents in the hands of an increasingly authoritarian government: as Sterling confirms in an interview, the Lord Byron character was based on "Reagan, the Great Communicator, a Thing who goes out and gives speeches" and Lady Ada "is a Margaret Thatcher" (Fischlin Interview). They also use the sub-genre to explore some of the more general implications of the computer revolution by removing computing from its original context so that readers can get a more distant perspective on it.

*See also* Cut Up

• *References and further reading*

Conte, Joseph. "The Virtual Reader: Cybernetics and Technology in William Gibson and Bruce Sterling's *The Difference Engine*." *The Holodeck in the Garden: Science and Technology in Contemporary American Fiction*. Ed. Peter Freese and Charles B. Harris. London: Dalkey, 2004. 28–52. Print.

Disch, Thomas. "Queen Victoria's Computers." New York Times.com, *New York Times*, 10 Mar. 1991. Web.

Genette, Gérard. *Narrative Discourse Revisited*. Trans. Jane E. Lewin. Ithaca, NY: Cornell University Press, 1988. Print.

Gibson, William. *The Difference Engine.* With Bruce Sterling. New York: Bantam Spectra, 1991. Print.

Gunn, Eileen. "A Difference Dictionary." *Science Fiction Eye* (1991): 40–53. Print.

Hellekson, Karen. "Looking Forward: William Gibson and Bruce Sterling's *The Difference Engine.*" *The Alternate History: Refiguring Historical Time.* Ed. Karen Hellekson. Kent, OH: Kent State University Press, 2001. 76–86. Print.

McHale, Brian. "Difference Engines." *ANQ: A Quarterly Journal of Short Articles, Notes, and Reviews* 5.4 (1992): 220–23. Print.

Spencer, Nicholas. "Rethinking Ambivalence: Technopolitics and the Luddites in William Gibson and Bruce Sterling's *The Difference Engine.*" *Contemporary Literature* 40 (1999): 403–29. Print.

Sussman, Herbert. "Cyberpunk Meets Charles Babbage: *The Difference Engine* as Alternative Victorian History." *Victorian Studies: A Journal of the Humanities, Arts and Sciences* 38.1 (1994): 1–23. Print.

## Dislocation

   Dislocation emerges as a prominent theme in much of Gibson's fiction, beginning with his very first short story, "Fragments of a Hologram Rose" (1977), which he wrote as an undergraduate at the University of British Columbia. To him, dislocation is a given, part of the human condition: his characters live fractured lives, largely because of social forces that are beyond their control. His narratives often center around the efforts of his characters to integrate themselves into larger society, something that generally proves impossible; thus dislocation is a product of modernity itself. His characters generally do manage to enter into meaningful relationships with others, however, somewhat mitigating their sense of alienation.

   That Gibson should so frequently address dislocation as a theme should not be surprising, given that he had little stability in his own life as a child. Born near Myrtle Beach where his family frequently vacationed, Gibson moved frequently as a young child since his father was assigned to construction sites throughout the South. His family finally settled in Norfolk, Virginia when Gibson was of school age. His life was soon disrupted by his father's sudden death by choking in a restaurant. Traumatized, his mother returned to Wytheville, Virginia, the small Appalachian town where she had grown up, to live with her mother. To Gibson, the sense of dislocation he felt because of the move was formative: he reports "feeling abruptly exiled ... to what seemed like the past" ("Since 1948"). Another time he comments that that he was "raised by Edwardians," that his grandmother was someone who "couldn't conceivably understand the world today," someone who referred to the Civil War as "the Northern Invasion" (Murray Interview). Gibson experienced dislocation again in his mid-teens when he was sent to boarding school in Arizona, beginning an existence there that was highly-structured and highly social. When his mother died, he left school, returning to Wytheville briefly before beginning an itinerant life, moving back and forth between the United States and Canada.

   It is not just sudden moves to very different places and the loss of both parents that gave Gibson a strong sense of dislocation: as an American teenager in the 1960s, he was part of a generation that came to see itself as being out-of-place. Unlike many of his contemporaries, Gibson never fully identified with the counterculture he participated in or thought of himself as part of a larger movement. He describes himself as just having "wandered though" the events of the late–1960s, adding that when "you're wandering through you're mainly thinking, wow that was a good breakfast or she's got a great ass" (Deuben Interview). Though he realized change was happening all around him, he never regarded himself as a "pivotal player" in it. His sense of dislocation was augmented by the fact that, since 1972 he lived in Canada as an exile of sorts, having left the United States initially so as to avoid the draft, at least ostensibly. Although appreciative of Canadian culture and society, he indicates that even after more than thirty years, he still doesn't "quite feel" Canadian, though he does not feel American either (Van Belkom Interview).

Having felt like an outsider himself for most of his life, Gibson was able to draw upon his own experiences of dislocation when he began writing fiction, his early works featuring not only back stories in which society is fractured by technological change, reorganization of the social order, and war but characters who themselves suffer great personal loss. *Neuromancer*, for example, is set in a post–World War III world in which the United States seems to no longer exist, corporations are largely unchecked, and new technologies have transformed everyday life. Henry Case, a console cowboy who can no longer enter cyberspace because of nerve damage induced by an employer he stole from, develops a "death wish" because of his abjection, a condition only exacerbated by the loss of Linda Lee, a woman he has come to love while living on the street. When presented with an opportunity to get his nerve damage repaired in exchange for doing a dangerous, highly-illegal cyberspace run, he takes it, even though doing so puts not only himself but humanity itself at risk since the run is intended to unite two artificial intelligences into a being that is entirely independent of its human makers. Ironically, in completing what can only be considered an anti-social mission, Case becomes a social being again, largely because of the relationship he develops with Molly Millions, another dislocated person. Once he heals both physically and mentally, he integrates himself back into society, finding both "work" and "a girl" and living happily ever after. In the novels that follow, the general pattern repeats itself, although the details vary greatly as characters who have been dislocated by forces much larger and more powerful than themselves attempt to re-enter society. Though his protagonists do not always succeed in this, the effort itself give shape and meaning to their lives, making their existences worthwhile, and most form important social connections, if only with one other person.

Familial dislocation is also a theme that runs through virtually all Gibson's work, beginning with the Tessier-Ashpool family. Marie-France Tessier and John Harness Ashpool, the founders of this family, use cryogenics to effectively abandon their children, only awakening themselves when they are needed for corporate business. Much of *The Sprawl Trilogy* focuses on story of 3Jane, a clone of one of the original Tessier-Ashpool children who is unable to make a meaningful life for herself without a real family and thus goes insane. She is not the only dislocated child to be featured in the *Trilogy*, of course: In *Count Zero*, Angelina Mitchell is quickly orphaned and Bobby Newmark presumes himself to be so after his mother's apartment is destroyed; when the two merge themselves into the fabric of the matrix towards the end of *Mona Lisa Overdrive*, effectively "marrying," they not only end their own sense of dislocation but resolve the *Trilogy*'s larger narrative as their merging enables the matrix itself to become whole again.

*See also Count Zero*; Counterculture; *Mona Lisa Overdrive*; *Neuromancer*; Tessier-Ashpool

• *References and further readings*

Gibson, William. *Count Zero*. New York: Ace, 1987. Print.
_____. *Mona Lisa Overdrive*. New York: Bantam Spectra, 1989. Print.
_____. *Neuromancer*. New York: Ace, 1984. Print.
_____. "Since 1948." *Source Code,* 6 Nov. 2002. Web.

## "Dougal Discarnate"

"Dougal Discarnate" (2010) is an unusual story for Gibson in that he makes himself a character in it. Written for Zsuzsi Gartner's anthology, *Darwin's Bastards*, "Dougal Discarnate" is set in the Kitsilano neighborhood of Vancouver where Gibson resides. The story concerns a man named Dougal whose mind becomes disembodied during an acid trip in 1972 while his body goes on to become an accountant. About ten years later, Dougal, who can only be seen or heard by people in the most extraordinary of circumstances, meets the narrator, a 33-year-old man, who is beginning to write fiction. The two become friends until Dougal, who until then has been limited to the Kitsilano neighborhood, becomes involved with a visiting Shaman who claims him as hers and makes him a familiar, taking him with her back to Okinawa.

Gibson identifies himself as the narrator concretely by having the latter refer directly to one of his own writings as "The New Rose Hotel," the name of one of Gibson's stories. As a result, the story can be read as semi-autobiographical, and the narrator's attitudes can be taken as Gibson's own. Certainly the narrator's opinion on utopias and dystopias resembles Gibson's, the narrator asserting that "one person's dystopia is another's hot immigration opportunity," meaning that what constitutes a dystopia is largely a matter of perspective. The story ends abruptly with the narrator reporting an email from Dougal, who indicates that he has found some measure of happiness with the Shaman, and he thought the film *Johnny Mnemonic* "had its moments" (241). In all, "Dougal Discarnate" is more of a sketch than a short story, albeit an interesting one because of its autobiographical elements. In particular, it suggests that after marrying, beginning a family, and becoming a writer in the 1970s, Gibson entered into a different kind of existence, one that involved distancing himself from the person he once was, a person like Dougal.

*See also* Counterculture; Dystopia; "Hippie Hat Brain Parasite"; Uncollected Stories

• *References and further reading*
Gibson, William. *Count Zero*. New York: Ace, 1987.
_____. "Fragments of a Hologram Rose." *Burning Chrome*. New York: Ace, 1986.
_____. *Mona Lisa Overdrive*. New York: Bantam Spectra, 1989. Print.
_____. *Neuromancer*. New York: Ace, 1984. Print.

## Dystopia

Although many people regard Gibson's work as dystopian, Gibson insists that it is not. As someone who grew up in a period where nuclear annihilation was considered to be not just possible but likely, he considers the work he wrote during the Cold War to be "wildly optimistic," the message being, "Hey, look—you do have a future. It's kind of harsh, but here it is" (Leonard Interview). Although conditions might be difficult for the large number of people who exist in what he calls "the street" in *The Sprawl Trilogy*, people still have a measure of freedom and control over their lives. The same is true in *The Bridge Trilogy* and the first two volumes of *The Bigend Trilogy*: conditions are difficult but remain tolerable, at least in the places Gibson depicts, and people still have agency. Gibson's most recent novel, *Zero History*, is arguably dystopian in the sense that it ends with humans on the verge of losing agency and therefore any hope for control of their lives. The novel is not a dystopia in the strict sense of the term, however, since the loss of agency is suggested rather than realized in the text.

As Claire Sponsler notes, the world the Sprawl sequence is set in is bleak, "one in which multinational corporations control global economies, urban blight has devoured the coun-tryside, crime and violence are inescapable events of urban life, and technology has shaped new modes of consciousness and behavior" (626). It is not a dystopia, however, since it is "a recognizable, near-future permutation of our own world" rather than a fully-real-ized alternative world that offers a space for rethinking existing social institutions and rela-tions. Moreover, many of the characters in the Sprawl sequence still possess agency, and resistance to the social order is possible, as evidenced by the actions of Henry Case, Molly Millions, Bobby Newmark, and others. Indeed, with the exception of "New Rose Hotel," the Sprawl sequence is comprised of narratives about successful resistance to authority since the protagonists generally succeed in beating the system, as it were.

The fictive world in which *The Bridge Trilogy* is bleak as well but not necessarily dystopian. Although many people's lives are difficult, the division between "haves" and "have nots" having grown, as evidenced by the San Francisco–Oakland Bay Bridge becom-ing a squatters' community, the novels' protagonists still have a large measure of control over their lives, and resistance is still possible from interstices such as the Bridge itself and virtual communities such as the Republic of Desire and the Walled City. Indeed, the final volume of the *Trilogy*, *All Tomorrow's Parties*, is a story about resistance as Colin Laney, the Walled City, Rei Toei, Berry Rydell, and others act collectively to prevent media baron Cody Harwood from manipulating the future to his benefit. Were Harwood to succeed in controlling the future, then the novel could be read as dystopian; Laney and his allies defeat Harwood, however, and people therefore retain agency and hope for a better future.

Though set in the period immediately following the September 11th attacks, *Pattern Recognition* is neither bleak nor dystopic since protagonist Cayce Pollard retains agency and is able to act in her own interests. Although she works for Hubertus Bigend, a char-acter who emerges as a villain over the course of the *Bigend Trilogy*, she is not controlled by him and, in the end, is able to leave his employ. The same is true of Hollis Henry in *Spook Country*: although manipulated by Bigend, she retains a significant measure of agency and largely controls her own life. Ultimately she recognizes the threat to human freedom that Bigend and people like him pose, expressing her fears by projecting of a holographic image of a Mongolian Death Worm onto the top of Blue Ant headquarters. In *Zero History*, the potential danger that Bigend represents is realized as he obtains the ability to determine "order flow," that is, advance knowledge of all stock market activity. In effect, he succeeds where Harwood fails, gaining the ability to shape the future to his advantage, thereby robbing others of their agency. As Voytek Biroshak, a character who came to Great Britain to escape totalitarianism, observes, we have reached a point where people are compelled to live with "Orwell's boot in face *forever*" (289). In answering a question at a reading from *Zero History* in New York City, Gibson himself seemed to confirm that the novel is dystopian, indicating that it is "the times themselves that are the villains" in his most recent work. To the extent that this is correct—that is, to the extent that the villain has become the world we live in—*Zero History* can be understood as a dystopia since agency itself is lost and all possibility of change is closed out.

*See also All Tomorrow's Parties*; Bigend, Hubertus; The Faust Legend; Laney, Colin; *Neuromancer*; *Pattern Recognition*; Politics; *Spook Country*; *Zero History*

• *References and further reading*

Gibson, William. *All Tomorrow's Parties*. New York: Berkley, 2003. Print.
_____. *Count Zero*. New York: Ace, 1987. Print.

_____. *Mona Lisa Overdrive*. New York: Bantam Spectra, 1989. Print.
_____. *Neuromancer*. New York: Ace, 1984. Print.
_____. *Pattern Recognition*. New York: Berkley, 2005. Print.
_____. *Spook Country*. New York: Berkley, 2009. Print.
_____. *Zero History*. New York: Putnam, 2010. Print.

## The Faust Legend

The Faust legend appears on some level or other in virtually all of Gibson's novels. Given that most of Gibson's work focuses on information technology, this should not be surprising: in the digital age, at least, information is power in a very real sense. Accordingly, Gibson's Faust-like characters—including Josef Virek, Cody Harwood, and Hubertus Bigend—actualize information, converting it into knowledge in order to gain an advantage over competitors or to transcend human limitations. Whereas in traditional versions of the Faust legend the person seeking omnipotence through omniscience is ultimately destroyed by overreaching, in *The Sprawl Trilogy* and *The Bridge Trilogy* the Faust figures, Virek and Harwood, are foiled by insignificant-seeming people who act decisively at critical times. In *Count Zero*, Virek hopes to incorporate his very being into the fabric of the matrix but is prevented from doing so by Marly Krushkova because she knows that "nothing that he wants can be good." Similarly, in *All Tomorrow's Parties*, Cody Harwood is prevented from shaping the future to his benefit by a combination of people that includes Colin Laney, a dying man living in a cardboard shanty who receives vital assistance at a critical moment from Silencio, an autistic-seeming child.

In *Zero History*, the final volume of *The Bigend Trilogy*, Gibson reworks the Faust legend, having Bigend ultimately succeed in acquiring the knowledge he seeks, in this case "order flow," "the aggregate of all the orders in the stock market" (177). Knowing "[e]verything anyone is about to buy or sell" gives Bigend the potential, at least, to control entire economies, an unprecedented amount of power. Ironically, he only succeeds with the help of people who neither like nor approve of him. Bigend's genius, it seems, is in hiring "people who'll go off the reservation, lead him somewhere new," in effect "[h]arnessing chaos" (176). Rather than try to control everything, as Faust figures do in traditional versions of the legend, Bigend not only allows for chaos but creates it: as Henry Hollis puts it, Bigend "erects his life, and his business, in a way guaranteed to continually take him over the edge. Guaranteed to produce a new edge he'll have to go over" (176–77).

The being that emerges as a result of the merging of two artificial intelligences, Wintermute and Neuromancer, in *The Sprawl Trilogy* can also be regarded as a successful Faust of sorts. Itself a product of the Faustian dreams of Marie-France Tessier, a founder of Tessier-Ashpool Corporation, who hoped to create a company hive-mind of sorts in conjunction with an artificial intelligence of unprecedented power, the resultant super–AI effectively becomes the matrix, incorporating itself into its very fabric. Although it fragments upon becoming aware of a similar being based in Alpha Centauri, it reconstitutes itself with the help of human agents and, at the very end of the *Trilogy*, prepares to make contact with the other matrix, a story that is left untold.

*See also* Bigend, Hubertus; *Bigend Trilogy*; *Bridge Trilogy*; Dystopia; *Sprawl Trilogy*

• *References and further reading*

Gibson, William. *Count Zero*. New York: Ace, 1987. Print.
_____. *Neuromancer*. New York: Ace, 1984. Print.
_____. *Zero History*. New York: Putnam, 2010. Print.

## "Fragments of a Hologram Rose"

Written in lieu of a final paper for an undergraduate course in science fiction at the University of British Columbia, "Fragments of a Hologram Rose" was published in *UnEarth*, a short-lived science fiction magazine, in 1977, and collected in *Burning Chrome* (1986). Although running less than 2,000 words, the story is complex in terms of both style and content, much like "Hinterlands." Set in a dystopic future governed by corporations rather than states, the protagonist, Parker, takes refuge in electronically-induced sleep and a virtual reality–based entertainment system after his girlfriend leaves him. As the story proceeds, the reader learns that Parker is not alone in his dependence on sleep inducers and virtual reality devices that allow him to live the experiences of other, idealized people: such machines have become commonplace and perhaps the only way for an oppressed people to cope with the nightmarish world in which they live. The story's title alludes to a hologram postcard of a rose that belongs to the woman who has left Parker, a postcard he shreds in the garbage disposal. Before re-entering induced sleep, he reflects on the fact that "each fragment" of the shredded postcard "reveal[s] the whole image of the rose"—a property characteristic of holograms. Identifying himself with the rose, "the scattered fragments" of which reveal "a whole he'll never know," he reflects upon his sense of alienation, only to remember that the whole rose can indeed be known from its fragments because each piece "reveals the rose from a different angle" (42). This insight, which represents a way out of his abject state, is almost instantly lost as he begins to sleep. The story's ending is thus very bleak, the protagonist unable to "ask himself" what the significance of being whole again might be in terms of his real life (42).

*See also Burning Chrome*; "Hinterlands"

• *References and further reading*
Gibson, William. "Fragments of a Hologram Rose." *Burning Chrome*. New York: Ace, 1986. Print.

## Gender

Gibson's representations of gender have been subject to much debate from the very beginning of his career. Some critics argue that his early work, like most cyberpunk fiction, is essentially masculinist in the sense that it not only plays into adolescent male fantasies but reinforces patriarchal gender norms, associating the masculine with activity, for example, and the feminine with passivity (Ross 1991a, 145). Others, however, like Dani Cavallaro, note that Molly Millions is hardly passive, and that in Gibson's later work, particularly in the novels comprising *The Bigend Trilogy*, female characters take leading roles, showing both initiative and independence (124). Gibson's representations of gender and technology have also been widely discussed, some critics suggesting that Gibson presents sex and gender as becoming increasingly irrelevant as technology makes both bodies and social relationships more plastic and others arguing that Gibson's work only reinforces existing norms (Cavallaro 121).

Gibson's first and best-known novel, *Neuromancer*, generally serves as the starting point for most discussions of gender in his work. As June Deery notes, it is hard to read Gibson's fictive world in the novel as being anything but male: "His is the world of macho, hardboiled console cowboys on the wild frontier, mercenary loners who try to outmaneuver each with the latest weaponry and gadgetry and even engage in old-fashioned saloon fights" (91). There are, however, powerful female characters in *Neuromancer* as well, most obviously Molly Millions, an independent-minded "street samurai" whose gender does not seem to be fixed along traditional lines or limit her in any way. Not surprisingly, perhaps, critics like Lauraine Leblanc and Nicola Nixon read Millions as a female man of sorts, Millions having altered herself so as to become more physically dangerous. She is also sexually aggressive in a way that is stereotypically associated with males, taking the lead in her first sexual encounter with Henry Case, for example: "Now she straddled him again, took his hand, and closed it over her, his thumb along the cleft of her buttocks, his fingers spread across her labia.... She rode him that way, impaling herself, slipping down on him, until they had both come" (33). Millions is the "cowboy" here rather than Case, "performing" a masculine identity in Judith Butler's sense of the term. Critics like Lance Olsen use the same sorts of evidence to argue that Millions is a *femme fatale* rather than a female man, a woman who, like Brigid O'Shaughnessy of *The Maltese Falcon* or Carmen Sternwood of *The Big Sleep*, is not just attractive and dangerous but attractive *because* she is dangerous. Others still regard her as someone who has transcended gender entirely, using money she earned as a "meat puppet," or high-tech prostitute, to become a cyborg for whom sex and gender are largely irrelevant.

Many of the novels that followed *Neuromancer* feature other, even more substantial, more fully drawn female characters as Deery concedes (91). Although some, like Angelina Mitchell and Chevette Washington, have a disturbing lack of agency, others, like Marly Krushkova and Chia Pet Mckenzie, demonstrate both initiative and independence, playing critical roles in the narratives in *Count Zero* and *Idoru* respectively, Krushkova by preventing Josef Virek from acquiring the ability to code himself directly into cyberspace and Mackenzie by keeping a nanotech assembler from Russian agents. Molly Millions, who reappears in *Mona Lisa Overdrive* as Sally Shears, is also much more developed as a character than she was in either "Johnny Mnemonic" or *Neuromancer*. Neither a female man nor a *femme fatale*, she identifies with other female characters and forms strong relationships with them, playing critical roles in the personal development of Kumiko Yanaka and Mona Lisa in particular (Palmer 232).

Ironically, as Gibson began to focus more of his narratives on female characters who are largely independent of men, he made his male characters more dependent upon females, as evidenced by Bobby Newmark, who is not only protected by women throughout *Count Zero* but learns to navigate the matrix from Jackie, a highly skilled female hacker. Indeed, he earns his hacker moniker, "Count Zero," simply by delivering information to another powerful female hacker, Jaylene Slade, who then takes decisive action and kills Conroy, ending the threat he poses to the novel's protagonists. In this, Newmark contrasts sharply with Case, the protagonist of *Neuromancer*, a self-sufficient loner who has little need of others. Slick Henry, a main character in *Mona Lisa Overdrive* and Milgrim in *Zero History*, also serve as examples of male characters who depend largely upon women for leadership and instruction.

In addition to giving women more important roles as characters in his later novels, Gibson increasingly presents things from a female perspective. Indeed, *Neuromancer* is the only novel of Gibson's to make exclusive use of a male narrative perspective through his protagonist, Case; his other novels employ multiple points of view, both male and female, with the exception of *Pattern Recognition*, which presented largely through the consciousness of its female protagonist, Cayce Pollard. As if to underscore the significance of this shift from male to female, the narrative indicates that "Cayce" is pronounced as "Case," suggesting that the protagonist of his first novel has been effectively supplanted.

THE CONSTRUCTION OF GENDER

Since much of Gibson's work, most notably the last two volumes of *The Sprawl Trilogy* and each of the novels that comprise *The Bridge Trilogy*, feature adolescents entering adulthood, Gibson's ideas on how gender is constructed can sometimes be discerned. On the surface, Gibson's work seems to affirm dominant stereotypes, males being presented as being essentially active and females as passive. In *Count Zero*, for example, Angelina Mitchell is passed from one protector to another, having little say or even interest in what happens to her. Though she shows more initiative in *Mona Lisa Overdrive* as she tries to free herself from Sense/Net's control, she is unable to do so, passing from the corporation's control to Molly Millions's and then back to the *loas*', who need her to incorporate herself into the fabric of the matrix so that they can again become a single entity. Similarly, Mona Lisa's effort to free herself from her abductors is also quickly thwarted, her escape being prevented by Molly Millions, who eventually passes her off to Sense/Net, where she replaces Mitchell, having been surgically altered to resemble her. Young women, it seems, have very little control of their own destinies, seemingly existing to be used by others, a point that seems to be affirmed by the fact that both Mitchell and Mona Lisa become simstim stars, entertainers whose neural input is used by others for enjoyment. It is important to note Gibson does not present the passivity of characters like Mitchell or Mona Lisa as being either inherent or necessary. Society may demand that women be docile objects of male desire but such demand can be resisted: it is at least possible for women to transcend the limitations that gender imposes upon them, most obviously in the case of Molly Millions, who goes from being a "meat puppet" to a powerful, independent-minded woman who defines herself rather than letting herself be defined by others (Palmer 237). Kumiko Yanaka, too, the thirteen-year-old daughter of a powerful Yakuza leader, goes from passive to active in *Mona Lisa Overdrive*, demanding that her father reveal the entire truth about her mother's death and insisting that he protect the people that have helped her.

A similar pattern can be seen in *The Bridge Trilogy*, where some female characters accept gender norms and others challenge them. As Gwyneth Jones notes, in *Virtual Light*, Chevette Washington is "essentially a passive prize and victim" (158), passing from Skinner's protection to Berry Rydell's. Although she demonstrates more independence in *All Tomorrow's Parties*, she still tends to react rather than act, her movements being largely determined by a former boyfriend who stalks her and then Rydell, who become her champion and protector, just as he was in *Virtual Light*. When she does finally take the initiative towards the end of *All Tomorrow's Parties*, slashing Konrad's hang glider as he launches himself from the top of the Bridge, it has no real effect, Konrad surviving the fall (321). In the end she remains a passive object, her sleeping form being described simply as that which Rydell "most desires, desires to cherish" (330). Rei Toei, in contrast, is able to transcend the limitations imposed upon her by gender in ways that Washington is not, a remarkable feat given that she is a computer construct based entirely on the desires of others. Unlike Washington, who is essentially a static character, Toei grows and changes, becoming more than she was originally programmed to be, a prescription, it seems, for escaping gender limitations that might apply to humans, too. At the end of *All Tomorrow's Parties*, Toei takes decisive action, not only thwarting Cody Harwood's efforts to shape the future for his own benefit but employing nanotechnology to reproduce herself as a corporeal being, copies of herself emerging from the nanofax machine of every Lucky Dragon convenience store in the world.

## Queerness and Heteronormativity

Gibson's work not only presents heterosexual relations as the norm but rarely even acknowledges the existence of queer identities, the exception being Webber, a lesbian character in *Count Zero* whom Gibson presents in positive terms. Significantly, Webber is part of a queer family, Webber and her partner having parented a child, combining their DNA through the use of technology. Since traditionally procreation is not only reserved for heterosexuals but also used to sanction heterosexuality as natural, Webber and her partner's success might be interpreted as a challenge to heterosexual norms. It could be argued, however, that Webber's death early in the novel reflects an unwillingness on Gibson's part to accept queerness (Childers et al 158). Certainly Gibson provides no examples of successful queer families in his work. Gibson's novels are also heteronormative in the sense that they frequently provide closure through male-female partnerships. As Tyler Curtain suggests, this is especially apparent in *Neuromancer*, which ends with Case pairing off with a virtual Linda Lee in cyberspace and a physical woman in the real world (137). Even then, however, the text's heteronormativity is arguably undercut by the fact that the woman Case meets calls "herself Michael." At the very least Gibson's use of a male name problematizes easy assumptions about what the sexual norms are in this particular fictive world.

## Gender, Technology, and Exploitation

As Gwyneth Jones indicates in *Deconstructing the Starships: Science Fiction and Reality* (1999), the degradation and exploitation females face in Gibson's early work reveal more "about the position of women," "the assumptions of society," and the conventions of mainstream science fiction than they do about Gibson's own attitudes about gender, Gibson representing the world as he sees it rather than as he would like it to be. Certainly the fictive world his characters inhabit is one in which women are exploited sexually and otherwise. To suggest that he celebrates such exploitation, however, is to ignore the dystopian tone of his work: exploitation and degradation are primary problems in Gibson's fictive worlds, problems that his protagonists address and frequently overcome. Molly Millions presents a particularly interesting case, she having allowed herself to be exploited as a meat puppet so that she can raise money to surgically alter herself and thereby escape exploitation in the long term; although she succeeds in this, transforming herself into a "razorgirl," her past is still a part of her and continues to inform her actions as evidenced by her violent reaction to Peter Riviera's exploitation of an image of her in a holographic performance he gives in Straylight. Rei Toei presents an interesting case as well since she goes from being simply a product of others' desires to a being who not only has desires of her own but is able to fulfill them, moving from the virtual to the real at the end of *All Tomorrow's Parties*. Although critics like Deery are critical of Gibson for failing to "explore in any depth the effect the effect of new technology on gender relations," he certainly raises it as an issue in *The Sprawl Trilogy* and suggests that technology has the potential to redefine such relations in *The Bridge Trilogy* through Toei.

*See also Count Zero*; Millions, Molly; *Mona Lisa Overdrive*; *Neuromancer*; Toei, Rei

• *References and further reading*

Butler, Judith. *Gender Trouble: Feminism and the Subversion of Identity*. New York: Routledge, 1990.
Chandler, Raymond. *The Big Sleep*. New York: Random House, 1939. Print.
Cavallaro, Dani. *Cyberpunk and Cyberculture: Science Fiction and the Work of William Gibson*. Athlone Press, 2000. Print.

Cherniavsky, Eva. "(En)gendering Cyberspace in *Neuromancer*: Postmodern Subjectivity and Virtual Motherhood." *Genders* 18 (1993): 32–46. Print.

Childers, Joseph, et al. "White Men Can't ... (De)centering Authority and Jacking into Phallic Economies in William Gibson's *Count Zero*." *Science Fiction, Canonization, Marginalization, and the Academy*. Ed. Gary Westfahl and George Slusser. Westport, CT: Greenwood, 2002. Print.

Curtain, Tyler. "'Sinister Fruitiness': *Neuromancer*, Internet Sexuality and the Turing Test." *Studies in the Novel* 28.3 (1996): 414–35. Print.

Deery, June. "The Biopolitics of Cyberspace: Piercy Hacks Gibson." *Future Females, the Next Generation: New Voices and Velocities in Feminist Science Fiction Criticism*. Ed. Marleen S. Barr. Lanham, MD: Rowman & Littlefield, 2000. 87–108. Print.

Gibson, William. *Count Zero*. New York: Ace, 1987. Print.

_____. *Idoru*. New York: Berkley, 1997.

_____. *Mona Lisa Overdrive*. New York: Spectra, 1997.

_____. *Neuromancer*. New York: Ace, 1994.

_____. *Pattern Recognition*. New York: Berkley, 2005.

Hammett, Dashiell. *The Maltese Falcon*. New York: Alfred A. Knopf, 1930. Print.

Jones, Gwyneth. *Deconstructing the Starships: Science Fiction and Reality*. Liverpool: Liverpool University Press, 1999. Print.

Nixon, Nicola. "Cyberpunk: Preparing the Ground for Revolution or Keeping the Boys Satisfied?" *Science Fiction Studies* 19.2 (July 1992): 219–35. Print.

Palmer, Christopher. "*Mona Lisa Overdrive* and the Prosthetic." *Science Fiction Studies* 31.2 (2004): 227–42. Print.

## "The Gernsback Continuum"

"The Gernsback Continuum" was the first of Gibson's stories to be published since "Fragments of a Hologram Rose" (1977), a story he wrote in lieu of a final paper for an undergraduate English class. First appearing in Terry Carr's *Universe 11* anthology in 1981, "The Gernsback Continuum" is one of Gibson's more widely discussed stories, not only offering social commentary but challenging the traditional norms of the science fiction genre. The story came into wider circulation upon appearing in both Bruce Sterling's influential cyberpunk anthology, *Mirrorshades*, and Gibson's own collection, *Burning Chrome*, in 1986. It was also included in Ursula K. LeGuin's widely used textbook, *The Norton Book of Science Fiction* (1997).

The story tells of a professional photographer, who, while traveling in the Southwest to document examples of the futuristic aesthetic that was popular in American pre-war design, begins entering into the world that was then being imagined — or at least he has delusions of doing so — seeing "a flying wing over Castro Street," for example (35). The story is told in the first-person in an almost cathartic manner as the narrator tries to recover himself and return to the world he is familiar with. Even though he fully recognizes that the real world is a "near-dystopia" marked by privation, war, pornography, and bad coffee, he prefers that to "perfect" future that was being promoted in the 1930s, a future that for all of its technological wonders has dark, totalitarian undertones (35).

Although relatively compact, running just 6,000 words, the story offers three distinct explanations for the narrator's seeming slippage into an alternative world — that he really entered into that world, penetrating "the membrane of probability" (27); that he is having a drug-induced fantasy; and that he is subject to "semiotic ghosts," that the "sci fi imagery" that permeated the culture in the pre-war period have "taken on a life of their own" in his unconscious" (33, 29). Ultimately, it is the last explanation, the one offered by his friend, Mervyn Kihn, that appears to be correct since the remedy Kihn's recommends ultimately succeeds: "Watch lots of television, particularly game shows and soaps. Go to porn movies. Ever see Nazi Love Motel? They've got it on cable, here. Really awful.

Just what you need" (33). As Kihn seems to suggest, as ridiculous as the present is, it is more real than any "futuropolis" imagined in the 1930s could ever be and therefore can put the ghosts to rest (24).

"The Gernsback Continuum" offers more than just an ideological critique of the pre-war, futuristic aesthetic, an aesthetic it repeatedly identifies with Nazism, for the story challenges futurism in general, that is, the notion that technological advances will lead to domestic prosperity. Written at a time when the Ronald Reagan administration was arming the United States in preparation for World War III, the story reminds us that rockets like those featured on the covers of Gernsback's various magazines in the 1930s "had fallen on London in the dead of night" in World War II (27). The implication, it seems, is that technology always has military applications, much of it be developed just for that purposes. In *Cyberfiction: After the Future*, Paul Youngquist pushes such a reading further, suggesting that perhaps the narrator really "a flying wing over Castro Street"— B-2 stealth bombers having been developed and tested in the West as part of Reagan's re-armament project: "If Gibson's hero *sees* an early B-2 prototype but *perceives* it as an obsolete flying wing, the sight blinds him to certain facts about the world he inhabits. A war machine looks like a quaint old luxury airliner"(52). He adds that Golden Age fantasies about a better, technologically-oriented future have "impede[d] the perception of a militarized present" (53). Youngquist supports this reading by observing that the insinuation of military elements into our everyday lives again becomes a subject for Gibson in his post–9/11 works (195).

As Bruce Sterling observes in his preface to *Burning Chrome*, "The Gernsback Continuum" also draws "a bead on the shambling figure of the SF tradition," targeting in particular the Pulp Age that immediately preceded science fiction's Golden Age. In a recent interview, Gibson conceded that the story serves as a manifesto of sorts, though it did not begin as such, the story being based on a review he wrote for a coffee table book on futurism entitled *The Streamlined Decade*. Angered when the review was rejected by an amateur science fiction magazine, Gibson indicates that he "rewrote it as a science fiction story," targeting the genre itself for "having rejected my arty little review of the coffee table book" (Clarke Interview).

*See also Burning Chrome*; "Hippie Hat Brain Paradise"; Science Fiction

• *References and further reading*

Bredehoft, Thomas. "The Gibson Continuum: Cyberspace and Gibson's Mervyn Kihn Stories." *Science Fiction Studies* 22.2 (1995): 252–63. Print.
Gibson, William. "The Gernsback Continuum." *Burning Chrome*. New York: Ace, 1986. Print.
_____. "Hippie Hat Brain Parasite." *Modern Stories* (Apr. 1983). Print.
Ross, Andrew. "Getting Out of the Gernsback Continuum." *Critical Inquiry* 17.2 (1991): 411–433. Print.
Westfahl, Gary. "'The Gernsback Continuum': William Gibson in the Context of Science Fiction." *Fiction 2000: Cyberpunk and the Future of Narrative*. Ed. George Slusser and Tom Shippey. Athens: University of Georgia Press, 1992. 88–108.
Youngquist, Paul. *Cyberfiction: After the Future*. New York: Palgrave Macmillan, 2010. Print.

# Hackers

In his early works such as "Burning Chrome," *Neuromancer*, and *Count Zero*, Gibson uses the term "console cowboy" and more often just "cowboy" to refer to hackers— that is, those who "hack" into computer systems and access data without proper authority. Although hacking is not necessarily illegal, if only because certain activities may not have yet been defined as criminal, it is widely regarded as such and therefore considered an out-law activity, one that Gibson glamorizes as a form of resistance to authority. In this sense, Gibson's "cowboys" parallel cowboys as they were represented in films such as *The Good, the Bad, and the Ugly* and *A Fistful of Dollars*—that is, as morally ambiguous characters who act in self-interest but nonetheless adhere to a certain ethic and are therefore moral if not lawful.

Gibson introduces readers to the hacker world in "Burning Chrome" through Auto-matic Jack and Bobby Quine, talented but as-yet unsuccessful hackers who team up for a "big score" that involves accessing the assets of an underworld figure named "Chrome." Even though the story is remembered today primarily for not only representing "cyber-space" in an accessible manner but introducing the term into the English language, it is an exceptional story in other ways as well, exploring, among other things, the moral impli-cations of data theft since, as Automatic Jack realizes, the "burning" of Chrome will result in her death since her money is the only thing that protects her from her enemies. Although set in the near future, the story is very much about the then present, Automatic Jack and Quine being based on phone phreaks and hackers that began coming into prominence in the 1970s—that is, people who found ways of to exploit weaknesses in technological sys-tems, particularly those employed by AT&T. Whereas phreaks like John Draper (also known as "Captain Crunch" because he discovered that a toy whistle included with the cereal could be used to manipulate the phone system because of its tone) purportedly broke into systems just for the sake of doing so, Gibson's Sprawl stories are set in a world in which hacking has become one of the few ways in which the socially and economically marginalized can gain some measure of control over their lives, or at least have the illu-sion of control (Levy 254). This is not to suggest that Gibson's hackers are simply petty criminals or opportunists, however. In *Neuromancer* Henry Case is represented as being an artist of sorts as well, and in the other two volumes of *The Sprawl Trilogy*, Bobby New-mark goes from being an ignorant child whose hotdogging in cyberspace almost gets him killed to an intellectually curious adult whose actins are motivated primarily by a desire to know exactly what cyberspace is and what it is becoming.

In *The Bridge Trilogy* Gibson focuses more on hacker communities than individual hackers. *Virtual Light*, for example, features the Republic of Desire, a shadowy hackers' collective that at first seems to be dedicated to pranks and isolated acts of resistance but in the end acts decisively to prevent quake-devastated San Francisco from being rebuilt as a seamless, gentrified twenty-first century city with no gaps in the infrastructure from which resistance can be based. Gibson provides a more in-depth depiction of a hacker com-munity in *Idoru* through Masakiko, an *otaku*—that is, a youth absorbed in computing to the point of seeming asocial to those who do not share his interests. Masahiko, it turns out, is neither disaffected nor a loner: as a member of the Walled City, a hacker collective that has created an interstice for themselves within the Net, he is part of a virtual com-munity that provides him with important social relationships. Unlike the hackers in Gib-son's earlier work, who are essentially antisocial and work alone or in small teams for personal gain, denizens of the Walled City like Masahiko have a sense of social responsi-bility not only towards its members but towards society at large. This becomes evident when, towards the end of *All Tomorrow's Parties*, the community acts decisively in con-junction with others to prevent Cody Harwood from shaping the future to his own advan-tage as nanotechnology becomes widely available.

Hacker communities are much less prominent in *The Bigend Trilogy*, hackers instead being represented as independent operators as they were in *The Sprawl Trilogy*. Hackers like Voytek Biroshak and Bobby Chombo are not petty criminals looking for a "big score" like Bobby Quine and Automatic Jack but rather artists of a sort who employ digital media. In *Pattern Recognition* Voytek is a likable, urbane man hoping to link together 300 early home computers, creating "some sort of lungfish-primitive connection machine" that can be displayed in a gallery, and in *Spook Country* the anti-social Bobby Chombo is a mash-up artist of sorts who uses his expertise in GPS technology to project projecting holographic images into public spaces. One important challenge they face is remaining independent of corporations as they pursue their art, something they both ultimately fail in, having become employees of the Blue Ant agency by the opening of *Zero History*. Both of them have seemingly given up on their artwork at this point, their skills instead being exploited by Hubertus Bigend for his own ends.

See also "Burning Chrome"; *Count Zero*; *Idoru*; *Neuromancer*; Newmark, Bobby; *Pattern Recognition*; *Spook Country*; *The Sprawl Trilogy*; *Virtual Light*; *Zero History*

• *References and further reading*
Childers, Joseph, et al. "White Men Can't ... (De)centering Authority and Jacking into Phallic Economies in William Gibson's *Count Zero*." *Science Fiction, Canonization, Marginalization, and the Academy*. Ed. Gary Westfahl and George Slusser. Westport, CT: Greenwood, 2002. Print.
Chun, Wendy. *Control and Freedom: Power and Paranoia in the Age of Fiber Optics*. Cambridge: MIT Press, 2006. Print.
Gibson, William. *All Tomorrow's Parties*. New York: Berkley, 2003. Print.
_____. "Burning Chrome." *Burning Chrome*. New York: Ace, 1986. Print.
_____. *Count Zero*. New York: Ace 1987. Print.
_____. *Idoru*. New York: Berkley, 1997. Print.
_____. *Mona Lisa Overdrive*. New York: Spectra, 1997. Print.
_____. *Neuromancer*. New York: Ace, 1994. Print.
_____. *Pattern Recognition*. New York: Berkley, 2005. Print.
_____. *Spook Country*. New York: Berkley, 2009. Print.
_____. *Virtual Light*. New York: Spectra, 1994. Print.
_____. *Zero History*. New York: Putnam, 2010. Print.
Heuser, Sabine. *Virtual Geographies: Cyberpunk at the Intersection of the Postmodern*. New York: Rodopi, 2003. Print.
Levy, Steven. *Hackers: Heroes of the Computer Revolution*. New York: O'Reilly Media, 2010. Print.

## Henry, Hollis

A primary character in both *Spook Country* (2007) and *Zero History* (2010), Hollis Henry is a bohemian, an artist by nature who brings her sensibilities to whatever project she is working on. Because she approaches things in an unpredictable, non-linear way, she is of great value to Hubertus Bigend, who, in *Spook Country*, hires her to write an article on locative art, that is, holographic art that is projected into highly-localized venues through the use of GPS technology. As it turns out, Bigend is much less interested in the art itself than in locating Bobby Chombo, a technology artist of sorts who produces the work of others. Ultimately, as an employee of Bigend, Henry has to make a moral choice similar to the one Marly Krushkova has to make in *Count Zero* when working for Josef Virek: in particular, she has to decide whether to withhold information from Bigend or honor her contract with him even though she distrusts him. She faces a similar situation in *Zero History* after again agreeing to work for him even though she has come to fear him and what he represents.

Although *Spook Country* is comprised of three narrative strands, only one of which centers on Henry, she ultimately emerges as the novel's protagonist, the novel being very much about her and her choices and actions. As the former leader singer of the now defunct post-punk band, the Curfew, Henry seems to have lost her sense of self since people treat her as a celebrity rather than as an individual. In taking an assignment from *Node*, an as yet unpublished technology-oriented magazine modeled on *Wired*, she is trying to establish a new identity for herself, one as a journalist. Ironically, *Node* apparently deems her suitable for the assignment not because her writing ability but because her celebrity will have a certain currency amongst locative artists. Even though she quickly realizes that she has been hired to acquire information rather than to write an article, she continues her work, in part because she needs employment and in part because she has become interested in locative art and those that create it. Eventually she learns that Bigend is using her to locate the expert in GPS technology, Bobby Chombo, who not only produces the art but has been tracking a mysterious shipping container in which Bigend has become interested. Upon discovering that Chombo is tracking the container for the "old man," a former government agent who is using it as part of a "cat and mouse" to torment those trying to profit from the U.S. invasion of Iraq, Henry decides that it is better not to fully disclose what she has learned to Bigend. She has decided, apparently, that Bigend is dangerous— or at least represents something dangerous— and that thwarting his desires can only be a good thing. Her negative attitude towards him is underscored at the very end of the novel when she arranges for a giant holograph of a Mongolian Death Worm to be projected from the top of his Vancouver headquarters, a symbol of "any major fear" that she cannot "quite get a handle on" (453).

The difficulties Henry faces in trying to escape her own celebrity are also highlighted toward the end of the book, the old man only telling her about the cat and mouse game because, as a celebrity, she is already "a part of the historical record" and therefore can be used as a "fireplace brick behind which" he can "leave an account" about what really is happening. As in the Rez storyline in the latter two volumes of *The Bridge Trilogy*, Gibson is very much interested in the ways in which celebrity fundamentally changes those who have it. Henry, it seems, is in danger of becoming *just* a celebrity, a person who is defined entirely by the public perception of her. She succeeds in reasserting her artistic identity at the end of *Spook Country* by commissioning a work of locative art that expresses what she fears most — people like Bigend gaining control of everything.

In *Zero History* Henry again enters the employ of Bigend, this time because she has lost most of her money in the economic recession that began in 2008. The fact that she does so even though she both dislikes and fears him introduces one of the novel's central themes: the world has become a place in which choice — ethical and otherwise — is a luxury to which few have access. As Gibson indicated in an interview with Amazon, in his view the twenty-first century is becoming increasingly Victorian as people become either "very, very wealthy" or "desperately poor," the desperately poor have little choice but to do the bidding of the more powerful. And it is not just Henry who is forced to work for him despite her misgivings: many of the characters that were introduced in the first two volumes of *The Bigend Trilogy* also now work for Bigend, including Milgrim, Voytek, Chombo, and even Inchmale, Henry's former bandmate. Difficult economic times might disempower most, but some, like Bigend it seems, become even more powerful.

As in *Spook Country*, in *Zero History* Henry is of value to Bigend not just because of her celebrity but because she approaches problems in a non-linear manner: he uses unpredictable agents like Henry to incorporate complexity into his operations, giving his agency a competitive advantage over others. Although he formally assigns Henry to identifying the designer behind an innovative new brand known as "The Gabriel Hounds," he is prepared to use anything she and other agents discover to his advantage. Learning that the designer in question is Cayce Pollard, the protagonist of *Pattern Recognition* who, like Henry, worked with Bigend despite strong misgivings, Henry must decide between honoring her contract with Bigend and protecting Pollard from him. That she ultimately chooses the latter seems to suggest that the world is still a place in where one can make decisions based on one's personal morality. The reader quickly learns that the significance of Henry's choice is symbolic at best because Bigend will soon learn the designer's identity anyway: we may still have choice, it seems, but the choices we make may not matter.

The notion that choice is increasingly becoming constrained when it is available at all is underscored by an even more important decision Henry has to make towards the end of the book — a decision Bigend forces upon her directly. Throughout the novel Henry, who began working for Bigend only because she felt that she had no choice but to do so because of her financial situation, has been considering leaving his employ. Once she finally decides to quit, however, she finds she cannot since doing so would result in harm coming to Milgrim. Bigend's rivals, it seems, have abducted Chombo, and are demanding Milgrim in exchange. When Bigend indicates that he is willing to sacrifice Milgrim for Chombo, Henry realizes that she must stay in Bigend's employ and rescue Chombo in order to protect Milgrim even though she knows that returning Chombo to him will result in an exponential increase in Bigend's power, making him even more dangerous. In a sense she has to choose between her personal loyalty to Milgrim and a social responsibility to thwart Bigend efforts to gain control of important financial markets with Chombo's assistance. In the end the fears of Bigend that she expressed in *Spook Country* by having a giant Mongolian Death Worm projected onto the top his headquarters are fully realized. The cruel irony is that she played a key role in bringing this about, by locating Chombo for Bigend in *Spook Country* and for helping Bigend recapture him in *Zero History*.

Taken as a whole, the narratives centering on Henry are about a woman trying — and ultimately failing — to retain control of her life. Initially she is presented as an artist who becomes defined by her celebrity. Realizing that others perceive her as the former lead singer of the Curfew rather than who she really is, she begins to lose her sense of self, regaining it only by creating a work of art in a new medium — the Mōngolian Death Worm she projects onto Bigend's headquarters. *Zero History* focuses less on her as a celebrity than on her a person who is living in a world where nearly everyone is losing control of their lives. Forced into Bigend's employ and then into helping him become nearly omnipotent, the novel ends with a nightmare rather than a work of art, Henry dreaming of Bigend as a ferret in a Klein Blue suit, his "muzzle rouged" with blood.

*See also* Bigend, Hubertus; *The Bigend Trilogy*; *Count Zero*; Milgrim; *Pattern Recognition*; *Spook Country*; *Zero History*

• *References and further readings*

Gibson, William. *Spook Country*. New York: Berkley, 2009. Print.
_____. *Zero History*. New York: Putnam, 2010. Print.
Youngquist, Paul. *Cyberfiction: After the Future*. New York: Palgrave Macmillan, 2010. Print.

## "Hinterlands"

First published in *Omni* in 1981 and then collected in *Burning Chrome*, "Hinterlands" is an atypical Gibson story in the sense that it is an example of early–1980s "soft" science fiction. Set in a space station about ⅛ of the way to Mars, the story features a first-person narrator, Toby Halpert, whose job it is to prevent astronauts returning from deep space from killing themselves before they can divulge any information they may have gathered. The astronauts, or "hitchhikers" as they are called in the story, are conveyed to another part of the universe by what is known as the "Highway," a singularity that is beyond human understanding. Although the returning astronauts are all suicidal, having encountered what is expressed only metaphorically in the story as "the Fear" of the "Big Night," some return with invaluable information, such as a cure for cancer. As Jeffrey Vincent Yule indicates, the story presents itself as a psychological study of Halpert, a man who has felt the Fear before but is nonetheless compelled to face it, albeit indirectly as a "surrogate" for returning astronauts. "Hinterlands" is more than just a character study, however, since it also indicts the supposedly advanced societies such as the United States and the Soviet Union for their arrogance and presumptions of superiority over other, "less-developed" societies. The story does this by likening the space-faring nations that use the Highway to the so-called primitives in places like Micronesia who developed "cargo cults" as a result of their contact with unfamiliar technologies. The Americans, Russians, and their allies who send person after person out into the unknown in the hopes of attaining some incomprehensibly advanced technology are like "[f]lies in an airport," having no understanding of the "Big Picture" or their place in it (72). The irony is that for all their ignorance, the leading powers claim dominion over the earth and are even willing to risk its destruction, Cold War rivalry continuing even at the space station.

Of all the stories collected in *Burning Chrome*, "Hinterlands" best exhibits the narrative complexity that became the norm in science fiction following the "New Wave" movement of the 1960s. As Yule observes, the story begins *in media res*, forcing the reader to accumulate detail until "the apparently unrelated elements of the story coalesce into a definable pattern" (96). The story also seems "New Wave" in the way that it psychologically rather than technologically oriented, standing in sharp contrast to the work of writers like Kim Stanley Robinson, David Brin, and Robert Forward, writers who came to characterize the "hard" science fiction revival that occurred in the 1980s.

If "Hinterlands" differs from the neo–Campbellian, hard science fiction stories of the Reagan era, it also differs from the those of the cyberpunk subgenre that Gibson himself helped establish with stories like "Johnny Mnemonic," "New Rose Hotel," and "Burning Chrome," all of which are also collected in *Burning Chrome*. Whereas Gibson's cyberpunk stories are written in a hard-boiled style reminiscent of 1930s writers like Dashiell Hammett and Raymond Chandler, "Hinterlands" is narrated by much more contemplative character who searches for but cannot find a meaning behind what is happening both to him and the world he has known.

See also *Burning Chrome*; Politics

• *References and further readings*

Gibson, William. "Hinterlands." *Burning Chrome*. New York: Ace, 1986. Print.
Yule, Jeffrey Vincent. *Contemplating the Diverse Beast: Analyzing Science Fiction's Marginalization*. Master's Thesis. Ohio State University, 1991. Print.

## "Hippie Hat Brain Parasite"

First appearing in Lewis Shiner's fanzine, *Modern Stories* in 1983 and then republished in Rudy Rucker's anthology *Semiotext[e]* in 1989, "Hippie Hat Brain Parasite" is one of just two stories in which Gibson presents himself as a character, the other being "Dougal Discarnate" (2010). Both stories explore the effects of drug use, highlighting potential dangers. "Hippie Hat Brain Parasite" centers on a phone conversation between Bill, the Gibson figure, and Mervyn Kihn, a character who is introduced in "The Gernsback Continuum" (1981) as "a free-lance journalist with an extensive line in Texas pterodactyls, redneck UFO contactees, bush-league Loch Ness monsters, and the Top Ten conspiracy theories in the loonier reaches of the American mass mind" (28). Kihn, it seems, has just seen what appears to be an alien — a brain parasite that takes the form of the heavily-laced, leather "hippie hats" that are still favored in "Sixties hipcult holdouts" like Ashland, Oregon or Santa Cruz, California (110); he speculates that the parasites "must've spread out from Haight-Ashbury" without anyone noticing since the people who wear such hats "look pretty zombie-out anyway" (111). The joke of the story is that Kihn, who publishes stories on subjects such as "menstruating Barbie Dolls" and "[l]uminous phantom Dachshunds" assumes that someone like Gibson will know more about the hippie-hat brain parasites than he does since Bill is the one who "write[s] about stuff like that" (112). In addition to implying that Bill's stories are even stranger than the ones he reports, Kihn's assumption suggests that Bill is familiar with drug culture and has perhaps even been a participant in it.

In "The Gibson Continuum: Cyberspace and Gibson's Mervyn Kihn Stories," Thomas Bredehoft connects Gibson's representation of cyberspace in his Sprawl stories to "Hippie Hat Brain Parasite" and "The Gernsback Continuum," arguing that all of them partake of a "hallucinatory iconography derived from literary representations of sixties-style acid trips." Bredehoft concludes that all of these stories — whether they center on cyberspace or drug use — warn against mistaking "escape for liberation," for "mistaking wishful thinking for reality." Such a reading seems consistent with Gibson's negative representation of not only drugs such as Wiz, Dancer, and Rize but of anything that prevents people from trying to improve their lives by offering them temporary escapes from it, including cyberspace, video games, television, and virtual reality systems such as simstim and apparent sensory perception (ASP).

*See also* Counterculture; "Dougal Discarnate"; "The Gernsback Continuum"; Uncollected Stories

- *References and further reading*

Bredehoft, Thomas. "The Gibson Continuum: Cyberspace and Gibson's Mervyn Kihn Stories." *Science Fiction Studies* 22.2 (1995): 252–63. Print.
Gibson, William. "Dougal Discarnate." *Darwin's Bastards*. Ed. Gartner Zsuzsi. Vancouver: Douglas & McIntyre, 2010. 231–40. Print.
_____. "The Gernsback Continuum." *Burning Chrome*. New York: Ace, 1986. Print.
_____. "Hippie Hat Brain Parasite." *Modern Stories* (Apr. 1983). Print.

## Hyperreality

Although Gibson addresses hyperreality and related ideas such as simulation and simulacra throughout his work, it is in *The Bridge Trilogy* that such concepts become subjects in themselves. Although in some ways Gibson's positions on hyperreality seem consistent with those of Jean Baudrillard — the person with whom the concept is most frequently associated — in *Idoru* and *All Tomorrow's Parties*, the final volumes of the *Trilogy*, Gibson suggests that Baudrillard's ideas on hyperreality do not fully account for the changes that are occurring in the digital age and that he does not adequately allow for their liberatory — or at least oppositional — possibilities. In *The Bigend Trilogy*, Gibson develops an alternative model of the hyperreal, one based on what William Burroughs termed the "cut-up" method.

Gibson explicitly introduces the hyperreal as subject in *Idoru*, the second volume of *The Bridge Trilogy*, through Rez, a character seemingly based on U2's Bono and other rock superstars, whose celebrity supplants his original self. As Ross Farnell observes, "Gibson constructs Rez *as* posthuman": Rez's life has become a fragmented and partially deified representation of the data —fan, corporate, and media — that surround him: he is a timeless, eternal present" (469). Indeed, in terms of information at least, Rez-the-person is less significant than Rez-the-celebrity; as Colin Laney, a data analyst working for Rez's security organization, notes, "the quantity of data accumulated" on Rez and his band is "greater than everything the band themselves have ever generated" (244). Accordingly, Rez becomes Baudrillard's simulacrum *par excellence* (Murphy 76): as Laney observes, he "is an iconified product packaged for mass consumption, the hyperreal patterns that circulate in, around, and through him indicate that *nothing but pattern* exists anymore."

Gibson pushes his representation of simulation, simulacra, and hyperreality even further through Rei Toei, a computer-generated simulation that becomes sentient. If Rez is a simulacrum, Toei is a simulacrum of simulacra, a copy of copies, the original itself being a simulation. Initially just a software agent designed to acquire information continually and redefine herself accordingly, Toei soon becomes "infinitely more than the combined sum of her various selves" (217). Indeed, as Laney eventually recognizes, though "created accidentally," she is an artificial intelligence, though largely unrecognized as such (263). Composed entirely of information, she is all signifier and thus, by definition, hyperreal; despite this, she is able to insinuate herself into the real, providing Chia Pet Mackenzie's location to Rez's security team at a critical moment, thus saving her from a Russian agent and enabling Rez to procure the nanotech device that serves as the novel's MacGuffin. For Gibson, it seems, the real and the hyperreal interpenetrate one another, making the latter a potential site for resistance to authority.

In *All Tomorrow's Parties*, the final volume of *The Bridge Trilogy*, Toei is given an even more important role, working with Laney and others to thwart Cody Harwood's efforts to shape the future to his benefit. The novel ends with her not only insinuating herself into the real but *becoming* real: Toei reproduces herself through the "nanofax" machines that have been installed in every Lucky Dragon convenience store in the world, each one issuing a living copy of her. Whether she still exists digitally as well is left as an open question, though the fact that every copy of her wears the same smile as it exits its Lucky Dragon store indicates that every copy of her is somehow linked.

As suggested above, *The Bridge Trilogy* can be read as a serious exploration of simulacra and hyperreal as it is being manifested in the digital age. On another level, however, it can be read as satire because of the seeming absurdity of Toei becoming a corporeal being through a combination of fax technology and nanotechnology. Although one must be cautious about identifying absurdities in science fiction because of the genre's openness to all possibilities, the fact that *All Tomorrow's Parties*, which was published in 1999, is set just ten years later or so suggests that Gibson did not mean for the world he represents to be

regarded as a viable future. Instead, Gibson may just be parodying post-structuralist theory in general and postmodern theories of the hyperreal in particular. Such an interpretation would not be inconsistent with the *Trilogy* as a whole, which is written in a satirical
vein, much like Thomas Pynchon's *The Crying of Lot 49* and Don DeLillo's *White Noise*.

In *Pattern Recognition*, the first volume of *The Bigend Trilogy*, Gibson again addresses
simulation, simulacra, and hyperreality through the novel's protagonist Cayce Pollard.
Pollard, it seems, is allergic to the hyperreal, as evidenced by her reaction to Tommy
Hilfiger products: "Some people ingest a single peanut and their head swells like a basket-
ball. When it happens to Cayce, it's her psyche. Tommy Hilfiger does it every time.... This
stuff is simulacra of simulacra of simulacra. A diluted tincture of Ralph Lauren, who had
himself diluted the glory days of Brooks Brothers, who themselves had stepped on the
product of Jermyn Street and Savile Row, flavoring their ready-to-wear with liberal lash-
ings of polo knit and regimental stripes" (18). Despite use of the term "simulacra" and
sustained exploration of concepts such as authenticity, homogenization, and the virtual
in *The Bigend Trilogy*, Gibson is less interested in post-structuralist accounts of the hyperreal than in the idea of remix — of making the old into the new. Indeed, he goes out of
his way to mock post-structuralism through Dorotea Benedetti, a character who hires an
American graduate student to seed her online postings with references to post-structural-
ists such as Fredric Jameson, Michel Foucault, and Jacques Lacan.

In *Pattern Recognition*, Gibson addresses remix — which corresponds to William S.
Burroughs's "cut-up method," a creative strategy Gibson has long been interested in —
primarily through discussions of film, the novel itself focusing on "the footage," seemingly related clips that have been posted anonymously on the net. In their efforts to
apprehend the whole that underlies the parts, "footageheads" — that is, those obsessed with
the footage — attempt to discern patterns in the clips, patterns that reveal meanings. As
Gibson indicates, however, human beings not only find patterns but create them, "Homo
sapiens" being "about pattern recognition," as one character puts it (23): patterns, whether
real or imagined, are how we make meaning. What is important here — what distinguishes
Gibson's sense of the hyperreal from that of post-structuralist theorists— is remix's creative potential. Copies of copies may be vapid and uninteresting — the Tommy Hilfiger's
use of remix merely for "flavoring" is Gibson's example of such — but they can also be
provocative and even, in a sense, original, as evidenced by the footage, which remixes
themes and styles drawn from classic film into something new and unique. Unlike Baudrillard and others, who seem to be essentially nostalgic about the "real," identifying the
hyperreal with a loss of authenticity, Gibson suggests that everything is remix, though
some may be of more value than others.

See also *All Tomorrow's Parties*; *Bridge Trilogy*; Cut Up; *Idoru*; *Pattern Recognition*; Pollard, Cayce; Toei, Rei

• *References and further reading*

Baudrillard, Jean. *Simulacra and Simulation*. Trans. Sheila Fraser. Ann Arbor: University of Michigan Press,
    1995. Print.
Childers, Joseph, et al. "White Men Can't ... (De)centering Authority and Jacking into Phallic Economies
    in William Gibson's *Count Zero*." *Science Fiction, Canonization, Marginalization, and the Academy*. Ed.
    Gary Westfahl and George Slusser. Westport, CT: Greenwood, 2002. Print.
Davidson, Cynthia. "Riviera's Golem, Haraway's Cyborg: Reading *Neuromancer* as Baudrillard's Simulation
    of Crisis." *Science Fiction Studies* 23 (1996): 188–98. Print.
Gibson, William. *All Tomorrow's Parties*. New York: Berkley, 2003. Print.
_____. *Idoru*. New York: Berkley, 1997. Print.

_____. *Pattern Recognition*. New York: Berkley, 2005. Print.
Jameson, Fredric. *Archaeologies of the Future: The Desire Called Utopia and Other Science Fictions*. New York: Verso, 2005. Print.
Lindberg, Kathryne V. "Prosthetic Mnemonics and Prophylactic Politics: William Gibson among the Subjectivity Mechanisms." *Boundary* 23.2 (1996): 47–83. Print.
Murphy, Graham. "Post/Humanity and the Interstitial: A Glorification of Possibility in Gibson's Bridge Sequence." *Science Fiction Studies* 30 (2003): 72–90. Print.
Schroeder, Randy. "Neu-Criticizing William Gibson." *Extrapolation: A Journal of Science Fiction and Fantasy* 35.4 (1994): 330–41. Print.
Sponsler, Claire. "Cyberpunk and the Dilemmas of Postmodern Narrative: The Example of William Gibson." *Contemporary Literature*. 33.4 (1992): 625–44. Print.

## *Idoru*

In *Idoru* (1996), the second volume of *The Bridge Trilogy*, Gibson turns from San Francisco, a quake-damaged twentieth-century city featured in *Virtual Light*, to Tokyo, a city that, following its own quake, has moved into the twenty-first century. Rather than simply rebuild after "Godzilla" strikes, Tokyo emerges in a new form, a digital-age city, its buildings "grown" through nanotechnology rather than simply rebuilt. As such, it provides Gibson with an ideal setting for exploring twenty-first century media as it is represented by Rez, a digital-age rock superstar who seems to becoming less "real" as his celebrity grows, and Rei Toei, an "idoru" or "virtual idol" who becomes more "real" as she becomes increasingly established in the datasphere. Thematically, at least, the novel centers itself primarily around the proposed marriage between the two, a marriage that symbolizes the merging of the real and the digital in the world at large.

The novel is comprised of two independent narratives that draw together as the novel proceeds. The first involves Colin Laney, who is hired by Rez's security team to help them better understand the marriage that Rez has proposed having with a digital being, Rei Toei. Laney, like Cayce Pollard in *Pattern Recognition*, is able to intuitively recognize patterns in "low-level, broad spectrum" data, an ability that gives him the potential, at least, to comprehend what exactly Rez and Toei are and what they are becoming. Although Laney has full access to data pertaining to Rez, he can find no trace of him as an individual until he accesses data from Rez's fan clubs, since that information contains not only reports of Rez's activities but also "the importance the event held for whoever had posted it" (300). In a sense, the fan reports contextualize the data on Rez, allowing Rez to "see celebrity ... as a paradoxical quality inherent in the substance of the world" (301). As Ross Farnell notes, "Gibson constructs Rez *as* posthuman," echoing "Marshall McLuhan's vision that the 'electronic man' would 'metamorphose' himself into abstract information" (469, 470).

If Rez is, in a sense, posthuman, Toei is postdigital, becoming not just an artificial intelligence but an artificial life, "an autonomous entity in the world's cyber-networks" (Farnell 473). She can only become a corporeal being, however, through the use of nanotechnology, more particularly through the use of a device like the nano-assembler that Chia Pet McKenzie accidently comes into possession of. As a number of reviewers and commentators have noted, the novel is vague about how exactly this might work, leading Andrew X. Pham, for example, to complain that "Gibson's unwillingness to delve further into his own suggestions of virtual life" results in a "void" that prevents the novel from being "truly thought-provoking." Gibson's refuses to present the postdigital and its implications in concrete terms in order to force the reader to participate in the conceptualization process, however; as he indicates in an interview with Salon.com, he "wanted to leave the reader with suggestions" as he did in *Neuromancer* (Salon Interview). Rather than indicate exactly what it is to be postdigital, Gibson hints at it through Laney, who, surveying the data pertaining to Toei, observes, "it had begun to acquire a sort of complexity. Or randomness.... The human thing" (331). Gibson reinforces Laney's basic insight by representing Toei in increasingly human terms as the novel proceeds, reporting her speech directly rather than in the third person and assigning her volition and even emotion.

Ironically, as Toei becomes more human, Rez becomes less so, turning into a simulacrum of sorts, as Graham Murphy observes (76). Although Gibson insists Lo/Rez is not based on U2, his representation of the celebrity of its larger-than-life "half–Irish" lead singer seems to be modeled at least in part on the experiences of Bono, lead singer of U2, whom Gibson came to know in the early 1990s, as his celebrity peaked. Gibson comments that he has always been intrigued by "the enormous mechanism" that surrounds rock superstars: "You go through this maze of smaller and smaller circles. And when you get to the center, there's just a guy. But it's a guy who's kind of charged with the energy of this system — and he isn't just a guy anymore, there's something else going on there" (Salon Interview). According to Gibson, the suggestion is that "there's already an aspect of Rez that is exactly what" the idoru is, that the celebrity Rez is "almost a vestigial organ" of the "real" one.

In structural terms, the novel is very simple, as Gibson alternates between the Laney and McKenzie storylines, employing hooks at the end of most chapters as though the book were a thriller. The stories themselves are anything but simple, however. Laney's story is told largely in retrospect as he is interviewed about his previous employment by Blackwood, Rez's security chief, and sociologist, Shinyu Yamazaki; McKenzie's is presented as if she were "a Judy Blume heroine" rather than the protagonist of suspense novel (Miller). She is more of an ingénue than even Chevette Washington and, like a number of Gibson's female protagonists, relies upon other characters to explain to her what is happening and what its implications are.

Although the novel has both satirical and humorous elements, targeting things ranging from fan communities to organized crime, *Idoru* does not read like a satire, in part because early on the Laney storyline focuses on the suicide of Alison Shires—a suicide Laney may have been an indirect cause of. Set in a world nearly indistinguishable from our own, the novel also lacks the displacement characteristic of satire: as one reviewer notes, the book "feel[s]" as if it were "set in a future that is no further away than the next revision of Windows." Finally, the novel's challenging intellectual content, at least when it comes to the posthuman/postdigital, and its refusal to provide the reader with "apparent closure" also give it a more serious tenor (Salon Interview).

## VIRTUAL REALITY AND VIRTUAL WORLDS

Even more so than *Virtual Light*, *Idoru* provides detailed accounts of what virtual experiences could be like, anticipating the development of virtual worlds such as *Second Life*, *Kaneva*, and *Onverse* in some ways. Chapter Four, in particular, offers a comprehensive account of a virtual experience through McKenzie as she enters her personalized virtual domain while on a flight to Japan. Like *Second Life* and many other popular virtual worlds of today, McKenzie's domain presents itself to her as an immersive, three-dimensional space in which she can navigate, perform certain actions, interact with others, and access materials ranging from school work to her collection of Lo/Rez material.

McKenzie's domain provides her with a much richer, more textured experience than is currently available, and she is able to interact with "software agents" based on real people such as Lo, the guitarist for Lo/Rez.

McKenzie's domain also differs from those available today in the sense that it is not just a personalized space within a virtual world but an independent space on the larger Web. Domains like hers are constructed at particular addresses and can be accessed by others. Although there is a certain amount of uniformity in the way such domains are coded, making it possible for people project their own avatar into someone else's domain, for example, there appears to be no set protocol to which they must absolutely conform, except, of course, for the protocols of the net itself. While this system affords users a great deal of control over their domains, it also creates certain vulnerabilities. McKenzie's domain, for example, is subject to repeated unauthorized entry, and Zona Rosa, a member of the Seattle chapter of the Lo/Rez fan club, hacks the site of the Tokyo chapter, announcing that Rez has died. Domains can even be appropriated by others, as Zona Rosa does, converting a website created and then "forgotten about" by a large corporation into her "secret place" in which she sets up "her own country" (242).

Gibson's presentation of immersive, fully-realized virtual domains is itself immersive, at least in literary terms, since he provides access to McKenzie's internal state through free indirect discourse as she enters her domain and presents her thoughts, words, and actions directly while she is there. He also presents her experiences directly rather than having the narrator frame them, and he provides specific detail in order to create a sense of immediacy. Through the use of these and other devices, Gibson is able to approximate a virtual reality experience for his readers, allowing them to feel what entering a virtual world might be like long before such worlds existed.

## Virtual Domains and Interstitiality

In *Idoru*, Gibson extends his ideas concerning the possibilities of virtual communities existing within the interstices of the net that he presented in *Virtual Light* through his representation of the Walled City, or Hak Nam. Like the Republic of Desire in the earlier novel, the Walled City is an unauthorized virtual space that serves as a point of resistance to the net, which has been almost completely corporatized. Gibson provides much more detail about the Walled City than he does about the Republic of Desire, indicating not only its purpose but how it was created and how it is maintained. Rather than expound upon these subjects directly, however, he conveys information about them in a diffuse manner, in effect, challenging the reader to figure out its secrets. In this sense, at least, *Idoru* is more sophisticated than earlier works like *Neuromancer*, where at one point, for example, Gibson uses a television program designed to explain cyberspace to children in the twenty-first century as a device for describing cyberspace to twentieth-century readers.

Modeled upon Kowloon the Walled City, an unincorporated urban space that existed on the outskirts of Hong Kong until it was demolished in 1993, the Walled City is an ungoverned virtual space where "[t]here are no laws ... only agreements" (276). In this sense it closely resembles the Bridge, a physical structure featured in the other two novels of the *Trilogy* that hosts a similar anarchical community. Whereas the Bridge just "happened" (*Virtual Light* 101), a community forming spontaneously on the Bay Bridge after an earthquake makes it unsuitable for traffic, the Walled City was created by people who were "angry" about the net, which "had been very free," becoming controlled by governments and corporations; its founders discovered a way to turn a "killfile" inside out, to "unravel" a part of the web so that they could utilize it without being regulated or surveilled (292). As Masahiko, a denizen of the Walled City, observes, it is "of the net, but not on it," a multi-user domain or "MÚD" that has no address (276).

By representing the actions of illicit virtual communities in positive ways, Gibson seems to be suggesting that in an increasingly seamless, digitalized world, people will have to either preserve existing interstices—as the Republic of Desire does in foiling plans for redeveloping San Francisco with nanotechnology—or creating new, virtual interstices as the Walled City does. In both cases the threat new technologies pose to liberty and freedom can only be resisted by employing technology, and hacker, along with their successors, the *otaku*, who become freedom fighters of sorts, heroes in the digital age. Ironically, even though the founders of the Walled City have created something new, they take care to incorporate features of the old, particularly imagery of the original Walled City near Hong Kong. They also integrate spatial relationships into their virtual domain, assigning members tiny spaces within the City so as to preserve a sense of the original's scale, the real Hak Nam having house thirty three thousand people in just 2.7 hectares (241).

## Virtual Identities

Although Neal Stephenson is rightly credited for popularizing "avatar" as both a concept and a term in his 1994 novel, *Snow Crash*, in *The Sprawl Trilogy*, the first volume of which appeared in 1984, Gibson's characters sometimes employ virtual representations of themselves when interacting with others in cyberspace. It is not until *Idoru*, however, that Gibson makes the use of avatars a subject in itself, exploring the ways in which people can use avatars to not only interact but to "live" in virtual domains. As Sherry Turkle demonstrates in her landmark study of multi-user domains, *Life on the Screen: Identity in the Age of the Internet* (1995) "screen personae" provide users with more than "an opportunity for self-expression" (185): they also allow people to explore alternative identities. As one person she quotes indicates, "You can be whoever you want to be. You can completely redefine yourself if you want ... you can just be whoever you want, whoever you have the capacity to be" (184). Although Turkle completed her study before avatars as they are known today were widely available, she addresses the same sort of issues Gibson does in his 1996 novel; the difference in *Idoru* is that Gibson imagines screen personae with visual and audio features designed by the user that can interact with other personae in virtual space.

Avatars first appear in the novel when three members of the Seattle chapter of the Lo/Rez fan club meet in a virtual domain that they designed to appear as a jungle clearing. Although the girls, McKenzie, Kelsey, and Zona Rosa, have met only virtually, they know each other well as evidenced by the fact that they are able to interact with one another on a non-verbal level as well as in words. Choices the girls make in their avatars' appearances are also significant, as are the voices they use. Kelsey, for example, employs "a saucer-eyed nymph-figure out of some old *anime*" that bears no resemblance to herself, at least in McKenzie's judgment, while the much more demure, introverted McKenzie uses an avatar that is very much like herself, only the nose and lips are "tweaked" (14).

In *Idoru*, avatars do more than project a sense of their users' identities: they also allow users to reinvent themselves, to be who they would like to be, something that becomes most evident in the case of Mercedes Purissima Vargas-Gutierrez, a "severely deformed" twenty-six-year-old who "has lived for the past five years in almost complete denial of her physical self" (376). Although physically incapacitated, Vargas-Gutierrez is able to present herself in a powerful manner through her personae, Zona Rosa, "the leader of a knife-packing *chilanga* girl gang" based in Mexico City (14). Employing a burning blue Aztec skull as an avatar, Vargas-Gutierrez is able to *be* Zona Rosa for all intents and purposes, eventually using the illegal virtual knife she wields to save McKenzie and others from "grave danger" (375). Gibson is able to underscore the extent to which Vargas-Gutierrez becomes Zona Rosa by presenting her only as Zona Rosa until the very end of the novel: in effect, it is the avatar who is a character in the novel, not the person who has adopted it.

See also *All Tomorrow's Parties*; *The Bridge Trilogy*; Hyperreality; Pollard, Cayce; Toei, Rei; *Virtual Light*

• *References and further reading*

Berressem, Hanjo. "'Of Metal Ducks, Embodied Idorus, and Autopoietic Bridges': Tales of an Intelligent Materialism in the Age of Artificial Life." *The Holodeck in the Garden: Science and Technology in Contemporary American Fiction*. Ed. Peter Freese and Charles B. Harris. London: Dalkey, 2004. 72–99. Print.
Farnell, Ross. "Posthuman Topologies: William Gibson's 'Architexture' in *Virtual Light* and *Idoru*." *Science Fiction Studies* 26.3 (1998): 459–60. Print.
Gibson, William. *All Tomorrow's Parties*. New York: Berkley, 2003. Print.
_____. *Idoru*. New York: Berkley, 1997. Print.
_____. *Pattern Recognition*. New York: Berkley, 2005. Print.
_____. *Virtual Light*. New York: Spectra, 1994.
Leaver, Tama. "Interstitial Spaces and Multiple Histories in William Gibson's *Virtual Light, Idoru*, and *All Tomorrow's Parties*." *Limina: A Journal of Historical and Cultural Studies* 9 (2003). Web.
Murphy, Graham. "Post/Humanity and the Interstitial: A Glorification of Possibility in Gibson's Bridge Sequence." *Science Fiction Studies* 30 (2003): 72–90. Print.
Stephenson, Neal. *Snow Crash*. New York: Bantam Spectra, 2000. Print.
Turkle, Sherry. *Life on the Screen: Identity in the Age of the Internet*. New York: Simon & Schuster, 1996. Print.

# Immediacy

Like many science fiction writers, Gibson creates a sense of immediacy by engaging readers directly in his fictions through invented idioms, references to future events and technologies, detail (or what Gibson calls "hyper-specificity"), and direct representations of the speech and thoughts of his characters, inducing readers to relate to the fictive world as if they were participating in it. He simultaneously maintains distance through a variety of other devices, using the resultant tension to control the level of the reader's identification with his characters, explaining that, like Thomas Pynchon, he reminds readers that characters are "cartoons" so that they do not get "completely sucked into the mechanism" or fictive world (Newitz Interview). He also gives most of his novels what he calls "That's all Folks" endings, closing out his stories in a way that makes any ongoing identification with characters difficult.

In *Neuromancer* and the other volumes of *The Sprawl Trilogy*, he creates immediacy by employing terms such as "simstim" and "hotdogger" without defining them, referring to the nuclear destruction of Bonn and Beograde as if they were well-known events, describing experiences such as entering cyberspace in different ways every time they occur, and frequently reporting the speech and thought of characters directly. At the same time, however, he consistently employs the past tense and distal language to maintain a certain distance between his readers and his characters. This is true even in the most physically and emotionally intense moments, such as in Henry Case's first sexual encounter with Molly Millions: "Now she straddled him again, took his hand, and closed it over her, his thumb along the cleft of her buttocks, his fingers spread across the labia. As she began to lower herself, the images came pulsing back, the faces, fragments of neon arriving and receding.... She rode him that way, impaling herself slipping down on him again and again, until they both had come, his orgasm flaring blue in a timeless space, a vastness like the matrix, where the faces were shredded and blown away down hurricane corridors" (33). By continuing to use the past tense and demonstratives like "that" even when providing both detail and direct access to the character's consciousness, Gibson helps readers maintain at least some critical distance from the characters and situations so that the reading experience remains intellectual as well as emotional.

The Bridge Trilogy employs similar devices to create a sense of immediacy while using tense and distal language to prevent readers from identifying too closely with characters and situations. The Trilogy's satirical tone and political overtones tend to augment this sense of distance, however. Virtual Light, for example, includes characters with unrealistic names like "Sublett" and "Lucius Warbaby," makes reference to places like "Nissan County" (once "Orange County") and "Skywalker Park" (once "Golden Gate Park"), and details the disastrous consequences of Reagan's "War on Drugs" and refusal to address AIDS in a comprehensive manner. Although hardly didactic, the novel conveys a sense of social and political consciousness on Gibson's part that partially offsets any sense of immediacy he creates through style. Idoru and All Tomorrow's Parties are less satirical than Virtual Light, allowing readers to identify more strongly with characters and situations. This is particularly true when it comes to Colin Laney, one of the Trilogy's more compelling characters. In describing Laney's meeting with two members of the Walled City in a virtual space, for example, Gibson uses the present tense, conveys Laney's thoughts directly, and employs words like "this" rather than "that" to create a sense of immediacy, allowing readers to experience the encounter through his characters consciousness: "It is not a construct, this place, an environment proper, so much as a knotting, a folding-in of information rooted in the substrates of the oldest codes. It is something like a makeshift raft, random pieces thrown together, but it is anchored, unmoving. He knows that it is no accident, that it has been put in his path for a reason" (214). Because of passages like this—passages that create a sense of immediacy—readers engage with Laney differently than they do with the Trilogy's other characters, ultimately making him more compelling: in a Trilogy featuring somewhat cartoonish characters like Berry Rydell, Chevette Washington, Chia Pet Mackenzie, Laney seems more fully human than the others.

Pattern Recognition, the first volume of The Bigend Trilogy, contrasts sharply with Gibson's earlier novels in that it consistently employs the present tense. As a result of that—and the fact that the novel focuses tightly on one particular character, Cayce Pollard—the novel generates a powerful sense of immediacy, drawing the reader into her consciousness, something that may have helped make the novel a mainstream best-seller. In Spook Country, however, Gibson returns to his previous form, providing detail and conveying the interior states of his characters to create immediacy while simultaneously maintaining distance through the use of the past tense and distal language, thereby keeping the reader more focused on his fictive world rather than the characters within it. As a consequence, the novel's social message about the perils facing post–Patriot Act America become more obvious, leading one critic to remark that the novel's "underlying political pre-occupation and detached narration came at the expense of character development" (Conover). Gibson adopts a similar strategy in Zero History, the final volume of the Trilogy, again balancing the proximal and distal to control the level of identification readers have with characters and keeping much of the focus on the novel's social message, in this case about consumerism and profiteering. At the very end of the novel he collapses all distance, however, closing out the *Trilogy* in the present tense as Hollis Henry awakens from a nightmare sleeping next to Garreth Wilson, her love interest. In doing so, Gibson avoids the "That's all, Folks" endings that mark so much of his earlier fiction, bringing the story into a present shared with the reader rather than relegating it to the past.

See also *All Tomorrow's Parties*; Henry, Hollis; *Idoru*; *Neuromancer*; *Pattern Recognition*; *Spook Country*; *Virtual Light*; *Zero History*

• *References and further reading*

Chafe, Wallace. *Discourse, Consciousness, and Time: The Flow and Displacement of Conscious Experience in Speaking and Writing.* Chicago: University of Chicago Press, 1994. Print.
Gibson, William. *All Tomorrow's Parties.* New York: Berkley, 2003. Print.
_____. *Idoru.* New York: Berkley, 1997. Print.
_____. *Neuromancer.* New York: Ace, 1994. Print.
_____. *Pattern Recognition.* New York: Berkley, 2005. Print.
_____. *Spook Country.* New York: Berkley, 2009. Print.
_____. *Virtual Light.* New York: Spectra, 1994. Print.
_____. *Zero History.* New York: Putnam, 2010. Print.

# Influence

In terms of overall influence, Gibson is arguably one of the most important writers of the late twentieth century since, as Stephen Poole observes, his representation of cyberspace — a term Gibson himself coined — "laid the conceptual foundations for the explosive real-world growth of virtual environments in videogames and the Web." At the very least, novels such as *Neuromancer, Count Zero,* and *Mona Lisa Overdrive* helped establish the idea of virtual domains as spaces that could be entered into and navigated, not only in the popular imagination but in the minds of those who were developing new technologies and/or seeking to exploit them commercially. Though Gibson did not invent cyberspace, he provided people with a way of thinking and talking about it and therefore had both a direct and indirect influence on the way it developed.

He is also important in terms of literary influence, being instrumental to the establishment of both cyberpunk and steampunk as viable subgenres of science fiction. His influence upon science fiction in general is even more significant, however. When Gibson began publishing in the early 1980s, science fiction readers generally valued linear, content-driven stories more than literary ones. *Neuromancer* and the novels that followed challenged the *status quo.* Although like most science fiction, Gibson's work featured new technologies, Gibson was less interested in future wonders themselves than in their effects on people, giving his novels a psychological depth usually associated with more literary fiction. He was also more of a conscious stylist than most science fiction writers of the time, using both detailed description and a variety of figures to convey novel ideas and sensations. As Dike Blair observes, Gibson succeeded in "captur[ing] the moods which surround technologies, rather than their engineering" (Blair Interview). The fact that *Neuromancer* swept the major science fiction awards and sold millions of copies demonstrated that so-called "soft" science was again viable, paving the way for a new generation of more literary science fiction writers such as Marge Piercy, Richard Paul Russo, and Neal Stephenson.

Gibson also had considerable influence on artists working in other media, particularly music, television, film, and video games. Sonic Youth's acclaimed 1988 album, *Daydream Nation*, which includes a song titled "The Sprawl," drew upon Gibson's *The Sprawl Trilogy*, and the opening track of the 2004 album, *Nurse*, is named for Gibson's 2003 novel, *Pattern Recognition*. Warren Zevon's 1989 album, *Transverse City*, was also inspired by Gibson's early work as was Billy Idol's *Cyberpunk* (1993), Idol commenting that he was "was revved up by the DIY energy of Gibson and the high-tech underground" when recording it (Ehrman). Gibson, who rarely offers public criticism of other people's work, disapproved of what he regarded as Idol's crass exploitation of cyberpunk, criticizing him in interviews and even basing Billy Prion, a washed-up rockstar who appears in *Pattern Recognition*, on him. U2 is probably the most prominent band to be influenced by Gibson and his work, the band's *Zooropa*/Zoo TV productions incorporating a number of elements from Gibson's work, including stage sets based on Gibson's cityscapes. At one point the band even considered incorporating the entire text of *Neuromancer* into their performances (Dalton). Gibson and the band became friendly in this period: Gibson interviewed them for *Details* magazine and the band provided a track for *Johnny Mnemonic* (1995). Bono and the Edge also provided interviews and music for *No Maps for These Territories* (2000), a documentary featuring Gibson.

Gibson's influence on film can be most clearly discerned in what might be called the "cyberpunk style" of the 1990s, epitomized in *The Matrix* (1999), where the lead characters wear leather, expensive sunglasses, and long jackets over tight, dark, well-tailored clothing and powerful firearms. The emphasis on fashion combined with hidden danger seems to be drawn directly from the Sprawl series, in which characters are very much preoccupied with both looks and weaponry, Gibson himself observing that "the wardrobe department had read *Neuromancer*" (Telegraph Interview). The cyberpunk aesthetic involved more than just clothes and guns, however: the menacing, claustrophobic grittiness of Gibson's Sprawl is reproduced in cyberpunk films like *Until the End of the World* (1991) and *Strange Days* (1995), films that offer "dirty, hyper-realistic 'lived in' looks at the near future" (SFAN). The popular television program *Dark Angel*, a number of *anime*, including *Ghost in the Shell*, and video games like *Cyberia, Deus Ex*, and *Bioshock* also draw upon the cyberpunk aesthetic Gibson helped popularize.

*See also* Cyberpunk

## Japan

Japan has figured prominently in Gibson's fiction from the very first, even though he had never actually been there until after *Neuromancer* was published in 1984. Like many Americans in the early 1980s, Gibson appears to have been both fascinated and frightened by a Japan that seemed poised to become a new kind of superpower. Gibson's early work, particularly the novels and stories set in the Sprawl, depict a world that has been "Japanified," to borrow Wendy Chun's term, both economically and culturally. Indeed, the global economy is structured around *zaibatsu*, a conglomeration of powerful corporations that govern not only themselves but their employees. Between them the *zaibatsu*— a Japanese word for the corporate system that dominated the Japanese economy from the late--nineteenth century until World War II —control official commerce, governments being largely subject to them rather than the reverse. Significantly, the corporations mentioned by name in the Sprawl narratives are largely Japanese: Hosaka, Sony, and Ono-Sendai, for example.

As Chun indicates, Gibson's representation of Japan in his early work can be understood in terms of "Orientalism," a critical concept developed by Edward Said to describe the ways in which Europeans constructed the so-called East as an exotic "Other." In Gibson's "hi tech Orientalism," the future is presented in binary terms in which Japanese corporatism, represented by the sinister *zaibatsu*, is opposed to American individualism, represented by console cowboys like Henry Case. Cyberspace is presented as a location where increasingly marginalized and disempowered individuals like Case can still triumph, a place where, to echo Chun, the Orient submits to Occidental penetration.

Not surprisingly, perhaps, the collapse of the Japanese economy in 1991 led to a change in the way Japan is represented in Gibson's work. Though still exoticized in *The Bridge Trilogy*, Japan is no longer presented as being threatening or antagonistic. Indeed, the evil corporations are generally American: Sunflower Corporation in *Virtual Light*; Slitscan in *Idoru*; and Harwood/Levine in *All Tomorrow's Parties*. Although there are still indications that the Japan of these novels has surpassed the United States technologically — post-quake Tokyo being rebuilt using nanotechnology while post-quake San Francisco is still under repair — both nations seem to be part of a post–Cold War, global system in which national boundaries are less significant than they were. If the United States is in decline, it because it is because its time as a superpower has passed, not because of any particular competition from Japan. As Shinya Yamazaki, a Japanese graduate student in sociology, observes in *Virtual Light*, the United States has become a "Thomasson," a "useless and inexplicable" monument to something that was. Japan, in contrast, is a part of what is coming into being, a technology-driven society in which change itself is the only constant.

Japan figures much less prominently in *The Bigend Trilogy*, being used as a setting for only a small part of *Pattern Recognition*. This fact alone seems indicative of how Gibson's — and arguably much mainstream America's — perception of Japan has changed because of Japan's economic collapse of the 1990s. Japan is presented as an interesting place but not a particularly important or threatening one. Although the novel's protagonist, Cayce Pollard, is assaulted while in Tokyo, it is by Italians who have followed her there from London, Tokyo itself being a cosmopolitan place that draws from many cultures but retains its own identify. The latter is perhaps best evidenced by a "Coca-Cola logo pulsing on a huge screen, high up on a building, followed by the slogan "NO REASON!"—a slogan that only adds to the sense of disorientation Pollard feels in a place that to her is at once familiar and alien.

Gibson has also written about Japan in a series of articles he wrote following a 2001 visit sponsored by *Wired* magazine. In "The Future Perfect," an article written for *Time*, he suggests that Japan is "the most inherently futuristic of all nations" because of its peculiar history, the Japanese, "after centuries of isolation, [having] "opened themselves ... to technologies as alien to their previous way of being and knowing as, say, reverse-engineered Roswell crash artifacts would be to us." Since then, Gibson argues, Japan has undergone similar shocks again and again, most recently because of the American occupation that followed World War II. As a result Japan effectively "lives in the future," the Japanese being the first to incorporate new technologies into their every day lives. He makes a similar argument in "Modern Boys and Mobile Girls," an article he wrote for *The Observer*, identifying the Japanese as the "ultimate Early Adapters." In the article he wrote for *Wired*, he adds an additional element to his historical explanation of what makes Japan "futurologically sexy," focusing on the "hybrid forms" that resulted from "American tissue" being "grafted" on to the "feudal-industrial core" that existed before the American occupation.

*See also All Tomorrow's Parties*; "Burning Chrome"; *The Bridge Trilogy*; Cyberspace; *Idoru*; *Neuromancer*; *Pattern Recognition*; *The Sprawl Trilogy*; *Virtual Light*

• *References and further reading*

Caesar, Terry. "Turning American: Popular Culture and National Identity in the Recent American Text of Japan." *Arizona Quarterly* 58.2 (2002): 113–41.

Chun, Wendy. *Control and Freedom: Power and Paranoia in the Age of Fiber Optics.* Cambridge: MIT Press, 2006. Print.

Gibson, William. *All Tomorrow's Parties.* New York: Berkley, 2003. Print.

_____. "Burning Chrome." *Burning Chrome.* New York: Ace, 1986. Print.

_____. "Future Perfect." TimeAsia.com, 30 April 2001. Web.

_____. *Idoru.* New York: Berkley, 1997. Print.

_____. "Modern Boys and Mobile Girls." Japan issue, Guardian.co.uk, *The Observer.* 1 April 2001. Web.

_____. "My Own Private Tokyo." Wired.com, *Wired* 9.9 (2001). Web.

_____. *Neuromancer.* New York: Ace, 1994. Print.

_____. "The New Rose Hotel." *Burning Chrome.* New York: Ace, 1986. Print.

_____. *Pattern Recognition.* New York: Berkley, 2005. Print.

_____. "Shiny Balls of Mud." *Tate Magazine,* 1 Sept/Oct 2002. Web.

_____. *Virtual Light.* New York: Spectra, 1994. Print.

Sanders, Leonard Patrick. *Postmodern Orientalism: William Gibson, Cyberpunk and Japan.* Doctoral Thesis. Massey University, 2008. Print.

Tatsumi, Takayuki. "The Japanese Reflection of Mirrorshades." *Storming the Reality Studio: A Casebook of Cyberpunk and Postmodern Science Fiction.* Ed. Larry McCaffery. Durham: Duke University Press, 1991. 366–73. Print.

## "Johnny Mnemonic" (novella)

After *Neuromancer*, "Johnny Mnemonic" (1981) is probably the most widely known of Gibson's works, largely because it is the first to be adapted for film and distributed as a major motion picture release. The original story, which was published in *Omni* in 1981 and then collected in *Burning Chrome*, was, according to Gibson, "perhaps the second piece of fiction" he had written (Salza Interview). Bearing this in mind, Gibson's use of the first person seems remarkably sophisticated in that he is able to employ an authentic-seeming voice, in this case that of the title character, without being limited by the adopted personae. The story also stands out for the way in which it establishes a sense of place through the use of specific but uncontextualized references and detail. As in most of his later work, Gibson is able to use the future as a setting without ever making the future his ostensive subject; though set in the future, the story is really about the present, something that Gibson insists is true of all of his fiction. The story was short-listed for the Nebula Award for best short story in 1981, establishing Gibson's reputation near the very beginning of his career.

The story centers on Johnny Mnemonic, a man sought by the Yakuza, a Japan-based crime organization, for stolen information he is storing in memory chips implanted in his head. He is saved first from Rafti, the person that originally hired him to steal information, and then from a ninja assassin by Molly Millions, a free-lance razorgirl, who insinuates herself into Mnemonic's employ (3). Millions, who herself has high-tech implants, defeats the latter in a distinctly low-tech way, luring him onto a trampoline-like "Killing Floor" maintained by the Lo Teks, a street gang that eschews most forms of high technology; there she performs a "mad-dog dance," undulating the floor and causing the assassin to cross the path of his own hi-tech weapon (20). Mnemonic and Millions then become partners, using a cybernetic dolphin designed by the military to extract traces of information Mnemonic has previously stored in his head to blackmail former clients.

Although set in the same world as *The Sprawl Trilogy*, the story differs from the later novels in terms of both style and content. Although *Neuromancer*, too, presents the perspective of only one character directly, it uses the third person to contextualize its protagonist's experiences and provide indications, at least, of what other characters are thinking and feeling, including Molly Millions, who appears in both works. "Johnny Mnemonic," in contrast, focuses tightly on the perspective of its protagonist, inflecting everything through him in a manner reminiscent of 1930s thrillers and detective novels. Indeed, Mnemonic's very words seem to be patterned after those of characters like Dashiell Hammett's Nick Charles or Raymond Chandler's Philip Marlowe, the story opening as follows: "I put the shotgun in an Adidas bag and padded it out with four pairs of tennis socks, not my style at all, but that's what I was aiming for: if they think you're crude, go technical; if they think you're technical, go crude" (1). By employing elements drawn from writers like Hammett, Gibson is able to not only establish gritty atmosphere but offset some of the strangeness of the story's other features, such as a cybernetic dolphin addicted to heroin or a ninja who fights with a monomolecular filament he keeps coiled within a prosthetic thumb.

Regarding content, the story differs from the Sprawl novels in that it does not concern itself with cyberspace, the matrix, or the implications of a global network of computers. Rather, as the very first sentence of the story suggests, it addresses how low technology can provide means of resistance in a high technology society. To the extent that it develops this theme by identifying high technology with the Japanese, the novel obviously reflects the attitudes of its time, most notably the American fear of and fascination with Japan in the 1980s as its economy expanded and it seemed to many to be poised to become a leading power. As Wendy Chun notes, during this period writers like Gibson engaged in what might be termed "hi tech orientalism," a process through which the Japanese are "othered" in an effort to contain the threat they represent. In "Johnny Mnemonic," the hi tech/low tech opposition is conflated with the Japan/United States opposition in the climactic battle between the ninja assassin and Molly Millions. The assassin himself seems to recognize that the battle represents more than just a struggle between two individuals, reacting "with pure aesthetic revulsion" to Millions's "mad-dog dance" and the drumming of the Lo Teks watching the fight. Although the ninja, a cyborg with a prosthetic weapon and a "jacked up" nervous system is represented as being physically more-than-human, he is simultaneously less-than-human in the sense that he is a "factory custom" rather than a man, and thus he is dehumanized in a manner similar to the way the Japanese were in World War II Allied propaganda (8).

*See also Burning Chrome*; *Johnny Mnemonic* (film); Millions, Molly

• *References and further reading*

Chandler, Raymond. *The Big Sleep*. New York: Random House, 1939. Print.
Chun, Wendy. *Control and Freedom: Power and Paranoia in the Age of Fiber Optics*. Cambridge: MIT Press, 2006. Print.
Gibson, William. "Johnny Mnemonic." *Burning Chrome*. New York: Ace, 1986. Print.
_____. *Neuromancer*. New York: Ace, 1984. Print.
Hammett, Dashiell. *The Maltese Falcon*. New York: Alfred A. Knopf, 1930. Print.

## Johnny Mnemonic (film)

Not surprisingly, perhaps, given the fact that it was produced more than a decade after the story, the 1995 TriStar Pictures film starring Keanu Reeves addresses different issues than the story, focusing on unethical corporations, overdependence upon digital technology, and the inability of traditional Christianity to address 21st-century issues in productive ways. Like the story, the film does suggest that low technology can be used to counter high technology, however, and it presents gaps in the infrastructure as points from which resistance can be effected. In making the latter point, Gibson imports a version of the broken bridge from *Virtual Light* to Newark, New Jersey, where most of the action takes place.

In a 1994 interview with Giuseppe Salza, Gibson described the production process as "the optimal screen experience," since he and director Robert Longo were given both the freedom and the budget to develop the film they wanted. According to Gibson, *Johnny Mnemonic* was re-edited after production, however, completely transforming it: "The film that was released is something like what you would have seen if the distributor had taken over post-production of David Lynch's *Blue Velvet* and made a whole-hearted, but very misguided attempt to turn it into a straight, irony-free thriller" (Van Belkom Interview). He adds, "The screenplay ... was meant to be sort of semi-comic, or in any case, very ironic movie that in a way was about B science fiction films as much as it was about anything else" (Van Belkom Interview). Although the final version presents itself as a cyberthriller, ironic elements still remain, and it is possible to regard it as a satire of what cyberpunk had become by the mid–1990s. For example, in a scene reminiscent of *Terminator 2: Judgment Day* (1991), the burnt corpse of the superhuman Street Preacher, played by Dolph Lundgren, appears to reanimate itself. The camera pulls back, however, revealing that it is being moved by pulley as J-Bone's lo-tech cohorts remove the detritus from the preceding battle. "Just garbage," J-Bone, played by Ice-T, comments: "Get that out of here."

The North American release of the film was neither a commercial nor a critical success, its box office gross falling far short of its $26 million production costs, and reviews were largely negative. The Japanese version, which runs more than ten minutes longer, not only adding scenes but also extending existing ones, adheres more closely to Gibson's screenplay and is widely considered superior. Takaheshi, a character played by popular Japanese actor Takeshi Kitano, is developed more fully in this version, and the Street Preacher seems to be a caricature of an Evangelical, charismatic minister as he preaches to his church. According to Gibson, the Street Preacher's sermon "bombastic, faux–Sterlingesque, literally balls [Lundgren was filmed naked] *sermon* on the virtues of posthumanity" was cut from the North American version "out of fear of offending the religious right" (blog 5/01/2000). Gibson adds that the Japanese release is a little closer to his and Longo's intention and that he agreed to have the screenplay itself published so that he could "demonstrate the difference between what I wrote, and what we shot, and what they [TriStar] released."

The release of the film coincided with *Johnny Mnemonic: The Interactive Action Movie*, a PC-based computer game in which player choices influence the story as it is being presented to them, the program drawing from 2,500 filmed scenes starring Christopher Russell Gartin as Johnny (Weiss). A *Johnny Mnemonic* soundtrack was also released in 1995, as were an audiobook and a pinball machine, Gibson reportedly having one of the latter in his basement (O'Hara Interview).

*See also* "Johnny Mnemonic" (story)

• *References and further reading*
Austin, Andrea. "Frankie and Johnny: Shelley, Gibson, and Hollywood's Love Affair with the Cyborg." *Romanticism on the Net: An Electronic Journal Devoted to Romantic Studies* 21 (2001). Web.

## Laney, Colin

A primary character in both *Idoru* and *All Tomorrow's Parties*, Colin Laney is a seemingly unimpressive, unassuming person, who, in the latter novel at least, behaves heroically—not only preventing megalomaniac Cody Harwood from shaping the future, but destroying himself in the process. Though an everyman of sorts, Laney emerges as the moral center of *The Bridge Trilogy*, becoming one of Gibson's most striking characters by the final novel. Laney, who intuitively perceives patterns in data because of 5-SB, an experimental drug he was given as a child, is introduced in *Idoru* as a data analyst hired to discern what he can about the potential for—and consequences of—a marriage between Rez, a rock superstar, and Rei Toei, a computer-generated pop star who has become self-aware. Previously he had worked for Slitscan, a media corporation that creates and destroys celebrities for profit, where his job was to identify "nodal points" in data, that is, to discern patterns in information pertaining to celebrities in an effort to exploit them. He is unable to remain detached from his work, however; realizing that a woman whose data he has been focusing on is suicidal, he tries to intervene, violating company rules and getting himself fired. Although no "hero," as he himself is quick to admit (79), Laney is a fundamentally decent person who tries to do what is right. As such, he serves as an emblem for Gibson of how people would be if the world was a better place. As in much of his later work, particularly *Pattern Recognition* and *Spook Country*, it is everyday people who can make a difference in thwarting even the rich and powerful like Harwood and Hubertus Bigend.

In *All Tomorrow's Parties*, Laney becomes a fully fledged hero, if only because in this case he succeeds in saving not just one person but, arguably, everyone. From within a cardboard shanty inside a Tokyo train station, Laney, who is terminally ill, challenges Harwood's effort to shape the future in his own favor. Harwood, it seems, has voluntarily dosed himself on 5-SB so that he, too, can identify nodal points: he hopes to use this ability to become even more rich and powerful as nanotechnology comes into everyday use in the twenty-first century. In what amounts to a sort of duel between the two—arguably one of the strangest, most abstract ones to be narrated in a mainstream work of fiction—Laney defeats Harwood by locating him in data so that his efforts can be neutralized. The effort overtaxes Laney, however, and he dies, sacrificing himself for others.

The fact that Laney so effectively counters Harwood's efforts from within a squatters' community built within a subway station is significant, the suggestion being that power can be resisted by even the most dispossessed, from interstices like the Cardboard City or the bridge that gives the *The Bridge Trilogy* its name. Just as importantly, the weak and disempowered can make a difference in shaping history. For this reason, it could be argued that Gibson uses Laney to express a post-punk sensibility: whereas the punk-like characters of *The Sprawl Trilogy* react to authority in anger and frustration, later characters like Laney, Cayce Pollard, and Hollis Henry resist it with a sense of purpose, taking action that is decidedly moral.

*See also All Tomorrow's Parties; The Bridge Trilogy; Idoru; Toei, Rei*

• *References and further reading*

Gibson, William. *All Tomorrow's Parties*. New York: Berkley, 2003. Print.

_____. *Idoru*. New York: Berkley, 1997. Print.

_____. *Virtual Light*. New York: Spectra, 1994. Print.

Leaver, Tama. "Interstitial Spaces and Multiple Histories in William Gibson's *Virtual Light, Idoru,* and *All Tomorrow's Parties.*" *Limina: A Journal of Historical and Cultural Studies* 9 (2003). Web.

Murphy, Graham. "Post/Humanity and the Interstitial: A Glorification of Possibility in Gibson's Bridge Sequence." *Science Fiction Studies* 30 (2003): 72–90. Print.

## Literary Influences

Like many writers, Gibson often seems reluctant to address influence questions, indicating in his blog that "if you know your own influences, your digestion's pretty sluggish." He is willing to discuss writers he likes, however, and acknowledges those that have shaped his worldview if not his writing: writers such as William S. Burroughs, J.G. Ballard, Thomas Pynchon, and Samuel Delany. He is quick to point out, however, that questions about literary influences are problematic since "they're usually framed to encourage you to talk about your writing as if you grew up in a world circumscribed by books," adding that he's "been influenced by Lou Reed, for instance, as much as I've been influenced by any 'fiction' writer" (McCaffery Interview 265). With this in mind, it should not be surprising that he frequently cites media such as film, sculpture, and even architecture as significant influences upon him.

In terms of literature, Gibson's early work is most obviously influenced by the *noir* detective fiction of writers like Dashiell Hammett and Raymond Chandler, largely because many of his characters correspond to the types featured in such writing, as do his plots and vernacular. As Lance Olsen observes, "He lifts lowlife sleuths and criminals, archetypical tough guys, mysteries solved through the collection and interpretation of clues, seedy underworld characters, clipped prose, and sparse dialogue from the hard-boiled detective genre" (33). Gibson himself acknowledges such influences from the very start, crediting Hammett in particular for developing a "cranked up, very intense, almost surreal" form of "American naturalism" that Gibson found very exciting (McCaffery Interview 269). In the same 1986 interview, however, he differentiates himself from Chandler, saying he always got "this creepy, puritanical feeling from his books." In his blog, Gibson again praises Hammett while distancing himself from Chandler, writing, "I've never read much Chandler either, another frequently supposed influence, adding that Dashiell Hammett is the "real deal": "[He] Invented the vehicle, as far as I know, though Chandler brought a classier chassis to it." Gibson continued incorporating a variety of *noir* elements into the fiction that followed *The Sprawl Trilogy*, as evidenced by characters such as arms dealer Michael Preston Gracie and his retinue in *Zero History* and the use of MacGuffins throughout *The Bigend Trilogy*. The dark tone is largely missing from works written after *Count Zero*, however, a notable exception being the narrative strand centering on Tito in *Spook Country*, which to some extent reproduces the air of pre-war thrillers like those of Eric Ambler and Graham Greene.

Gibson also counts Thomas Pynchon as "a major influence," not only on his own work but also on the whole "cyberpunk thing, the SF that mixes surrealism and pop culture imagery with esoterical historical and scientific information" (McCaffery 272). Although Pynchon's influence can be discerned in most of Gibson's work, it is in the first two volumes of *The Bridge Trilogy* that it becomes most evident, at least in terms of plot and characterization. *Virtual Light*, in particular, seems Pynchonesque as Chevette Washington, who corresponds to Pynchon's Oedipa Maas, becomes increasingly ensnared in what amounts to a conspiracy amongst certain real estate developers to rebuild San Francisco with high-tech high rises. Like Pynchon's novel, *Virtual Light* has a baroque plot and flat characters with overtly symbolic, unrealistic names like Sublet, Loveless, and Lucius Warbaby. More importantly, perhaps, it has the feel of a Pynchon novel, employing humor and satire to undercut any *gravitas* as soon as it emerges. *Idoru*, too, has many Pynchonesque elements, but the satire is more muted, and Gibson avoids making easy jokes like renaming Orange County "Nissan County" and calling a Madonna impersonator "McDonna." The novel, like *All Tomorrow's Parties*, is also heavier in tone than *Virtual Light*, and it introduces Colin Laney, one of Gibson's most serious-minded characters.

Pynchon's influence on Gibson was not only literary; like William S. Burroughs, Pynchon had a powerful effect on Gibson's worldview, something that is most obviously reflected in the way Gibson depicts multinational corporations as replacing nations as governing authorities in novels ranging from *Neuromancer* to *All Tomorrow's Parties*. Even novels set in the present like those of *The Bigend Trilogy* suggest that nation-states are giving way to corporations, as evidenced by Winnie Tung Whitaker, a U.S. government agent who has to go through the Blue Ant agency to thwart Michael Preston Gracie's efforts to secure military contracts for clothing in *Zero History* since the government gives her no authority to do so. Gibson credits *Gravity's Rainbow* for helping him realize that a single corporation can profit from both sides in a war, that they are "entities" that exist "outside of national boundaries" with loyalties towards no particular state. The sense of paranoia that suffuses much of Gibson's work is also arguably Pynchonesque, though in Gibson's novels, seeming coincidences are sometimes just that, and *Pattern Recognition*, at least, suggests that it is sometimes better to let go of one's paranoia and just live. Gibson also distinguishes his work from Pynchon's in terms of characterization, observing that in Pynchon's case, "you're never allowed to believe in characters. He's making moves all the way to remind you that these are cartoons" (Newitz Interview). Gibson concedes that he has "a little bit of that," too—that he does not want "people to get completely sucked into the mechanism," that they "should remember that they're riding on a roller coaster," but he insists that his characters are fully realized rather than cartoons. As Dave Itzkoff suggests, such a strategy makes Gibson more of a realist than a postmodernist since he presents his characters as real.

Burroughs was another primary influence on Gibson, most obviously in the way Gibson adopted and adapted Burrough's cut-up technique in works like "The Gernsback Continuum" and *The Difference Engine*, and in the way he creates rhetorical matrices or "collages" to convey ideas that cannot be easily expressed descriptively. Burroughs's greatest influence may have been upon Gibson's sense of "what SF — or any literature, for that matter, could be" (McCaffery Interview 278). Gibson continues: "What Burroughs was doing with plot and language and the SF motifs I saw in other writers was literally mind expanding. I saw this crazy outlaw character who seemed to have picked up SF and gone after society with it, the way some old guy might grab a rusty beer opener and start waving it around." In effect, Burroughs taught Gibson that writing was more than just entertainment, that conventions could be violated not just for the sake of doing so but also to offer both social and cultural criticism.

In addition to Hammett, Pynchon, and Burroughs, Gibson often lists Alfred Bester, J.G. Ballard, and Samuel Delany as primary influences. Ballard and Bester merit special attention, though their impact is more general than specific, influencing Gibson's world-view more than his prose. Like Gibson, Bester and Ballard rejected Golden Age science fiction and its attendant ideologies of material progress, focusing instead on the psychological and sociological effects of technology (Youngquist 45). He has also been influenced in obvious ways by his friends and co-authors Bruce Sterling, John Shirley, and Jack Womack. He consistently denies that Philip K. Dick had any influence, other than "the distilled paranoia" that he found "in most of his work" (Cyberpunk Interview). He seems to be carefully neutral about Neal Stephenson, though Chevette Washington, a bike messenger he introduces in *Virtual Light* seems to parody Y.T., a skateboarding courier who appears in *Snow Crash*. In general, Gibson rarely comments on his contemporaries, insisting that he reads no new fiction when writing.

    *See also* Counterculture; Cut Up

## Milgrim

    As a person who has no sense of his own past and therefore lives entirely in the present, Milgrim is one of Gibson's most original, interesting characters, serving as a mirror of sorts for the post 9/11 world in which he lives. Milgrim (no other name is ever provided for him) is introduced in *Spook Country* as an Ativan addict who has come under the control of Brown, a quasi-official government agent who needs Milgrim to translate a particular Russian vernacular for him. Despite remembering almost nothing of his life before he became an addict, Milgrim is nonetheless able to draw the language skills he learned while a student at Columbia University, and he retains elements of his old personality, presenting himself as a introverted person with somewhat refined tastes. Though he is entirely dependent upon Brown for Rize, a Japanese drug similar to Ativan, Milgrim, who reads the *New York Times*, looks down upon him for being an uneducated, dull-minded, Fox News–watching man and thus he serves as vehicle for what amounts to an attack upon the neo-conservatives Gibson held responsible for the wars in Afghanistan and Iraq and the erosion of civil liberties under the Patriot Act. At the end of the novel he escapes Brown's control, and, with $5,000 he finds in Hollis Henry's purse, he has an opportunity to begin a new life for himself in Vancouver. Having seen what the world has become while translating for Brown, he rejects it, choosing to retreat into a 1961 paperback on revolutionary Messianism he found in the pocket of a Paul Stuart raincoat he stole earlier.

    To an extent, Milgrim as he appears in *Spook Country* can be understood as an every-man of sorts, his condition being the postmodern condition, a condition in which one is controlled by one's desire, being entirely alienated from oneself. Depicted in the "flat" manner characteristic of postmodern writers like Thomas Pynchon and Don DeLillo, Milgrim's two-dimensionality is more a quality than a lack: he is presented as the type of person we are becoming as the rich and powerful consolidate their control over every aspect of existence.

    In *Zero History*, the final volume of *The Bigend Trilogy*, Milgrim emerges more fully as a protagonist, his story being one of the two main narrative strands, along with that of Hollis Henry. Now in the employ of Hubertus Bigend, who has paid for eight months of treatment in an exclusive treatment center for drug addicts, Milgrim begins to recover not only elements of his past self but the opportunity to grow: he is no longer the static character he was *Spook Country*, increasingly demonstrating initiative and even forming close relations with others. A Rip Van Winkle type character in the sense that he awakens in a world that is contiguous with the one he knew before he became an addict and yet alien, Milgrim provides readers with an outside perspective on the world they themselves are living, a world that, with the advent of digital technology, has changed in fundamental ways. What he discovers as he becomes a becomes a more fully-rounded person is that the world itself has flattened, the differences between London and Paris, for example, becoming almost negligible, being occupied by the same sorts of people doing the same sorts of things. Finally pronounced cured by Bigend at the end of the novel and afforded "full human status," Milgrim discovers that there is no point in being fully human in a world controlled by people like Bigend, people who use new technologies to promote a monoculture, if only because a monoculture represents not only a larger market but one that is easier to manage. Upon learning that he has fully recovered at the end of the novel, the medications he had been using for detoxification having long been placebos, Milgrim remarks, "But I *like* a placebo," his words registering his discomfort with what the world has become.

*See also* Bigend; Hubertus; *The Bigend Trilogy*; *Count Zero*; Henry, Hollis; *Pattern Recognition*; *Spook Country*; *Zero History*

• *References and further reading*
Gibson, William. *Pattern Recognition*. New York: Berkley, 2005. Print.
\_\_\_\_\_. *Spook Country*. New York: Berkley, 2009. Print.
\_\_\_\_\_. *Zero History*. New York: Putnam, 2010. Print.

## Millions, Molly (aka Sally Shears)

Although one of Gibson's earliest characters, being introduced in "Johnny Mnemonic" (1981) as a seemingly one-dimensional, street-hardened "razorgirl," Molly Millions develops into one of Gibson's most complex, taking a leading role in both *Neuromancer* and *Mona Lisa Overdrive*. Modeled physically on Chrissie Hynde, lead singer of the Pretenders, as she appeared on the cover of her first album, Millions is initially presented as a sexy, dangerous mercenary with leather pants, mirror shade implants, surgically enhanced reflexes, and blades that project from under her fingernails. Like many of the characters in Gibson's early work, she seems to be designed to appeal to readers looking for thriller-like adventures rather than provocative ideas, though the fact that she uses low-tech to defeat a high-tech ninja at the climax of the story underscores a serious point Gibson makes about strategies for resisting authority. Although not exactly a punk, Millions exudes a certain punk sensibility, being aggressive, self-assured, and insistent upon making her own way.

In *Neuromancer*, Gibson's first novel, she becomes a much more complicated, interesting character. Although still referred to as a razorgirl, she is much more than just a bodyguard or a street punk looking for excitement: indeed, she is as essential to the success of the "Straylight run" as Henry Case, being responsible for acquiring the code that will allow the two AIs, Wintermute and Neuromancer, to merge. More of a backstory is provided for her as well, giving her more depth. Millions, it turns out, earned the money she needed to become a razorgirl by being a "meat puppet"—that is, a high-tech prostitute whose body is integrated into virtual reality-based sex fantasies. Although such prostitutes were not supposed to know how their bodies were being used, Millions becomes increasingly conscious of the fantasies she is being involved in until she wakes up in the middle of one, finding herself with a woman's corpse and a Senator, whom she immediately kills. Having been used in the most heinous of ways, she refuses to be used anymore, either personally or professionally, becoming an independent contractor who regards her employers as potential antagonists and poisons the drug supply of fellow employee Peter Riviera because he is a sociopath.

Even though the novel's action is presented primarily through Case's consciousness, because of a simstim link that allows him to experience what Molly does, readers have access to Millions' consciousness through him. On one level, of course, Gibson's use of such a device provides him with a means of titillating certain readers by describing what if feels like to Case when Millions caresses her own nipple or walks in high heels; on another level, however, the simstim link allows Case to appreciate Millions for her professionalism, drive, and physical and psychological strength. By sharing not only her experiences but sensations and emotions directly, Case learns more about not just her but women in general, something that helps him come to terms with his earlier loss of Linda Lee and to enter into a satisfying relationship with another woman at the end of the novel. It is not just Case who learns from Millions, however, or benefits from their personal and professional relationship. Like Case, she is able to come to terms with the loss of a significant other — in her case, Johnny from "Johnny Mnemonic" — because of what she has learned from her partnership with Case. Once she and Case complete their mission, she is able to move on not only from her past but from being a razorgirl: we learn in *Mona Lisa Overdrive* that after spending the money she is paid for her role in the Straylight run, she leaves the street, becoming a businesswoman of sorts.

The resolution of Millions and Case's relationship is also significant since Gibson reverses what one might expect of a *noir* thriller, a detective genre that he consistently drew from in much of his early work. In stories by Dashiell Hammett or Raymond Chandler, it is typically the male protagonist who moves on, his love interest being only a small part of a larger narrative centered on him. In *Neuromancer*, it is Millions who moves on, Case having been her love interest. The note she leaves him seems to confirm this: she tells him she is leaving, indicating that the relationship is "taking the edge off" her "game" (267). Accordingly, as Dani Cavallaro observes, although "[r]eminiscent of the *tough dame* of that mean-streeted genre traceable back to Chandler's crime fiction, she may be alternatively read as an image of a liberated woman" (123).

In *Mona Lisa Overdrive*, the action of which is set fourteen years later, Millions, who now calls herself "Sally Shears," has become a completely different person. No longer a razorgirl, she runs a casino she partially owns, only returning to her previous life because she is being coerced by 3Jane, who knows of Millions' criminal past. 3Jane forces Millions to kidnap Angelina Mitchell, and to use the body of Mona Lisa — who has been surgically altered to look like Mitchell — to make it look as if Mitchell has been killed. Not surprisingly, perhaps, Millions cooperates with 3Jane's agents as little as she dares, ultimately finding a way to save Mitchell and Mona Lisa. What is surprising is the types of relationships Millions develops with other women. Whereas in *Neuromancer* and "Johnny Mnemonic," Millions is presented as a woman among men, in *Mona Lisa Overdrive*, Millions primarily connects with women, not only protecting Mitchell and Mona Lisa but becoming almost maternalistic towards Kumiko Yanaka, the daughter of a Japanese crime boss who sends her to England because of dangers in Japan. As Lance Olsen observes, Millions teaches Yanaka how to navigate a "patriarchical system" that exploits and destroys women, Molly representing "at least some degree of hope for liberation from the male system" (104). At the end of the novel, she retakes control of her life, explaining to Slick Henry, "Wanna be by my fucking self for a change" (302).

 *See also* Gender; "Johnny Mnemonic"; *Mona Lisa Overdrive*; *Neuromancer*; *The Sprawl Trilogy*

• *References and further reading*

Bukatman, Scott. *Terminal Identity: The Virtual Subject in Postmodern Science Fiction*. Durham: Duke University Press, 1993. Print.

Cavallaro, Dani. *Cyberpunk and Cyberculture: Science Fiction and the Work of William Gibson*. Athlone Press, 2000. Print.

Cherniavsky, Eva. "(En)gendering Cyberspace in *Neuromancer*: Postmodern Subjectivity and Virtual Motherhood." *Genders* 18 (1993): 32–46. Print.

Fair, Benjamin. "Stepping Razor in Orbit: Postmodern Identity and Political Alternatives in William Gibson's *Neuromancer*." *Critique* 46.2 (2005): 92–103. Print.

Gibson, William. "Johnny Mnemonic." *Burning Chrome*. New York: Ace, 1986. Print.

\_\_\_\_\_. *Mona Lisa Overdrive*. New York: Spectra, 1997. Print.

\_\_\_\_\_. *Neuromancer*. New York: Ace, 1984. Print.

Leblanc, Lauraine. "Razor Girls: Genre and Gender in Cyberpunk Fiction." *Women and Language* 20 (1997): 71–76. Print.

Youngquist, Paul. *Cyberfiction: After the Future*. New York: Palgrave Macmillan, 2010. Print.

## Mitchell, Angelina

 A primary character in *Count Zero* and *Mona Lisa Overdrive*, Angelina Mitchell represents one of Gibson's first efforts to represent female consciousness directly. She is introduced in, the second volume of *The Sprawl Trilogy*, as the seventeen-year-old daughter of a leading biotech researcher who been raised entirely at the Maas Biolabs facility in Arizona. Her father, who has implanted biochips in her brain at the behest of the Tessier-Ashpool AI, arranges to defect to another company but sends Angelina in his place, killing himself immediately afterward. Because of these implants, Angelina is able to enter into the matrix unconsciously, saving Bobby Newmark from a lethal security program just before the action of the novel begins. She quickly becomes the book's focal point: a New Jersey–based Vodou organization identifies her as Ezili Freda, the Virgin of Miracles, and tries to locate her; then Josef Virek, a cancer-ridden billionaire who can experience things only virtually, tries to abduct her. Possessed by Legba, a Vodou *loa*, she directs Turner, the man hired to help her father defect, to the Sprawl, where she meets Newmark and members of the Vodou organization. Virek's efforts to abduct her are foiled, and she and Bobby go to New Jersey as a couple to learn more about Vodou. The novel ends with a coda that indicates she has become a simstim star — that is, a performer whose sensations and experiences are recorded so that they can be perceived by others.

 Although much of *Count Zero* focuses on Angelina, she is a static character, being acted upon rather than acting, the exception being the saving of Bobby, something she does almost unconsciously. Rather than act for herself, she passes from father's control to Turner's, then the Vodou organization, and finally Sense/Net. In this sense, she contrasts sharply with Marly Krushkova, a protagonist who acquires agency over the course of the novel, ultimately regaining control of her own life. Indeed, in *Count Zero*, at least, Angelina functions as a MacGuffin, that is, as an object of desire that drives the plot, much like the Maltese falcon in the Dashiell Hammett novel by that name. Angelina's essential passivity is further underscored by the fact that she becomes a simstim star whose life is controlled by Sense/Net and whose body and mind provide entertainment for others.

In *Mona Lisa Overdrive*, the third volume of *The Sprawl Trilogy*, Angelina, now a major simstim star, is just out of rehab, Sense/Net's Artificial Intelligence, Continuity, having had her drugged in order to disable her biochip implants. She is abducted by Sally Shears (Molly Millions) at the behest of 3Jane, the last surviving member of the Tessier-Ashpool clan, who envies her ability to enter directly into the matrix. Shears, who has also abducted Mona Lisa, an Angelina look-alike whose corpse is supposed to be used to replace Angelina's in an effort to fake her death, brings her to Bobby, who has died but whose consciousness continues in 3Jane's personal universe, or "aleph." Angelina dies as well, but her consciousness is integrated into the aleph, her biochip-based special abilities giving the aleph a level of consciousness that makes it possible for it to contact the "other" matrix that has been located in the Centauri system. As in *Count Zero*, she is constantly in the control of others, her biochip implants making her the object of others' desires.

Although a more dynamic character in *Mona Lisa Overdrive* than in *Count Zero*, Angelina is still essentially passive, passing from the control of Sense/Net to Sally Shears to the artificial intelligence controlling the aleph. Her dependence upon others is underscored by the way her body is positioned when she dies, "her legs folded under her like a statue, her arms around him [Bobby]" (293). Even though she accompanies Bobby and the others in their effort to contact the other matrix, she has little comprehension of what is happening, worrying that they are "teasing her," that it's all just "some joke" of Bobby's (308).

See also *Count Zero*; Gender; *Mona Lisa Overdrive*; Newmark, Bobby

- *References and further reading*

Cavallaro, Dani. *Cyberpunk and Cyberculture: Science Fiction and the Work of William Gibson*. Athlone Press, 2000. Print.
Gibson, William. *Count Zero*. New York: Ace, 1987. Print.
_____. *Mona Lisa Overdrive*. New York: Spectra, 1997. Print.
_____. *Neuromancer*. New York: Ace, 1984. Print.
Palmer, Christopher. "*Mona Lisa Overdrive* and the Prosthetic." *Science Fiction Studies* 31.2 (2004): 227–42. Print.
Rapatzikou, Tatiani G. *Gothic Motifs in the Fiction of William Gibson*. Amsterdam: Rodopi, 2004. Print.

## Mona Lisa Overdrive

Unlike *Count Zero*, which makes only nominal references to the storylines of the book that preceded it in the series, *Mona Lisa Overdrive* (1988) follows up on characters such as Molly Millions, Finn, 3Jane, Angelina Mitchell, Bobby Newmark, and even Henry Case, providing *The Sprawl Trilogy* with closure, at least in terms of its primary storylines. It also provides a certain amount of thematic closure, following up on "the Change" that occurred in cyberspace when it became self-aware as a result of the merging of two specially-designed artificial intelligences, as related in *Neuromancer*, and its ensuing fragmentation into constituent parts that present themselves as *loa*, as related in *Count Zero*. *Mona Lisa Overdrive* reveals what is only hinted at in the novels that precede it — that cyberspace has indeed become has become a nearly omniscient form of consciousness whose "center failed" when it became aware of "*another* matrix," a counterpart to itself based in the Centauri star system (257, 308). The final novel of the *Trilogy* goes on to relate how cyberspace reforms itself into a whole, preparing itself to make contact with "the other" (307).

Despite the closure *Mona Lisa Overdrive* provides on both the narrative and thematic level, a number of critics, including Lance Olsen and Thomas Disch, find the novel to be an unsatisfying conclusion to the *Trilogy*, since its ending "generates inconclusiveness at the very moment of apparent conclusion" (Olsen 111). Both Olsen and Disch go on to suggest that the novel was written with a sequel in mind, implying that Gibson hoped to profit from at least one more "clone" of *Neuromancer* (Disch 1988). Responses like these to the novel's open-endedness seem to represent humanist reactions to Gibson's refusal to present a totalizing truth at the end of the *Trilogy*: like William Burroughs, Thomas Pynchon, and the other postmodern writers who influenced him, Gibson thematizes questions of truth, something even Olsen acknowledges, writing that the novel's ending "reminds the reader that the goal of the quest is the quest itself, that at best one must yet again deal with pieces in the absence of wholes" (107).

As in *Count Zero*, in *Mona Lisa Overdrive* Gibson creates multiple storylines that draw together but never quite become one as the novel proceeds. The first concerns Kumiko Yanaka, aged thirteen, the first child to appear at any length in Gibson's work. Sent to London for safety by her father, a powerful member of the Yakuza, a Japanese criminal organization, she is accompanied by Colin, a computerized companion of sorts that at first appears to have limited abilities but has actually been altered and is sentient. There she meets Sally Shears, aka Molly Millions, who is being extorted into abducting Angelina Mitchell at the behest of 3Jane, who, having failed in her efforts to exist both within and without cyberspace, has developed a pathological hate for Mitchell because of her direct link into the matrix. Although the Kumiko strand has little to do with the novel's main action, it does, as Olsen notes, help advance one of the novel's main themes as Kumiko comes to terms with the death of her mother, and, more generally, with her past. At the very end of the novel, Kumiko moves from childhood to adulthood, learning to act rather than just be acted upon, as evidenced by her demanding of her father that he protect those who protected her during her adventures.

The second strand, which centers on Slick Henry, is essential to the novel's main action only in the sense that Henry's relationships with primary characters such as Gentry and Bobby Newmark serve as a means for bringing them together. In this sense, Henry resembles characters like Rosencrantz and Guildenstern in *Hamlet*, characters who advance the action but neither understand the larger drama or partake in it consciously. A convict-turned-artist who works through his trauma by creating robot-like kinetic sculptures that represent elements of his ordeals, Henry is a passive character, one who is acted upon rather than acts. Like Kumiko, however, he has a story of his own, one of growth and development that relates thematically to the novel's larger story about the "Change" that occurred when cyberspace became self-aware. Indeed, in "erecting anew the forms of pain and memory" in his artwork, he closely parallels the shattered artificial intelligence in *Count Zero* that fashions Cornell-like boxes out of scraps from the past. Like the AI, he recuperates himself by working through his trauma symbolically, ultimately regaining agency, an event that is represented in the novel by him handing the controls of one his most important statue to Sally Shears as he leaves his home for Cleveland with Cherry-Lee Chesterfield.

A third strand focuses on Angelina Mitchell, now a major simstim star, who has not been in communication with either Bobby or the *loa* for some time. Just out of a drug rehabilitation program, she is contacted by Mamman Brigitte, who informs her that her employer, Sense/Net, a company directed by an advanced AI named Continuity, has been using drugs to prevent her from using the biochips grafted into her brain from entering the matrix. Mitchell, who was essentially a passive character in the previous novel, takes more initiative in *Mona Lisa Overdrive* but still has little control over her own life: ultimately, she is brought to the altar by Brigitte and Continuity to be married to Newmark, who, having linked the "pocket universe" created by 3Jane to the matrix, emerges as the novel's hero since his action not only saves Slick Henry, Chesterfield, and others but enables the *loa* to reintegrate themselves into the larger, fully sentient being they once were. In the novel's resolution, Mitchell is, quite literally, brought along for the ride, as Finn, Colin, and Newmark drive to encounter the "other" matrix in a long, low, grey car.

The fourth strand also centers on a character, Mona Lisa, who is also essentially passive. A sixteen-year-old prostitute who is surgically altered to resemble Mitchell so that her corpse can be used to fake Mitchell's death, she is passed from person to person, beginning with her pimp and ending with Porphyre, who has her assume Mitchell's identity and become a simstim star. Of all the characters in Gibson's novels, it is Mona Lisa who is perhaps accorded the least agency, her only significant effort to take control of her life being thwarted by Shears, who abducts her just as she is about to attempt an escape from Prior following her surgery. Although hardly a feminist, Gibson depicts Mona Lisa in a way that seems to be critical of the way in which patriarchy can entirely subject women, allowing them virtually no agency. His representation of her moving from prostitution to simstim sex object also can be interpreted as a critique of the way women are objectified in the media, a form of objectification that powerfully reinforces patriarchal values.

*Mona Lisa Overdrive* is perhaps Gibson's most ambitious work, at least in terms of narrative structure, since he develops highly abstract themes through a series of narrative strands that center on largely peripheral characters who lack agency. Moreover, Gibson refuses to explain what is happening to cyberspace, the ostensive subject of the *Trilogy*, in descriptive terms, instead relying upon consciousness metaphors and symbols such as the *loa*. To an extent, such indirect exposition — which some see as self-conscious artistry — led to frustration on the part of readers. Thomas M. Wagner, for example, asserts that Gibson tries too hard "to push his own envelopes," resulting in "a hell of a mess, a convoluted literary Rubik's Cube whose sides stubbornly refuse to match up no matter how much you play with it." As Wagner concedes, however, Gibson is able to induce readers into "*wanting* to solve it," something that, in addition to testifying to Gibson's talent as an entertaining writer as Wagner would have it, suggests that Gibson involves readers in the meaning-making process, just as he does in *Count Zero*.

## LITERARINESS

Although reviews of *Mona Lisa Overdrive* were mixed, the novel was nominated for both the Hugo and Nebula awards, and seems to have helped establish Gibson's literary reputation: even the most negative reviews, like the one published by Disch in the *New York Times* acknowledge his skill as a writer, Disch highlighting the "flash" of his prose, that is, the "quick, high-intensity glimpses that linger on the retina of the imagination." Literary theorists also began to address Gibson's work, increasingly identifying him with postmodernism. Fredric Jameson, for example, cites *Mona Lisa Overdrive* on the first page of his celebrated theoretical text, *Postmodernism or, the Logic of Late Capitalism* and goes on to note that Gibson's "representational innovations ... mark his work as an exceptional literary realization within a predominately visual or aural postmodern production" (38). Claire Sponsler, too, identifies the novel as postmodern, although, as she notes, it also marked his entry into mainstream fiction, being the first of his books to be published as a quality paperback by Bantam Books rather than as an Ace Science Fiction Special (626).

## TRAUMA AND RECUPERATION

Trauma and recuperation are themes that bring the novel's disparate parts together since they figure largely not only in the strands centered on Kumiko, Slick Henry, Mitchell, and Mona Lisa but also in the stories of Newmark and the now-sentient cyberspace, the latter of which are told only indirectly. All of the novel's primary characters have been traumatized in some way and work toward recuperation, their stories providing a means for understanding the more abstract form of trauma cyberspace undergoes when it becomes sentient and moves from what a Lacanian might call the "imaginary" to the "real." In the case of cyberspace, the consciousness that is achieved with the unification of Wintermute and Neuromancer is almost immediately shattered when it becomes aware of "the other," a matrix based in the Centauri system that, in Lacanian terms, represents radical alterity (257). It is only through the aleph, which corresponds to the Lacanian notion of the superego/ego-ideal, that cyberspace is able to recuperate, overcoming the trauma it has been subjected to by the big Other: in effect, by linking the aleph to cyberspace, Newmark gives it a superego, providing it with a means of adapting itself to requirements of the socio-symbolic order.

This is not to suggest that Lacanian analysis is necessary to understanding Gibson's representation of trauma or that Gibson is sympathetic with or even interested in Lacanian theory. Since Gibson explains cyberspace's emerging sentience in terms of human psychology, however, psychoanalytical approaches seem appropriate when discussing it. They also seem appropriate to discussions of trauma and recuperation in relation to human characters such as Kumiko, who must come to terms with her mother's suicide, and Slick Henry, who has been adversely affected by treatments he received while in prison. As Christopher Palmer indicates, they and the other traumatized characters need other things or people to serve as "transitional objects or prostheses" in order to recover (227). Ironically, it is Sally Shears, a woman who herself has suffered from both sexual exploitation and romantic loss, who serves as a prosthesis for not only Kumiko, Mona Lisa, and even Mitchell. As mentioned earlier, Slick Henry's kinetic sculptures serve as prosthesis for him just as the Cornell boxes do for the AI in *Count Zero*. For Gibson, it seems, art can be therapeutic since it involves working out trauma symbolically, a subject he revisits in even more detail in *Pattern Recognition* (2003).

See also *Count Zero*; Gender; Millions, Molly; *Neuromancer*; Newmark, Bobby; *The Sprawl Trilogy*; Tessier-Ashpool Family

## • *References and further reading*

Bukatman, Scott. *Terminal Identity: The Virtual Subject in Postmodern Science Fiction.* Durham: Duke University Press, 1993. Print.

Gibson, William. *Count Zero.* New York: Ace, 1987. Print.

_____. *Mona Lisa Overdrive.* New York: Spectra, 1997. Print.

_____. *Neuromancer.* New York: Ace, 1984. Print.

Jameson, Fredric. *Postmodernism, or, the Logic of Late Capitalism.* Durham: Duke University Press, 1991. Print.

Palmer, Christopher. "*Mona Lisa Overdrive* and the Prosthetic." *Science Fiction Studies* 31.2 (2004): 227–242. Print.

Schroeder, Randy. "Neu-Criticizing William Gibson." *Extrapolation: A Journal of Science Fiction and Fantasy* 35.4 (1994): 330–41. Print.

Sponsler, Claire. "Cyberpunk and the Dilemmas of Postmodern Narrative: The Example of William Gibson." *Contemporary Literature* 33.4 (1992): 625–44. Print.

## Music

In a 1986 interview with Larry McCaffery, Gibson indicates that musical influences were as important to his work as literary ones (265). In some cases, such influences are easy to discern: the name "Linda Lee," a character in *Neuromancer*, for example, is drawn from the Velvet Underground song "Cool It Down," and a space tug is named for "Sweet Jane," one of their better known songs. *All Tomorrow's Parties* is also named for a Velvet Underground song, and the surname for Rikki Wildside, a character in "Burning Chrome," comes from Reed's song "Take a Walk on the Wild Side." The influence of Lou Reed and the Velvet Underground goes beyond just naming, however: as Leonard Patrick Sanders suggests, the influence of their music can be discerned in "a diffuse but potent postmodern mix of character types, scenes, mood, affect, identification, and styles" (139). Indeed, Gibson's early work presents readers with a futuristic "walk on the wild side" with its "combination of lowlife and high tech," to borrow a phrase Bruce Sterling used in his introduction to *Burning Chrome*. Gibson himself seems to make this connection, suggesting that *Neuromancer* can be understood as a Lou Reed album (Van Belkom Interview).

That Gibson should be so influenced by Lou Reed and the Velvet Underground should not be too surprising, given the fact that Gibson was an artistically oriented teenager in the 1960s who regarded the Beatles as being too mainstream (Thill Interview). Gibson continued listening to the Velvet Underground and other alternative bands through the 1970s and 80s, reporting that *Neuromancer* (1984) was written "to a soundtrack that consisted mainly of equal parts Joy Division and vintage Velvets" (Blair Interview). He also lists Steely Dan and David Bowie as important influences, indicating that the futurism of albums like *Diamond Dogs* was "the hip science fiction of our age" and that he wanted "to write up to that standard, rather than trying to write up to Asimov" (van Bakel Interview). He also listened to Patti Smith and other performers associated with the New York City punk scene in the late 1970s, noting that the American strain of punk, which actually "predated what happened in London," was "subversively retro in a really irony-free way," being rooted in 1960s street culture rather than 1970s "art school" nihilism and ironic self-awareness (Murphy Interview). In addition to the music, which he "enjoyed immensely," Gibson appreciated what he calls the punk "attitude," consciously bringing it to science fiction: "That attitude was so perfectly counter to what I saw happening in the mainstream of the genre that it couldn't have been more perfect for my purposes. It wasn't that I wanted to tear the genre down, but I wanted to return it to something of my idea of what it had been when I was 15 or 16 years old, which had been my heyday for reading Science Fiction" (Gutmair Interview). He seems to have found punk's DIY (Do It Yourself) response to overproduced mainstream, commercialized music particularly appealing, incorporating a similar attitude into his work through characters like Henry Case, Bobby Newmark, and Zona Rosa. As Charles Gimon explains, "Gibson's techno toys are things that readers could imagine themselves owning someday. Few people expect to own their own private spaceship anytime soon, but an Ono-Sendai cyberspace deck seems like a natural evolution from today's notebook computer. This is the 'punk' in 'cyberpunk,' the same do-it-yourself ethos that pushed the Sex Pistols and the Clash to prominence while Gibson started writing, or as anti-hero Johnny Rotten said: 'Anyone can pick up a guitar and be just like us.'"

Although punk elements can still be discerned in Gibson's later work, particularly in his representations of street culture and characters like Sammy Sal of *Virtual Light*,

Fontaine in *All Tomorrow's Parties*, Damien in *Pattern Recognition*, and even Garreth Wilson in *Zero History*, by the time he wrote *Idoru* in the mid–1990s, his interests had generally shifted to the music industry and the nature of celebrity, as evidenced by his representation of rock superstar Rez, a character based loosely on U2's Bono, and Billy Prion, a character based on Billy Idol. He addresses the recording industry and celebrity again in the last two volumes of *The Bigend Trilogy*, making Hollis Henry, former lead singer of a well known post-punk band, and Reginald Inchmale, a guitarist-turned-producer, important characters. In a 2007 interview he acknowledges that his focus has changed significantly: "I have no idea what Hollis's band would have sounded like but at some point I had it worked out in my head what labels they would have been on, and that was what mattered to me rather than what they sounded like" (Parker Interview).

*See also* Counterculture; Cyberpunk

• *References and further reading*

Gibson, William. "Steely Dan's Return." *Addicted to Noise* 6.3 (1 Mar. 2000). Print.
Sanders, Leonard Patrick. *Postmodern Orientalism: William Gibson, Cyberpunk and Japan*. Doctoral Thesis. Massey University, 2008. Print.

## Neuromancer

*Neuromancer* (1984) is Gibson's first and by far most acclaimed novel, being the only work to have won the Hugo, Nebula, and Philip K. Dick Awards. It has sold approximately 7 million copies and was named by *Time* magazine as one of the most important English-language novels to be published since 1923 despite the fact that it was reviewed only belatedly by the *New York Times* and received very little press outside of the science fiction community (Grossman). Even though the novel is dated in certain respects, with characters still using pay phones, for example, many of the issues the novel raises are still important, and the novel still seems relevant to twenty-first century readers, as evidenced not only by appreciations written on 25-year anniversary celebrations of its publication but by recent online reviews and commentary. As Randy Schroeder observes, the novel "continues to engage emergent tropes" decades after it was first issued (17).

The novel is significant in cultural terms, being widely credited with giving shape to cyberspace as it was being realized in the 1980s and 1990s. Although Gibson had little if any technical knowledge of how virtual domains were being developed in the 1980s, his representation of "cyberspace," a neologism that was introduced in "Burning Chrome" (1982) and popularized in *Neuromancer*, enabled computer scientists and engineers to communicate their ideas about the virtual. According to Gibson, "They had this idea, but they'd never been able to explain to anybody what it was. Once they had *Neuromancer*, they could just go around with a suitcase full of copies, and when people said, 'I just can't fathom what you're talking about,' they'd say, 'Read this. It's sort of like this'" (Murray Interview). Although it is difficult to assess in concrete terms the influence Gibson had upon the development of human-computer interfaces, there is no question that, as Sabine Heuser puts it, "cyberspace" has had "a far-reaching and lasting effect well beyond Gibson's specific usage, since it has infiltrated other domains of discourse and passed into common English speech" (100).

*Neuromancer* is also credited with establishing cyberpunk as a subgenre and revitalizing science fiction in general. Although as Larry McCaffery, Bruce Sterling and others observe, *Neuromancer* was by no means the first cyberpunk novel, it quickly became its most representative text. Indeed, one could argue it became the subgenre's *urtext*, effectively erasing everything that came before it and becoming a starting point for everything that came after. As Rob Latham put it in his review of *Fiction 2000: Cyberpunk and the Future of Narrative* (1992), for many people "Cyberpunk = Gibson = Neuromancer" (266). The novel has had an impact on science fiction as a whole, not only because it has attracted an outside audience as Peter Fitting notes (308) but because it challenged the *status quo* (308). Larry McCaffery argues that in this sense, at least, cyberpunk is analogous to punk rock: both created new spaces within existing industries for innovation and change, leading to revitalization (13). In particular, it challenged the "cause-and-effect narrative development" that was then standard in science fiction and the genre's general though by no means universal optimism about the advance of knowledge (14). Although it is easy to overstate the originality of both *Neuromancer* and cyberpunk in general since in many respects they developed out of the work of "New Wave" writers like Philip K. Dick, Ursula K. Le Guin, and Samuel R. Delany, it is hard to overstate their impact upon the genre, since they brought experimental, literary science fiction writing both unprecedented critical attention and increased sales.

The fact that *Neuromancer* was so influential a novel is perhaps surprising, given that Gibson had not previously written a novel or even fully established himself as a writer. According to Gibson, the novel is very much an apprentice text, a product of the "[b]lind animal panic" that came from signing a contract with Ace Books before he felt ready to complete a novel (McCaffery Interview 268): "*Neuromancer* is fueled by my terrible fear of losing the reader's attention," a fear that resulted in "a hook on every page." He also borrowed plot elements and characterization from the detective novels of writers like Dashiell Hammett and Raymond Chandler, mixing in "offbeat language" he learned in Toronto's "soft-core version of the hippie/underground scene in the late 1960s" (283). In terms of story, he reports drawing upon "what had worked for me before," incorporating Molly Millions from "Johnny Mnemonic" into the world of "Burning Chrome" (1982), short works that themselves employed themes and motifs of classic detective novels and thrillers. Despite such influences, as a whole *Neuromancer* does not seem derivative or formulaic, largely because it is dynamic rather than static, particularly in terms of characterization. Unlike Hammett's Sam Spade, who is essentially unchanged at the end of every novel, Gibson's protagonist, Henry Case, is transformed by his experiences, beginning anew in a sense; indeed, even "the Dixie Flatline construct"—a human mind recorded in ROM (Read Only Memory)—is not entirely static since his needs and desires seem to change over the course of the novel. *Neuromancer* also differs from detective novels in the way that it addresses social issues overtly. Although novels like *Maltese Falcon* and *The Thin Man* have certain implicit social attitudes and positions, they are not Hammett's ostensive subject. *Neuromancer*, however, is as much *about* the social implications of new technologies as it is about Case, something that becomes evident at the end of the novel when Gibson provides closure to the Case narrative but leaves the consequences of the merger between two artificial intelligences, Wintermute and Neuromancer, open. As James Schellenberg observes, "The story turns out to be about AI and corporate power."

The novel's protagonist, Henry Dorsett Case, is typical of both *noir* detective fiction and cyberpunk in the sense that he is a marginalized figure seeking reintegration into society, making the novel modernist to the extent that it addresses the alienation associated with the changing modes of production, distribution, and consumption that developed under global capitalism (Armstrong 200–5). A former "console cowboy," Case is prevented from jacking in to cyberspace by nerve damage inflicted upon him by a client he stole from. Addicted to the "bodiless exultation of cyberspace" (6), he agrees to do a particularly dangerous "run" in exchange for having his nerve damage reversed. As the action proceeds, he begins to form attachments again, first with Molly Millions, a "razorgirl" hired to assist him on his run, and then with Finn, Dixie Flatline, and even Wintermute, the AI who arranges the run in an effort to become fully sentient. Case also manages to come to terms with the death of a woman he had loved, who died as a result of her love for him (259). Most importantly, perhaps, he comes to terms with his physical self, which, as a console cowboy, he has come to think of as "meat." Indeed, an injury to Millions forces him to become an action hero of sorts, to leave his computer deck and not only save her physically but complete the mission (216). The novel ends with him completely reintegrating himself back into society: he returns home, marries, and finds regular employment, never to see "Molly again" (271).

The novel's "fairy-tale ending," with Case successfully incorporating himself back into "the system," makes the novel seem humanist as well as modernist, something that gives pause to Tony Myers and others who try to read Gibson's work as postmodern (905). According to Myers, although the novel has many postmodern characteristics, most particularly its use of cyberspace "as a representational strategy for domesticating what Jameson terms 'postmodern space,'" its focus on Case and his redemption ultimately undercuts the conceit that under capitalism, "subjectivity is reduced to a function of the system" (905). Similarly, Claire Sponsler argues that the novel, like its sequels, is ultimately a failure, at least as a postmodern work, since Gibson is unable "to shape plot and agency in a way that matches the postmodern ideology and aesthetic" that his work "embraces" (640, 627). She is particularly troubled by the way in which Gibson invests "first human agents, then machines, and finally cyberspace itself ... with a heroic and romantic power that ultimately undermines the resolutely unromantic surface world he has set up" (639). Although both Myers and Sponsler operate from the assumption that Gibson's early work is part of a postmodern project, their points are still relevant to those who regard the work as modernist or humanistic, since they reveal seemingly conflicting impulses in the novels' construction.

Sponsler also criticizes Gibson "for refusing to propose a progressive politics even though its dystopian future opens up a considerable space for resistance to the logic of late capitalism" (640) and Andrew Ross chastises Gibson for "evad[ing] the responsibility to imagine futures that will be more democratic than the present" (150). As Nobuo Kamioka observes, however, Gibson's use of a "traditional frame" drawn from popular fiction makes it impossible for him to be "subversive enough" to satisfy progressive critics (64). The fact that the novel presents itself as a dystopia also seems to limit its potential to present alternatives to the *status quo*: one is unlikely to find "utopian impulses" in a dystopian novel (Ross 150). Gibson does create spaces for resistance against the dominant culture in *Neuromancer*, most notably the Ninsei area of Chiba City, which hosts a number of "techno-criminal subcultures" and Zion, a "makeshift" Rastafarian space colony "founded by five workers who refused to return" to Earth (6, 103). Although Gibson's representation of spaces such as these are not nearly as developed as the "outlaw zones" of his later novels, the freedom of action they allow characters like Case and Millions is essential to their very survival as they challenge both government authorities and multinational corporations.

## STYLE AND "LITERARINESS"

One thing that differentiates Gibson from most other science fiction writers of his time is his overt literariness, something that becomes most evident in his use of extended metaphors, describing an encounter between some missionaries and some office workers, for example, in the following terms: "A pair of predatory looking Christian Scientists were edging toward a trio of young office techs ... the techs licked their perfect lips nervously and eyed the Christian Scientists from beneath lowered metallic lids. The girls looked like tall, exotic grazing animals, swaying gracefully and unconsciously with the movement of the train, their high heels like polished hooves against the gray metal of the car's floor." By depicting what Case sees in such terms, Gibson is able to express not only Case's state of mind at that particular point in the novel but his attitudes towards women. Passages like this led reviewers to praise *Neuromancer*, perhaps overly so, for its literary qualities. *The Washington Post*, for example, described the novel as "an amazing virtuoso perform-ance," and the *San Francisco Chronicle* touted its "exceptional texture," adding that it is marked by "a number of literary ... inventions." Certainly the novel stands out for its use of figurative language to convey a sense of what "cyberspace" might be like to readers who in 1984 would have little if any access to the Internet, and Gibson's use of fine-grained detail provides readers with a sense that they are experiencing the future. As Iain Rowan indicates, however, Gibson sometimes provides too much detail, particularly when it comes to providing brand names: "It's not enough for Gibson to describe the artificial sunlight on Farside, the orbital colony; instead the reader has to be informed in the space of just a few pages that Case 'knew that sunlight was pumped in with a Lado-Acheson system,' that the 'narrow band of the Lado-Acheson system' smoulders, and that Case is dazzled by 'the Lado-Acheson' sun."

Commentators have also criticized Gibson's characterization, arguing that it lacks nuance and that his representations of Peter Riviera and Armitage/Willis Corto are uncon-vincing. As Rowan points out, however, the sometimes flat characterization "actually works to *Neuromancer*'s benefit" since "the superficiality merely amplifies the dehumanised atmosphere of an impersonal world." Gibson's uneven characterization also serves to high-light Case's rehumanization: in effect, he goes from being a caricature reminiscent of 1930s detective fiction to the sort of fully fledged character one might expect to find in a more self-consciously literary work. Gibson's portrayal of Millions, however, is arguably less suc-cessful, in part because Gibson makes little effort to present her interiority, at least in *Neu-romancer*. In *Mona Lisa Overdrive*, a novel in which Millions appears as Sally Shears, Millions is a more fully rounded character whose perspectives are represented directly by Gibson rather than refracted through other characters.

## 1980s, SOCIAL ISSUES, AND TECHNO-ORIENTALISM

According to Peter Fitting, one of the reasons Gibson's early work remains culturally significant is because it offers readers "a poetic evocation of life in the late eighties." Although Gibson makes only indirect references to the 1980s, primarily through the men-tion of corporations such as Sony, Hitachi, and Braun that have survived into the twenty-first century, the novel is very much of that time in the sense that it is preoccupied with the same sorts of issues that Americans were in the Reagan era, namely the decline of nation states in general and the United States in particular, the disappearance of the mid-dle class, and the impact new technologies will have on everyday life.

The novel also addresses the emergence of Japan as a dominant power, as evidenced not only by events such as Mitsubishi's takeover of both the Bank of America and Genentech, but the "Japanification" of world culture in general (Chun 201): in effect, Japan is subjected to a "techno-orientalism," to borrow David Morley and Kevin Robins's term — that is, it is presented as an object of both desire and fear, a threat to be at once contained and exploited. As Wendy notes, economic tensions between "West" and "East" are largely played out in cyberspace, with Case and his associates representing "American ingenuity" and individualism. Her suggestion that their corporations such as Tessier-Ashpool are supposed to represent "Japanese corporate assimilation" is less convincing, however, since Tessier-Ashpool is hardly based on a Japanese corporate model. Although Japanese corporations are certainly presented as being powerful if not pre-eminent, at least in the area of technology, Gibson seems to be identifying corporatization in general as a problem, possibly in response to the Reaganist policies of the 1980s that deregulated industries, according corporations more power. Certainly Gibson regarded Reaganism as a problem, commenting in his blog, "Reagan's presidency put the grit in my dystopia.... His smile was the nightmare in my back pocket."

## Cyberspace as It Is Represented in *Neuromancer*

Although Gibson was not the first writer to depict either virtual reality or cyberspace (though he was the first to use the latter term, according to the *OED*), he did bring such concepts into the mainstream through *Neuromancer*, which was not only a popular success but gradually came to be recognized by critics as an important novel. As both literary critics and computer scientists have noted, however, cyberspace as presented in *Neuromancer* is very different from cyberspace as it has been realized in the real world. Gibsonian cyberspace is experienced differently than present-day cyberspace in the sense that it is totally immersive: an as-yet unavailable technology based on sensory stimulation ("simstim" in the novel) allows cyberspace to be experienced as a place, "the cyberspace matrix" being "a drastic reduction of the human sensorium, at least in terms of presentation" (55). Although like today's Internet, Gibson's matrix is largely visual, the eyes themselves are apparently bypassed as "dermatrodes" send signals directly to the brain. The difference this makes in how one experiences the virtual becomes clear when Case, who has been fully immersed in cyberspace removes "the trodes from his forehead" and looks at his computer screen, which presents itself very much like a contemporary display, with Molly Millions, whose progress he has been following, appearing simply as a "pulsing red cursor" moving through a space that has simply been "outlined" (65).

The fact that his version of cyberspace is a much more realized form of virtual reality than anything available on the Internet today allows Gibson to explore the social implications of new technologies long before they are actually introduced. Rather than present cyberspace as being distinct from physical space, thereby affording people an opportunity to experiment with alternative identities, Gibson focuses on the ways in which actions in virtual domains carry over into the real and vice versa. At the beginning of the novel, Case is the least admirable of people, a self-destructive man who, in his weakness destroys others, having killed not only three people over petty sums but indirectly brought about the death of Linda Lee, a women he loves but neglects. Cyberspace provides him an opportunity to remake himself, to be a hero rather than a villain. Although the "runs" he makes against Sense/Net and then Tessier-Ashpool are hardly altruistic, they do involve moral choices and they force him to make connections with others again. They also restore his sense of empowerment and self-worth and afford him an opportunity to find closure in his relationship with Lee, since Neuromancer incorporated her personality into a virtual domain before she died. The fact that, at the end of the novel, Case seems to be fully recuperated suggests that what happens in cyberspace is, indeed, real in a very important sense.

Because it represents a plastic space in which almost anything can happen, cyberspace also functions as a "meta-device" in that it allows Gibson to work in other genres such detective fiction, the Western, and even erotica without violating the integrity of his story (Heuser xxii). As Gibson himself puts it, cyberspace allows for a lot of "moves" since "characters can be sucked into apparent realities—which means you can place them in any sort of setting or against any backdrop" (McCaffery Interview 272). As Gibson recognized, such "freedom can be dangerous because you don't have to justify what's happening in terms of the logic of character or plot." In *Neuromancer*, he manages this danger by restricting the virtual domains Case enters to ones based upon experiences that he has already had, the exception a domain based on a stereotypical isolated tropical beach. He also offers an explanation as to why the virtual domains are drawn from Case's experiences—Wintermute needs to draw on what is familiar to Case in order to communicate with him. As a result, the virtual domains Gibson presents seem to be integral to the story rather than gratuitous or contrived. Even though the technologies being represented are fantastic, they are treated in a naturalistic sort of way.

See also *Count Zero*; Cyberspace; Gender; Hackers; Molly Millions; *Mona Lisa Overdrive*; Politics; *The Sprawl Trilogy*; Tessier-Ashpool Family

• *References and further reading*

Brouillette, Sarah. "Corporate Publishing and Canonization: *Neuromancer* and Science-Fiction Publishing in the 1970s and early 1980s." *Book History*. Ed. Ezra Greenspan and Jonathan Rose. University Park: Pennsylvania State University Press, 2002. 187–208. Print.

Bukatman, Scott. *Terminal Identity: The Virtual Subject in Postmodern Science Fiction*. Durham: Duke University Press, 1993. Print.

Cavallaro, Dani. *Cyberpunk and Cyberculture: Science Fiction and the Work of William Gibson*. Athlone Press, 2000. Print.

Cherniavsky, Eva. "(En)gendering Cyberspace in *Neuromancer*: Postmodern Subjectivity and Virtual Motherhood." *Genders* 18 (1993): 32–46. Print.

Chun, Wendy. *Control and Freedom: Power and Paranoia in the Age of Fiber Optics*. Cambridge: MIT Press, 2006. Print.

Csicsery Ronay, Istvan, Jr. "The Sentimental Futurist: Cybernetics and Art in William Gibson's *Neuromancer*." *Critique: Studies in Contemporary Fiction* 33.3 (1992): 221–40. Print.

Fair, Benjamin. "Stepping Razor in Orbit: Postmodern Identity and Political Alternatives in William Gibson's *Neuromancer*." *Critique* 46.2 (2005): 92–103. Print.

Fitting, Peter. "The Lessons of Cyberpunk." *Technoculture*. Ed. Constance Penley and Andrew Ross. Minneapolis: University of Minnesota Press, 1991. 295–315. Print.

Gibson, William. "Burning Chrome." *Burning Chrome*. New York: Ace, 1986. Print.

_____. *Count Zero*. New York: Ace, 1987. Print.

_____. *Mona Lisa Overdrive*. New York: Spectra, 1997. Print.

_____. *Neuromancer*. New York: Ace, 1984. Print.

Hammett, Dashiell. *The Maltese Falcon*. New York: Alfred A. Knopf, 1930. Print.

Jameson, Fredric. *Postmodernism, or, the Logic of Late Capitalism*. Durham: Duke University Press, 1991. Print.

Myers, Tony. "The Postmodern Imaginary in *William Gibson's Neuromancer*." *MFS: Modern Fiction Studies* 47.4 (2001): 887–909. Print.

Schroeder, Randy. "Neu-Criticizing William Gibson." *Extrapolation: A Journal of Science Fiction and Fantasy* 35.4 (1994): 330–41. Print.

Sponsler, Claire. "Cyberpunk and the Dilemmas of Postmodern Narrative: The Example of William Gibson." *Contemporary Literature*. 33.4 (1992): 625–44. Print.

Yu, Timothy. "Oriental Cities, Postmodern Futures: *Naked Lunch, Blade Runner*, and *Neuromancer*." *Melus* 33.4 (2008): 45–71. Print.

## "New Rose Hotel"

Published in *Omni* in 1984 and collected in *Burning Chrome*, "New Rose Hotel" is arguably Gibson's last true cyberpunk story in the sense that it focuses entirely on a "combination of lowlife and high tech," to borrow Bruce Sterling's formulation. A first-person narrative told by a man awaiting his death at a coffin-style hotel near the Narita International Airport, the story concerns an effort by the unnamed narrator, a corporate mercenary named Fox, and a *femme fatale* named Sandii to induce a brilliant researcher, Hiroshi Yomiuri, to defect from Maas Biolabs to Hosaka Corporation. Although they initially succeed, Sandii ultimately betrays the narrator, who is in love with her, infecting Yomiuri and Hosaka's top researchers with a deadly virus. Believing that Fox is part of the conspiracy, they kill him and pursue the narrator, who knows he will eventually be found.

Like "Johnny Mnemonic," "New Rose Hotel" is reminiscent of 1930s detective novels both in terms of plot and narrative voice, and though Sandii is Gibson's first *femme fatale*, such characters are certainly a part of the detective tradition. "New Rose Hotel" differs from "Johnny Mnemonic" and the other Sprawl stories in its focus on *zaibatsus*, which, according to the narrator, have developed structures "independent of the individual lives" that comprise them — "Corporation as life form" (107). Although *zaibatsus* are a key part of the dystopian future that serves as a setting for all of the Sprawl narratives, "New Rose Hotel" is the only of the stories to suggests that the corporations cannot be effectively resisted, making it one of his darkest works.

The story has received scant critical attention, even though it is relatively well known because it was adapted for a film by the same name, starring Christopher Walken, Willem Dafoe, and Asia Argento. In expanding the 4,500-word short story into a 93-minute film, screenwriters Abel Ferrara and Christ Zois added a great number of characters and situations and present Sandii as an opportunistic prostitute rather than as a ruthless mercenary who uses her sex appeal to her advantage. The film also presents her as Italian rather than as "Eurasian, half gaijin" (104) and therefore avoids engaging in the same form of "high-tech orientalism" that is evident in much of Gibson's early work as he conflates Japanese technology and desire (Chun).

*See also Burning Chrome*; Japan

• *References and further reading*

Chun, Wendy. *Control and Freedom: Power and Paranoia in the Age of Fiber Optics.* Cambridge: MIT Press, 2006. Print.
Gibson, William. "The New Rose Hotel." *Burning Chrome.* New York: Ace, 1986. Print.

## Newmark, Bobby (aka "Count Zero")

Bobby Newmark, a hacker who appears in both *Count Zero* and *Mona Lisa Overdrive*, is among the most fully developed of Gibson's characters, going from being a disaffected yet cocky adolescent to an intellectually engaged adult, who ultimately sacrifices his life for the sake of knowledge. In this he represents the hacker ideal: as Thomas Gentry indicates in *Mona Lisa Overdrive*, Newmark hacks into the matrix not to "steal" but to "learn" (228). Bobby also behaves heroically in a more conventional sense, remaining behind during the siege of the Factory to create a diversion at the end of that novel (272).

Newmark is introduced in *Count Zero*, the second volume of *The Sprawl Trilogy*, as an aspiring console cowboy living with his mother in Barrytown who is nearly killed by a security program as he tests unknown software. He is saved from the "black ICE" by an unknown entity, who later proves to be Angelina Mitchell, and then becomes involved with a New Jersey–based Vodou organization that identifies Angelina Mitchell as Ezili Freda, the Virgin of Miracles (58). With the help of Jackie, a priestess of Danbala and potential love interest, Newmark learns to navigate the matrix and is instrumental in saving Mitchell from Josef Virek, a rich and powerful man who hopes biochips like those implanted in Mitchell will make him immortal. The novel ends with Newmark, who has earned his "Count Zero" hacker moniker, becoming romantically involved with Mitchell, never to return to the suburbs.

To the extent that the novel centers on Newmark's growth and development, *Count Zero* can be considered a *bildungsroman*, if not a *erziehungsroman*, as Lance Olsen suggests (89). Certainly, along with Marly Krushkova, Newmark is the character the narrative seems most invested in, much of it being presented from his perspective. More importantly, perhaps, his actions, along with Krushkova's, prevent Virek from incorporating himself into the very fabric of the matrix and thus changing it irrevocably. Newmark is not presented as being particularly heroic, however, or as someone who is destined for extraordinary things; rather, he is an ordinary person who, though caught up in great events, is not great himself but merely competent. In this sense he is different from characters like King Arthur or Luke Skywalker, Gibson's suggestions seeming to be that history often turns on the action of everyday people. Ultimately, Newmark is simply a boy who becomes a man, accepting adult responsibilities and doing what might reasonably be expected of him.

In *Mona Lisa Overdrive*, the third volume of *The Sprawl Trilogy*, Newmark is presented in very different terms. Having become estranged from Mitchell, the novel opens with him being jacked into an aleph, or "pocket universe," he has stolen, his all-but-catatonic body being attended to by Slick Henry, Cherry-Lee Chesterfield, and others in the Factory, an abandoned-building-become-artists'-enclave in Cleveland. Newmark, it seems, has become obsessed with understanding the nature of the "Change" that occurred in the matrix fourteen years earlier when the Tessier-Ashpool artificial intelligences merged, and the aleph provides him with a potential means of comprehending it. He dies while the Factory is besieged by agents hoping to recover the aleph, but his consciousness continues in the aleph, where it is joined by Mitchell's, Mitchell also having died. Ultimately he appears to have found the knowledge he has sought, and along with Mitchell, the Finn, and Colin, an artificial intelligence based on the very latest technology, he is poised to take part in the contacting of "other matrix" that is based in Alpha Centauri.

The complex relationship between Newmark and Mitchell gives him more depth that is evident in other early characters such as Bobby Quine and Henry Dorsett Case. Although the novel begins with Newmark and Mitchell estranged from one another, it is clear that their relationship is unfinished, creating a tension which is resolved only when we learn that he has left her so that he could enter the aleph and learn from it. Although obsessed with knowledge, he is not Faust-like in the sense that he seeks knowledge for its own sake and not to acquire power. Ironically, it does give him power, however — the power to not only save his companions but to help the matrix, which had attained consciousness in *Neuromancer*, to reconstitute itself. It is in utilizing this power that Newmark becomes heroic, since he is forced to sacrifice himself in doing so. Whereas in *Count Zero* he is essentially passive, acquiring agency only in the end, in *Mona Lisa Overdrive* he has agency from the very start, ultimately using it to do heroic things. In this regard, Newmark anticipates the more dynamic heroic characters of his later novels such as Colin Laney, Cayce Pollard, and Hollis Henry.

*See also Count Zero*; Cyberspace; Hackers; Millions, Molly; *Mona Lisa Overdrive*; *The Sprawl Trilogy*

• *References and further reading*

Cavallaro, Dani. *Cyberpunk and Cyberculture: Science Fiction and the Work of William Gibson*. Athlone Press, 2000. Print.
Csicery-Ronay, Istvan, Jr. "Antimancer: Cybernetics and Art in Gibson's *Count Zero*." *Science Fiction Studies* 22 (1995): 63–86. Print.
Gibson, William. *Count Zero*. New York: Ace, 1987. Print.
_____. *Mona Lisa Overdrive*. New York: Spectra, 1997. Print.

## No Maps for These Territories

*No Maps for These Territories* (2000) is a feature-length, independent film featuring Gibson that was written and directed by Mark Neale and filmed primarily in a car driven by Neale. Presented as a visionary of sorts, Gibson speaks from the backseat at length on a variety of topics, sometimes speculating broadly on issues ranging from the ubiquity of cyberspace to becoming post-human. At times he seems almost like a mystic, though his sense of irony generally comes through. When asked, *What is going to save us?* for example, Gibson replies: "Acceptance. Acceptance of the impermanence of being, and the acceptance of the imperfect nature of being. Or, possibly, the perfect nature of being, depending on how one looks at it.... Basically, I don't know. You know, all the 'fridge magnets of the New Age' have a certain, a kernel of truth in them, I think." Although Gibson often undercuts his own statements with jokes or laughs, the film seems to take these statements very seriously. Indeed, it seems almost reverential at times, the interviewer never challenging Gibson's position and Neale using archival footage in support of Gibson's various pronouncements about what the future might hold. For example, as Gibson speaks of how "a synergism between computation and genetic research" could lead to "immortality," Neale splices in clips of chromosomes seeming to separate and combine.

Gibson does not always speak in such broad, speculative terms, of course, sometimes providing autobiographical information about his youth or describing his beginnings as a writer. It is not just what Gibson says that makes the film interesting, however: we also see how he reacts to things, giving us a sense of what he is like. For example, when Gibson hears his friend and fellow writer, Jack Womack, describe him as a visionary who changed the world in a marked way, we see just how uncomfortable the unassuming Gibson becomes because the camera is trained on him: his half-smile becomes pained and he fumbles for a cigarette, looking like he wishes he were somewhere else.

The film is also notable because it highlights Gibson's connection with Irish band U2, the Edge providing both music and commentary and Bono reading from *Neuromancer*, *All Tomorrow's Parties*, and another work. Although Neale, who worked with both Gibson and U2 in conjunction with the latter's *Zoo TV* project, is responsible for bringing members of U2 into the project, the two certainly would not have agreed were they not friendly with Gibson, whom they met in 1992. Having said that, there seems to be a certain arbitrariness to featuring the band so prominently, something Neale concedes: "Music and rock 'n' roll is a part of Gibson's books, there is a very rock 'n' roll, adolescent side to it all and so it didn't seem too out of place. But the bottom line is that [Bono and Edge] are there because I could get them in there" (Pancella Interview).

The film, which opened at the Vancouver International Film Festival in October, 2000, was screened at various film festivals in the United States and Great Britain in the year that followed and released on DVD in 2003. Critical response was generally positive, and the film is valued today for the insight it provides into Gibson's character. Despite his obvious discomfort with being cast as some sort of guru, something Gibson registers not only in the Womack sequence but in many of his book tour interviews, Gibson himself gives the film his "seal of approval" on his blog, adding that it is "probably as close to autobiography as you're likely to get from this particular writer" (blog 1/09/2003).

## Pattern Recognition

Set in 2002, *Pattern Recognition* (2003), the first volume of Gibson's third trilogy, is a 9/11 novel not only because it represents the world as having fundamentally changed after the attacks but because it addresses the events of that day directly through Cayce Pollard, the protagonist, who lost her father at the World Trade Center. Gibson had completed about 100 pages of the book by September 10 and, returning to the manuscript after a three-week hiatus, realized that the world he was writing about had changed in a fundamental way, that "the meaning of everything, *ever* that had gone before had to be reconsidered in the light of something that had happened" (Leonard Interview). The novel reflects this change through the consciousness of its protagonist, Cayce Pollard, who struggles not only to reorient herself in the post–9/11 world but come to terms with her father's disappearance.

The novel's plot centers on Pollard's personal and professional quest to find the creator of the "footage"—a series of short, seemingly simple film clips that have been anonymously posted onto various parts of the Internet, developing a large cult following. A "footagehead" herself, Pollard is approached by Hubertus Bigend, owner of the Blue Ant agency, to search out the creator of the mysterious clips, ostensibly so that he can better understand how footage is creating a market for itself without being overtly promoted. As her quest proceeds, the narrative becomes increasingly Pynchonesque, not only because Pollard's adventures parallel those of Oedipa Maas in *The Crying of Lot 49*, but also because, like Pynchon, Gibson depicts the emergence of a new aesthetic, something Frederick Jameson addresses at length in *Archaeologies of the Future* (2005). As Jameson observes, in Gibson's novel "the posthorns and the other telltale graffiti" of Pynchon's Tristero conspiracy have been replaced by the bits of footage, which are painstakingly collected, collated, and analyzed by the footageheads, who form a secret society of sorts, communicating in hushed conversations, exchanged glances, and postings on the Fetish:Footage:Forum website (388). Whereas Pynchon heralds the emergence of a consumerist aesthetic, however, Gibson marks the emergence of a post-consumerist one, an aesthetic that privileges the generic over the branded. Pollard, who has a fashion "allergy," reacting viscerally to certain types of branding in a way that, ironically, makes her invaluable to the fashion industry, embodies this aesthetic, dressing in as brand-neutral a manner as she can, even removing the trademarks from her clothing.

Following a series of adventures that lead her from London to Tokyo, then back to London, and finally Moscow, Pollard ultimately discovers that the footage's creator is Nora Volkova, a former film student who has been critically injured in a bombing and can now only express herself through the footage, which she builds up, almost pixel by pixel, from found video. Because of security concerns of her uncle, a "New Russian" billionaire, Andrei

Volkov, Nora's footage is anonymously distributed by her twin sister, Stella, who tracks it by digital watermarks that are encrypted into it—watermarks that correspond to those that appear on postage stamps in *The Crying of Lot 49*. The digital watermarks, which are collectively organized into a pattern that resembles a city map, seem also to correspond to Tyrone Slothrop's city map in *Gravity's Rainbow*, another of Pynchon's novels that serves as an intertext, connecting Pynchon's critique of post-war corporate capitalism to Gibson's of post–9/11 syndicate capitalism. The connection between Gibson's 9/11 novel and Pynchon's World War II novel is underscored by the fact that the footage itself appears to many footageheads to be set in London in the 1940s just as *Gravity's Rainbow* is (175). Gibson's suggestion seems to be that in the aftermath of 9/11, the world cannot be rebuilt as it was anymore than it could after World War II, because things have fundamentally changed: corporate capitalism has given way to syndicate capitalism, with money and power amassed in the hands of syndicates, organized crime, and individuals like Bigend and Volkov, the latter of whom Pollard identifies with Adolf Eichmann (345).

As in *The Bridge Trilogy*, in *Pattern Recognition* Gibson is often satirical and sometimes humorous, for example basing one character, Billy Prion, on pop singer Billy Idol, complete with silver hair and a botox-induced sneer, and describing Hubertus Bigend as "a nominal Belgian who looks like Tom Cruise on a diet of virgin's blood and truffled chocolates" (20). The book takes on a more serious and sometimes even sentimental tone, however, when addressing the events of 9/11 and their aftermath, as in the following passage which describes Pollard copying pictures of her missing father to post near Ground Zero: "She had, while producing her own posters, watched the faces of other people's dead emerging from the adjacent copiers at Kinko's, to be mounted in the yearbook of the city's loss. She had never, while putting hers up, seen one face pasted over another, and that fact, finally, had allowed her to cry, hunched on a bench in Union Square, candles burning at the base of a statue of George Washington" (192).

Gibson succeeds in blending the satirical, the humorous, and the sentimental by refracting them through a "single point-of-view" narrative, one in which "you would be with the point of view character from top of the chapter to the bottom" (Owens Interview). He also employs the present tense almost exclusively, inviting readers to experience events as Pollard does, and makes frequent use of free indirect discourse. Utilizing such devices enables him to convey a sense of Pollard's consciousness in all its complexity, unifying the novel's various tones and registers in a manner reminiscent of Virginia Woolf and other high modernists.

## PATTERNS, MEANING, AND APOPHENIA

*Pattern Recognition* addresses the human propensity for identifying patterns, for finding order in chaos, if not imposing it. As one of the characters in the novel, Parkaboy, indicates, this propensity can be "both a gift and a trap" (23), not only because those who correctly identify patterns have an advantage over those who misidentify them but because those expecting to find meaning in the random may become effectively paralyzed, unable to act until a meaning can be discerned (23).

As Pollard herself recognizes, as a "coolhunter," her vocation is "to recognize a pattern before anyone else does," something she is able to do instinctively because of her fashion allergies (88). She is initially unsuccessful in identifying patterns in the events in her own life, however, unable even to discern whether they exist or not. Her obsession with the footage reflects her need to impose order onto chaos, to find meaning in what may be random: along with the other footageheads, who include Parkaboy and Dorotea Benedetti, she analyzes the clips as they appear in an online forum, convinced of a "nascent meaning" (118). On a more personal level, her obsession with the footage relates directly to her need to find meaning in the disappearance of her father, Wingrove: to her, the feeling of loneliness and loss the footage conveys relates directly to her own feelings (111). Ultimately, her success in finding the maker of the footage provides her with closure since she learns enough about her father's last day in New York to accept the fact that he is, indeed, gone. In addition, her quest enables her to connect with the Volkavas, two young women who also lost their fathers to a bombing and feel a similar sense of loneliness and loss.

Pollard's quest to discover the meaning of the footage by finding its maker also enables her to go from being passive to active. At the beginning of the novel she is undirected and unable to take much initiative, being victimized by Dorotea Benedetti and dominated by Bigend. She gradually acquires agency, however, pursuing her own agenda, defending herself against Benedetti and her agents, and defying Bigend's efforts to manipulate and control her. As she becomes empowered, she also becomes better able to address the loss of her father, working through her grief, and eventually moving beyond it. In a sense, she gets her father back, or at least her memories of him and the things he has taught her; he is no longer "ungrieved" (133). Eventually, she receives what appear to be directions from him in her dreams, enabling her finally to discern the pattern around the footage and locate its maker.

Pollard's mother, Cynthia, too, seeks the meaning behind Wingrove's disappearance, endlessly analyzing the "noise" in sound recordings taken at and near Ground Zero since she believes those who have passed to "the other side" communicate through it (191). Not surprisingly, perhaps, Pollard regards her mother's efforts as an example of apophenia, "the spontaneous perception of connections and meaningfulness in unrelated things" and finds discussing it with her unpleasant, refusing to open emails on the subject for much of the novel and dismissing their contents when she finally does (117–18). Ironically, the messages that her mother passes on to her do seem to relate to her quest to find the maker of the footage, one of them, for example, apparently referencing the "T-bone"–shaped fragment of a Claymore mine that has been lodged in the head of Nora Volkova, an injury that Pollard at the time is unaware of (192). By having Pollard eventually come to terms with the loss of her father despite missing such messages, Gibson suggests that even though there may be patterns to be discovered, identifying them is not always necessary or even beneficial.

## TECHNOLOGY, COMMUNICATIONS, AND HUMAN RELATIONSHIPS

By setting the novel in the near past rather than the future, Gibson is able to address the ways in which new technologies affect everyday lives, technologies ranging from search engines to security systems. *Pattern Recognition* concerns itself in particular with communication technologies and the ways they impact Pollard's relationships with others. Although email and online communities are not ostensive subjects of the novel, the ways in which the characters utilize them offer *de facto* commentary on such media.

A number of the novel's characters connect through the Fetish: Footage: Forum website, not only to discuss the footage itself but to connect socially. Together, the footageheads form a subculture based on shared interest in the footage but extending beyond it as evidenced by the relationship that develops between Pollard and Parkaboy, even though Pollard "knows almost nothing about him, other than that he lives in Chicago and, she assumes, is gay" (40). Although their relationship is only virtual at this point, Pollard and Parkaboy share a certain intimacy, one that allows Pollard to "get away" with chiding him for "flaming" Mama Anarchia on the forum and to take comfort in his online presence when she is unnerved by the actions of Dorotea Benedetti and her agents (50). Gibson uses the fact that "Mama Anarchia" eventually proves to be the username of Benedetti to further demonstrate how virtual lives and physical ones are merging, becoming what Gibson terms a "blended reality" (Leonard Interview 2007).

Gibson also uses the relationship between Pollard and Parkaboy to explore how virtual relationships can develop into romantic ones. At the beginning of the novel, the two are online friends only, something Gibson makes clear by identifying Parkaboy as Pollard's "favorite," then immediately qualifying the statement by adding "on F:F:F" (40). Although they become closer as they work together to discover the maker of the footage, Parkaboy still identifies himself by his username when they first speak on the phone, only revealing his given name, "Peter Gilbert," when she needs it to purchase an airline ticket for him (288). Even though their first phone conversation is awkward, with Pollard observing that Parkaboy "sounds quite unlike he 'sounds' on the screen, whatever that means," such differences prove to be superficial as the real Parkaboy proves to be the same as the virtual one (149). Pollard soon realizes how "deeply" she "values" his friendship, and by the time they meet, they seem to have a romantic connection (287). Significantly, the novel's closing line indicates that their relationship has become physical, with Pollard kissing his back as they lie in bed together, and in *Zero History* we learn they marry and start a family (367).

Gibson's depiction of how intimate virtual relationships can become is all the more powerful because he uses a potential romantic relationship between Pollard and Boone Chu to serve as a counterpoint. Pollard is immediately attracted to Chu, "a very good-looking young Asian man" when they meet, seemingly randomly, on the street, looking after him, "feeling a wave of longing, loneliness" (96–97). As the narrative proceeds, her physical attraction to him continues but they never become emotionally intimate, in part because trust never develops between them as it does between her and Parkaboy. The differences between Pollard's relationships with the two men also become evident when Pollard opens emails from the two of them in succession. Chu's terse email leads her to observe that Chu is not "the most eloquent of correspondents" while Parkaboy's displays the usual humor, intimacy, and openness (231–32). That Pollard ultimately prefers Parkaboy, a "middle-aged white guy" with a "receding hairline" to the more sexually attractive Chu suggests that virtual relationships can be as intense as physical ones, if not more so.

*See also* Bigend, Hubertus; *The Bigend Trilogy*; Pollard, Cayce; *Spook Country*; *Zero History*

• *References and further reading*

Easterbrook, Neil. "Alternate Presents: The Ambivalent Historicism of *Pattern Recognition*." *Science Fiction Studies* 33 (2006): 483–503. Print.

Gibson, Williams. *Pattern Recognition*. New York: Berkley, 2005. Print.

_____. *Spook Country*. New York: Berkley, 2009. Print.

_____. *Zero History*. New York: Putnam, 2010. Print.

Hollinger, Veronica. "Stories About the Future: From *Patterns of Expectation* to *Pattern Recognition*." *Science Fiction Studies* 33 (2006): 452–82. Print.

Jameson, Fredric. *Archaeologies of the Future: The Desire Called Utopia and Other Science Fictions*. New York: Verso, 2005. Print.

Konstantinou, Lee. "The Brand as Cognitive Map in William Gibson's *Pattern Recognition*." *Boundary 2: An International Journal of Literature and Culture* 36.2 (2009): 67–97. Print.

Link, Alex. "Global War, Global Capital, and the Work of Art in William Gibson's *Pattern Recognition*." *Contemporary Literature* 49.2 (2008): 209–31. Print.

Palmer, Christopher. "None of What We Do Is Ever Really Private." *Science Fiction Studies* 33.3 (2006): 473–82. Print.

Pynchon, Thomas. *The Crying of Lot 49*. New York: Perennial, 1966. Print.

_____. *Gravity's Rainbow*. New York: Viking, 1973. Print.

Wegner, Phillip E. "Recognizing the Patterns." *New Literary History: A Journal of Theory and Interpretation* 38.1 (2007): 183–200. Print.

Youngquist, Paul. *Cyberfiction: After the Future*. New York: Palgrave Macmillan, 2010. Print.

Zeidner, Lisa. "*Pattern Recognition*: The Coolhunter." New York Times.com, *New York Times*, 19 Jan. 2003. Web.

# Politics

Although Gibson insists that he has "always tried very hard not to be a 'political' novelist," as one might expect of any socially engaged writer, his political attitudes come through in his fiction, particularly in his most recent work, which, set in the present, is critical of neoconservatives and the Bush agenda (blog 10/01/2004). Even then he is indirect in his criticism, if not always subtle, in *Spook Country*, for example, identifying the slow-witted neoconservative operative Brown as a FOX news viewer. Describing himself as "vaguely Left of center" in the mid–1990s and more recently as "more or less a centrist," Gibson rarely comments on particular politicians or issues other than those related directly to his work, with the exception of George W. Bush and the consequences of the so-called War on Terror, which he is openly critical of.

It is not just Gibson's recent work that has political overtones, however. Even very early works such as "The Greensback Continuum" (1981) challenge what Gibson sees as the essential conservatism of Golden Age science fiction, a conservatism that he found to be still ambient in the early 1980s when he became a professional writer. Fortunately for Gibson, a like-minded group of writers was emerging at the same time, a group that was then called "the Movement," and later termed "cyberpunk." These writers, which included people like Pat Cadigan, John Shirley, and Bruce Sterling, challenged the status quo of not only science fiction but of Reagan-era politics. In "Hinterlands" (1981) and in "Red Star, Winter Orbit" (1983) the latter being a story co-authored with Sterling, Gibson suggests that the Cold War is not only unwinnable but unsustainable — points he makes again in *Neuromancer* and the other volumes of *The Sprawl Trilogy*— by having it culminate in a nuclear exchange, neither the United States nor the Soviet Union remaining superpower status afterwards. The novels, which Gibson indicated in interviews were really "about the Reagan eighties" also address the gap between the haves and the have-nots, a gap that expanded in the 1980s in part because of Reagan's policies (Blair Interview). Gibson comments, "When I wrote *Neuromancer*, I was conscious of writing about Reaganomics. I was writing about the outcome of that kind of political philosophy. One of those outcomes was that in *Neuromancer*, the United States is like Mexico City" (Gutmar Interview).

In *Virtual Light*, the first volume of *The Bridge Trilogy*, Gibson's work takes on a satirical edge, targeting things such as televangelism, celebrity culture, and American litigiousness. Like the volumes that follow, however, it offers little in the way of direct political commentary other than quick references to things such as an Oliver North elementary school and the disastrous consequences of the "War on Drugs." The *Trilogy* does offer sustained commentary on the economic climate of the "roaring '90s," however, with capitalism running amok, the novel being set in a world overrun by convenience stores, media corporations, and private security forces. Even cyberspace has become commercialized, with major corporations developing it as if it were real estate. Gibson's politics also become evident in his representations of interstices such as the Bridge and the Walled City — spaces at once inside and outside of the dominant culture that serve not only as refuges but as sites of resistance: the protagonists of these novels are insignificant-seeming people who, sometimes unknowingly, act to prevent the rich and powerful from extending their control into new domains, including the interstices themselves.

Gibson is much less reticent about his politics in his interviews and on his blog, particularly recently. For example, in a high-profile interview with *Rolling Stone*, which was published in their 40th-anniversary issue, he says of the 2000s, "It's been an extraordinarily painful decade or so. I just never in my wildest dreams could have imagined that it could get as fucked up as this guy [George Bush]." In his blog, which becomes increasingly political at the peak of election cycles, he is even more explicit, writing in October, 2004, for example, that "The Republican Party has been hijacked by extremists" and that "The idea that Kerry and Bush are merely two sides of the same bad coin is both ludicrous and all too potentially tragic." During the 2008 elections, he openly encouraged people to support Barack Obama: "Are you planning to vote for Obama? Let me advise you to do what it takes, Tuesday, to do that. Don't be a part of that part of the electorate that, for whatever reason, intends to vote, but doesn't. Whichever way this election goes, you will not want to journey into your personal future, the future of the United States, or the future of the world, without having cast your vote in this election. If I know anything about the future, I know that."

In his most recent novel, *Zero History*, Gibson makes only a passing reference to Obama, though Garreth Wilson's observation that there is "more free-floating ambiguity" about the War on Terror under Obama seems to register a certain disappointment that the administration failed to act more decisively in ending the war (293). Although he does not mention the Tea Party in the book, he did speak of it in some of the interviews he gave while on his 2010 book tour. Asked about the Tea Party's apparent success in becoming a popular movement, he replied: "It helps to have a black guy in the White House. Any Black guy. If you want to do an old, grumpy white folks party, get a black guy in the White House. You get your old grumpy white folks to turn out" (Gallagher Interview). He adds that the movement will ultimately harm the Republican Party: "They're going to have to find a different way to operate or they'll go the way of the Whigs. Not like next year, but eventually. You can do all sorts of crazy shite when you're not in power to interrupt what the guy in power is doing. But it costs you down the line if it really was crazy shit."

*See also* Counterculture; Dystopia

• *References and further reading*

Gibson, William. "The Gernsback Continuum." *Burning Chrome*. New York: Ace, 1986. Print.
_____. "Hinterlands." *Burning Chrome*. New York: Ace, 1986. Print.
_____. *Neuromancer*. New York: Ace, 1984. Print.
_____. *Spook Country*. New York: Berkley, 2009. Print.
_____. *Virtual Light*. New York: Spectra, 1994. Print.
_____. *Zero History*. New York: Putnam, 2010. Print.
Youngquist, Paul. *Cyberfiction: After the Future*. New York: Palgrave Macmillan, 2010. Print.

## Pollard, Cayce

The main character of *Pattern Recognition*, the first volume of *The Bigend Trilogy*, Cayce Pollard is one of Gibson's most striking characters, largely because the story of her personal recovery following the 9/11 attacks represents the story of Americans at large as they tried to redefine themselves in a world that has become permanently altered. To a large extent, Pollard's story is a 9/11 story, the novel presenting us with Pollard's efforts to come to terms with the loss of her father, Winthrop Pollard, who disappeared in New York on the day of the attacks. On another level, however, the novel addresses the more general need people have to come to terms with a world that is increasingly unknowable, a world replete with simulacra. Ultimately, Pollard's issues seem to resolve themselves as she realizes that her situation is, in fact, the human condition, the world having become a place marked not just by loss but an absence of anything real.

Ironically, as someone working in the fashion industry, Pollard is in part responsible for bringing the hyperreal being. As a "coolhunter," she tries "to recognize a pattern before anyone else does" and "point a commodifier at it" so that it can be reproduced en masse as a consumer good. Fully cognizant of her complicity in the flattening of a once diverse world into a monoculture, Pollard despises her profession but nonetheless feels she has no choice but to continue in it out of economic necessity. Her professional activities are made even more difficult for her because she has "a morbid and sometimes violent reactivity to the semiotics of the market place," an allergic reaction to certain logos and brands, particularly those that seem to her to be entirely derivative like Tommy Hilfiger and that which is overly derivative.

Pollard's two issues— her need to address the loss of her father and her need to address the guilt she feels for being a coolhunter —come together when she is hired by media mogul Hubertus Bigend to identify the maker of some mysterious footage that has been appearing on the Net, acquiring a cult following. For Pollard the quest to find the maker is both professional and personal because she herself has been obsessed with the footage since the loss of her father, the footage resonating deeply with her for reasons she cannot explain. One of the many things she learns along the way is that the professional cannot be separated from the personal because what we do largely determines who we are. The problem, Pollard learns, is that people have little choice in their place in society, their abilities and skills determining it rather than their preferences and inclinations.

Ultimately Pollard succeeds in identifying the maker of the footage, thereby succeeding in her quest for the "real." As it turns out the maker, Nora Volkova, and her sister, Stella, who is responsible for the innovative way in which the footage is disseminated, are very much like Pollard, the two of them having lost their parents in a bombing. Nora, who was incapacitated by the explosion, can only express herself by constructing a "real" for herself pixel by pixel in her footage. The lesson that she learns from the Volkova sisters is essentially an existentialist one: in a world in which public meanings are endlessly deferred, one can still make private meaning for oneself. With this realization, she gains a measure of control over her own life, something marked by the disappearance of her fashion allergies. More importantly, perhaps, she finally becomes able to grieve for her father, accepting the fact that he is dead even though she can never know exactly how he died since his body was not recovered.

In *Zero History*, the final volume of *The Bigend Trilogy* we learn that Pollard has indeed found a way to create meaning for herself. Ironically, she does so not by leaving the fashion industry but by becoming a designer herself. As the founder of The Gabriel Hounds line of clothing, Pollard is able create the "real" not only for herself but for others by designing what she likes rather than what she thinks will sell and by avoiding all of "the bullshit" involved with promotion (337). Rather than advertise her brand, she keeps her brand a secret, the branding becoming the secret itself: the only ones who can acquire her brand are those who know to, the knowledge they bring to the transaction making the brand real.

One of the most impressive things about Pollard as a character is the fact that Gibson is able to use her to articulate a theoretical position on the nature of the "real" without employing theoretical terms or otherwise appearing didactic. Indeed, both Pollard and Parkaboy, whom she meets online in a forum dedicated to the footage, express hostility to theorists like Jean Baudrillard and "the other Frenchmen" who were largely responsible for introducing terms such as the "real" and "hyperreal" into discourse about the nature of reality (*Pattern Recognition* 50). As in *Idoru*, Gibson seems to be at once exploring the ideas of such theorists and satirizing them, Gibson seemingly having a problem with the idea of theorizing becoming an end in itself. In *Zero History* Pollard and Parkaboy, who eventually marry, move beyond theory by putting their ideas into practice through the Gabriel Hounds line.

*See also* Bigend, Hubertus; *The Bigend Trilogy*; *Idoru*; *Pattern Recognition*; *Spook Country*; *Zero History*

• *References and further reading*

Baudrillard, Jean. *Simulacra and Simulation*. Trans. Sheila Fraser. Ann Arbor: University of Michigan Press, 1995. Print.
Easterbrook, Neil. "Alternate Presents: The Ambivalent Historicism of *Pattern Recognition*." *Science Fiction Studies* 33 (2006): 483–503. Print.
Gibson, William. *Pattern Recognition*. New York: Berkley, 2005. Print.
_____. *Zero History*. New York: Putnam, 2010. Print.
Hollinger, Veronica. "Stories About the Future: From *Patterns of Expectation* to *Pattern Recognition*." *Science Fiction Studies* 33 (2006): 452–71. Print.
Jameson, Fredric. *Archaeologies of the Future: The Desire Called Utopia and Other Science Fictions*. New York: Verso, 2005. Print.
Palmer, Christopher. "*Pattern Recognition*: 'None of What We Do Is Ever Really Private.'" *Science Fiction Studies* 33.3 (2006): 473–82. Print.

## Science Fiction

Gibson has long insisted that science fiction — or, at least, any science fiction worth reading — is "never about the future"; that, instead, it "uses the conceit of the imaginary future to examine the present" (Blume Interview). As such it is among the most socially engaged of genres, a genre that has the potential to affect the ways in which people think and act. In his view, science fiction writers, like all writers, have certain responsibilities when it comes to their work, including an obligation to take both their work and its readers seriously. To an extent, it was his disappointment in the science fiction of the late 1970s and early 1980s for refusing those responsibilities that led him to begin writing. As he explains in an interview, when he resumed reading science fiction in the 1970s after having given it up as a teenager, he found it to be "a viable, traditional 20th-century pop art form that is bankrupt in a really interesting way. That was one of the things that attracted me to it" (Gross Interview). He also seems to have been motivated in part by a sense of perversity, indicating in another interview that in his early work, at least, he wanted to write things that "would bug the science fiction community to no end" (Gross Interview). He adds: "I was tired of unicorn fantasies and I was tired of this sort of endlessly recycled pseudo–Heinleinean stuff, you know, male power and fantasies, and the future is the United States, and so I thought I'm gonna come in here and do the old, put the double-whammy on this stuff," and, as a result, "be roundly ignored."

In the very first story he wrote as a professional writer, "The Gernsback Continuum" (1981), Gibson challenged the *status quo*, suggesting that the futurism that dominated American science fiction from the 1930s through its Golden Age in the 1950s promoted views that were essentially militaristic if not fascistic. Although the story was initially ignored, at least by the science fiction establishment, it did help establish Gibson's position as part of a movement within the science fiction community that was later termed "cyberpunk," and the stories that followed were heavily promoted by Bruce Sterling in his fanzine, *Cheap Truth*. Although Gibson's work hardly needed such promotion, "Johnny Mnemonic" (1981) and "Burning Chrome" (1982) being nominated for Nebula Awards, being a part of an artistic community gave him a critical sense of belonging early in his career as well as a sounding board for his work as he continued to experiment within the genre. Though very much appreciative of the warm reception he received from the science fiction community at large, he nonetheless remained critical of its mainstream, which he regarded as "inherently conservative" (Brave New World Interview).

It was not just Gibson's content that was radical, of course: Gibson was more self-consciously an artist than most fiction writers of the 1980s, plotting his stories carefully and constructing complex rhetorical matrices in order to convey abstract ideas such as cyberspace. Critics were quick to recognize his facility with language, and Gibson was widely regarded as the most literary of science fiction writers. To an extent, however, Gibson considered himself as a literary artist who happened to write science fiction, something that should not be too surprising given that Gibson is not particularly science-oriented and did not even own a computer while writing *Neuromancer*. As he explained to Leanne Harper, writing science fiction enabled him to reach "exactly the same audience I would have wanted to reach, plus the science fiction audience as well" (30). In other words, science fiction afforded him both a popular audience and a literary one.

For all its literariness, *The Sprawl Trilogy* is still instantly recognizable as science fiction: though the novels are certainly not about spaceships or aliens, they do include them, much of the action taking place in orbit and the *Trilogy* ending with a group of characters trying to contact a cyberspace matrix located in Alpha Centauri. The same cannot be said of *The Bridge Trilogy*, which not only lacks aliens and spaceships but is set in a near future that could not possibly happen: even the most credulous reader could hardly believe that within fifteen years California would be split into two states, the United States would form a federation with Canada, and a quake-damaged Tokyo would be rebuilt with nanotechnology. Were *Virtual Light* not written by someone already labeled a "science fiction writer," it might have been categorized as literature or mainstream fiction and placed alongside the works of writers like William Burroughs, Thomas Pynchon, and Margaret Atwood. Indeed, the marketplace seemed to recognize this on some level, *Virtual Light* being the first of Gibson's novels to become a *New York Times* best seller. With *The Bridge Trilogy*, it seems, Gibson finally succeeded moving from science fiction to the mainstream "without losing a sense of what it is [he is] ... doing" (McCaffery Interview 283).

Given the fact that *The Bigend Trilogy* is set in the near past rather than the future, it might seem difficult to argue that Gibson's most recent work qualifies as science fiction at all. Reviews of his work often to refer to him as a science fiction writer who has recently turned to mainstream fiction, and he is no longer nominated for major awards within the science fiction community. With all this in mind, it may seem surprising, perhaps, that Gibson still considers himself as much a science fiction writer as he ever was, indicating that he "never believed in the separation," adding: "It's a matter of where you're allowed to park. If you can park in the science fiction bookstore, that's good. If you can park in the other bookstore, that's really good" (Amazon Interview). More recently, he remarked that in *Zero History* and other novels set in the near present, he was just using the "toolkit" he got from science fiction "to examine a present that becomes increasingly fantastical and more peculiar with each passing day" (Handlen Interview). To him, there is no reason to set novels in an imaginary future when "the actual 21st Century is richer, stranger, more multiplex, than any imaginary 21st Century could ever have been" (blog 5/31/2010).

   *See also* Cyberpunk; "The Gernsback Continuum"

• *References and further reading*

Christie, John R.R. "Science Fiction and the Postmodern: The Recent Fiction of William Gibson and John Crowley." *Essays and Studies* 43 (1990): 34–58. Print.
Gibson, William. "The Gernsback Continuum." *Burning Chrome*. New York: Ace, 1986. Print.
_____. *Neuromancer*. New York: Ace, 1984. Print.
_____. *Virtual Light*. New York: Spectra, 1994.
_____. *Zero History*. New York: Putnam, 2010. Print.
Huntington, John. "Newness, *Neuromancer*, and the End of Narrative. *Essays and Studies* 43 (1990): 59–75. Print.
McCaffery, Larry. *Storming the Reality Studio: A Casebook of Cyberpunk and Postmodern Science Fiction.* Durham: Duke University Press, 1992. Print.
Ross, Andrew. "Getting Out of the Gernsback Continuum." *Critical Inquiry* 17.2 (1991): 411–33. Print.
Sterling, Bruce. Preface. *Burning Chrome*. New York: Ace, 1986. xi–xvi. Print.
Youngquist, Paul. *Cyberfiction: After the Future.* New York: Palgrave Macmillan, 2010. Print.

# "Skinner's Room"

   "Skinner's Room" (1990) is less a story than a somber sketch of an aged man and young woman who share a makeshift plywood dwelling built near the top of one of the towers of the Bay Bridge. The man, Skinner, is one of the squatters who claimed the bridge years ago, the displaced and homeless taking it over spontaneously; very old now, he is prompted by the young woman who has stayed with him for three months to remember how the Bridge came to be what is, how those on the margins claimed a space for themselves, finding an interstice in which they could be unregulated and unsurveilled. The story's primary action takes place in Skinner's memory as he recollects fragments from his past so that he can articulate them to the woman. The unnamed woman, who herself has been displaced, drifting down to San Francisco from the Northwest, seems to identify with Skinner and the other Bridge people who have formed an alternative community, a counterculture of sorts. That they have succeeded in doing so seems to be confirmed at the very end of the story when Skinner describes to the woman how he and others had scaled the towers, climbing above the circling news helicopters and finally seeing the city from the outside rather than from within.

   Although relatively unknown, having first been published as part of a 1990 art exhibition at the San Francisco Museum of Modern Art and then being rewritten for *Omni*, where it appeared in 1991, "Skinner's Room" is arguably one of Gibson's most successful stories, at least in artistic terms. Rather than rely upon action or romance to hold the reader's interest, Gibson juxtaposes events, encounters, and descriptions in a way that reveals not only the psychological complexity of his characters but offers social commentary if not social criticism. The story is also of note because it provided a basis for *The Bridge Trilogy*. Parts of *Virtual Light* are set in Skinner's room and other parts of the Bridge, and both Skinner and the woman, who is named "Chevette Washington" in the novel, play key roles. Washington also appears in the final volume of the trilogy, *All Tomorrow's Parties*, Skinner having died, and the novel ends with Washington and Berry Rydell on the roof of Skinner's room, where they took refuge when Cody Harwood's agents set the Bridge aflame.

   *See also All Tomorrow's Parties; The Bridge Trilogy; Virtual Light*

• *References and further reading*

Gibson, William. *All Tomorrow's Parties*. New York: Berkley, 2003. Print.
_____. *Virtual Light*. New York: Spectra, 1994.

## Spook Country

   Like *Pattern Recognition*, the volume that precedes it in *The Bigend Trilogy*, *Spook Country* (2007) is set in the recent past rather than the future, allowing Gibson to address contemporary issues and events in a more direct manner. As Gibson acknowledged in a speech he gave at the 2010 Book Expo America Luncheon and later published on his blog (May 31, 2010), the novel centers on what he calls "the deep end of the Bush administration," referencing particular events such as George W. Bush's ill-advised "Mission Accomplished" landing on the *U.S.S. Abraham Lincoln* in 2003 and the disappearance of 363 tons of American currency during the invasion of Iraq. Accordingly, like *Pattern Recognition*, the book reads more like reality-based thriller than a work of science fiction, even though it addresses the ways in which technology affects us much in the same manner his earlier works do. As Steven Poole notes in his review of *Spook Country* for the *Guardian*, the novel also functions as satire, targeting "advertising, music, and the geekocracy" (Poole 2007). Because of the satire, which is sometimes pointed, the book seems to lack *gravitas*, at least according to some reviewers, with Thomas M. Wagner of *SF Reviews*, for example, complaining that "the story ought to have amounted to more than it does" (Poole 2007). Other reviewers, like Dave Itzkoff of the *New York Times*, regard the novel's satirical elements as strengths since they are consistent with the attitudes the novel's protagonists find they must adopt in order to cope with twenty-first century life — a sense of the ridiculous evidenced by the prank the novel ends with. Although Gibson himself seems to acknowledge a certain lightness to the book, at least in generic terms, referring to it as a "a caper novel" (Amazon Interview), in the interviews he has given following its release, he indicate that he takes the subject matter itself seriously, noting that post 9–11 Patriot Act America is radically different from the country it was, even though many do not recognize it, and that, indeed, the entire nation seems to be suffering from Stockholm syndrome, sympathizing with those that control them rather than resisting them (Owens Interview).

   The novel's primary narrative centers on Hollis Henry, a singer turned freelance writer working on story on locative art — that is, virtual art that employs GPS technology so that it can be broadcast at precise locations—for *Node*, an as-yet unpublished European magazine modeled on *Wired*. She quickly learns that in researching the story, she has become a *de facto* operative of Hubertus Bigend, an advertising magnate who believes that

Bobby Chombo, a technician who helps locative artists produce their work, holds the key to locating a mysterious cargo container that has been on the high seas for three years. Secondary narratives center on Milgrim, a drug addict who has been kidnapped by an operative known only as "Brown," who also seeks the container, and Tito, a private operative of Chinese-Cuban descent who acts as a courier for "the old man," a mysterious figure who seems to be somehow connected to the container. As in most Gibson narratives, seemingly unrelated narratives come together as Hollis learns the secret of the container, which, it turns out, contains $100 million in currency meant to facilitate the U.S. occupation of Iraq. The old man, it seems, is a disaffected former U.S. operative who, disgusted with the new world order, has been playing cat and mouse with the currency, giving Brown and his affiliates the runaround just for the sake of doing so (318). Ultimately, he employs Tito and his cohorts to mark the bills with cesium so that those in possession of the container will be exposed when they try to smuggle the money back in to the United States. The novel ends with Hollis lying to Bigend about what she has learned and then commissioning a work of locative art herself — a Disney-like image of a giant scarlet Mongolian Death Worm wrapped around the top of Bigend's headquarters in Vancouver.

In terms of style, the novel differs from Gibson's earlier, speculative work in its commitment to what Itzkoff calls "modernist realism," that is, representations of the human condition that are neither idealized nor abstracted. Even though the novel's realism is undercut at certain points by its satirical elements, for the most part Gibson tries to present the world as it is rather than as it might be. At the same time Gibson also suggests that the world is ultimately unknowable, a characteristic he identifies with "an emergent, new kind of realism" in which writers "are willing to admit to themselves — and to some extent the reader — that they don't know what the hell is going on" (Murray Interview).

The novel's satirical elements are most apparent in its representation of Brown, a FOX News–watching, low–IQed operative for a Blackwater-like company, who, for all his affectations of being a master spy, proves to be ineffectual if not incompetent, losing track of Tito, Milgrim, the old man, and the container — and breaking his leg in the process. As noted earlier, the novel also satirizes the advertising industry through Bigend and his megalomania, just as *Pattern Recognition* does, and the music industry through Hollis, who uses her star power as lead singer for a now defunct post-punk band, the Curfew, to navigate a celebrity-worshipping culture.

In *Spook Country*, as in *Pattern Recognition*, Gibson uses figurative language more to express emotions and internal states than technological wonders as he does in his speculative fiction, for example describing a character's feeling of nakedness "as an occult aura of preternaturally intense awareness, as though the wearer were a vampire in an Anne Rice novel, or a novice cocaine user" (77). Gibson also uses figurative language to highlight the sublime — and sometimes the absurd — that can be found in everyday experiences and objects, describing a dirty Sunset Boulevard sidewalk as "a pointillist abstract in black chewing gum" (7). He also makes skillful use of free indirect discourse, both individuating the consciousnesses of his primary characters and inviting readers into them. In this sense at least, *Spook Country* is arguably Gibson's most sophisticated novel.

## "Karain" as an Intertext

To an extent *Spook Country* appears to be patterned on "Karain: A Memory" (1897), one of the Joseph Conrad short stories that Gibson references when he talks about the Aceh region of Sumatra as "Prime Conrad territory" (114). Conrad's story focuses on a Malay chief, Karain, who is haunted by the ghost of a friend he has betrayed; he hopes to travel to England with the smugglers who provide him with guns since he thinks of England as being a land of neither conscience nor ghosts. Rather than transport Karain to Europe, however, one of the Englishmen, Hollis, provides him with a charm made out of gold sovereign with the image of Queen Victoria on it, claiming that it will ward off ghosts; Conrad's implication seems to be that imperialism and the capitalist system that underlies it have no more conscience and are thus immune to ghosts. Conrad's story ends many years later when the story's unnamed narrator and another crew member, Jackson, encounter each other before a gunshop in London, and Jackson wonders whether ghosts, being manifestations of conscience, are real, and whether England is really free of them.

The connection between "Karain" and *Spook Country* go beyond just the specific reference to Gibson's reference to "Conrad territory" and the fact that Gibson appears to name one of his protagonists, Hollis, after the Conrad character who equates imperialism and capitalism with a lack of conscience. As the word "spook" suggests, *Spook Country*, like "Karain," is a ghost story of sorts, a story about people haunted by conscience. In *Spook Country*, however, the ghost is an ex-spook, a former U.S. operative who manipulates the cargo container in order to torment Brown and those he works for, people he finds unconscionable because they are trying to profit from the war in Iraq. Gibson's novel can thus be read as an indictment of George W. Bush's neoconservatism in the same way that Conrad's story served as an indictment of British imperialism and capitalism. Accordingly, *Spook Country* is perhaps the most overtly political of Gibson's novels.

## SPOOKS IN POST 9-11 AMERICA

Gibson's title, *Spook Country*, is more than just an allusion to the ghost-ridden imperial metropolis of Conrad's story, of course, for "spook" is also a slang term for spy or secret agent. For Gibson, post 9-11 America is a nation haunted by spooks, a nation in which people have come to assume that their every action, their every word, is being recorded if not observed, a sensibility that manifests itself in the text when Hollis, sitting in a Starbucks, realizes that the most terrifying thing about post–9-11 America is that she is "afraid to trust her phone and the net stretching out from it."

Spooks like Brown and his associates, operatives of private corporations that are contracted to do intelligence work, pervade the novel as well, representing a different kind of threat since, like the private companies such as Blackwater contracted to assist in the occupation of Iraq, they provide the government with a means of distancing themselves from any violations of law and convention even as they benefit from them. The fact that Brown in particular is at once malevolent and incompetent makes him seem all the more threatening, something that becomes clear when, about to lose track of Tito, he simply tries to run him down.

Cold-War era spooks such as the old man and the members of Tito's family are treated by Gibson much more sympathetically: indeed, Gibson represents the old man's cat-and-mouse game with the shipping container as a positive moral action, albeit an insignificant one taken by itself. Like the giant Mongolian Blood Worm Hollis has projected upon the top of Bigend's building, the old man's game is an act of resistance as well as a prank. Accordingly, as Itzkoff notes, *Spook Country* "is arguably the first example of the post–post–9/11 novel, whose characters are tired of being pushed around by forces larger than they are — bureaucracy, history and, always, technology — and are at long last ready to start pushing back."

## PARANOIA, COINCIDENCE, AND CHOICE

Like *Pattern Recognition*, *Spook Country* addresses the paranoia concomitant with living under surveillance and potential means for addressing it. Both novels feature protagonists who recognize that their every word and action may be known but refuse to be paralyzed by such knowledge. Indeed, both Cayce Pollard and Hollis Henry attempt to retain control over information themselves, Pollard by withholding information from Bigend and others in order to protect Nora Volkova, and Hollis Henry by doing the same to prevent the contamination of the currency with cesium from being known. If Bigend is correct in asserting to Hollis at one point that "possession of information amounts to involvement," Hollis largely succeeds in determining how she is involved (254).

The protagonists of both novels also refuse to let unlikely seeming coincidences prevent them from taking action out of fear that they are being manipulated. In *Pattern Recognition*, Gibson addresses this issue overtly through Pollard, who reflects upon coincidences and their likelihood, ultimately drawing upon her father's advice: "There must always be room for coincidence.... When there's not, you're probably well into apophenia, each thing then perceived as part of an overarching pattern of conspiracy. And while comforting yourself with the symmetry of it all ... you stood all too real a chance of missing the genuine threat, which was invariably less symmetrical, less perfect" (304). In *Spook Country*, coincidences abound as well, occasionally giving Hollis and other characters pause at times but never paralyzing them. Even though she knows that coincidence is never "a safe concept" in a world dominated by spooks (254), in the novel's final chapter Hollis accepts an unlikely encounter with Tito as being "entirely by accident," an attitude that suggests that she has made a conscious decision not to be paranoid, even though she may have good reason to be so (476). This decision is in a sense existential since she chooses the terms by which she defines her existence.

See also Bigend, Hubertus; *The Bigend Trilogy*; Henry, Hollis; Japan; Milgrim; *Pattern Recognition*; Politics; *Zero History*

• *References and further reading*

Conrad, Joseph. "Karain: A Memory." *Tales of Unrest*. New York: Doubleday, Page, 1920. 3–55. Print.
Gibson, William. *Spook Country*. New York: Berkley, 2009. Print.
_____. *Virtual Light*. New York: Spectra, 1994.
_____. *Zero History*. New York: Putnam, 2010. Print.
Itzkoff, Dave. "Spirits in the Material World." New York Times.com, *New York Times*, 26 Aug 2007. Web.
Jameson, Fredric. *Archaeologies of the Future: The Desire Called Utopia and Other Science Fictions*. New York: Verso, 2005. Print.
Jones, Steven. "Second Life, Video Games, and the Social Text. *PMLA: Publications of the Modern Language Association* 124.1 (2009): 264–72. Print.
Youngquist, Paul. *Cyberfiction: After the Future*. New York: Palgrave Macmillan, 2010. Print.

## The Sprawl Trilogy

*The Sprawl Trilogy* is comprised of Gibson's first three novels, *Neuromancer* (1984), *Count Zero* (1986), and *Mona Lisa Overdrive* (1988). Named for "the Sprawl," an urban area that stretches from Boston to Atlanta, the novels are set in a near future where global corporations dominate, orbital space has been commercialized, and information is a commodity. Japan, it seems, has emerged as an economic superpower following a limited nuclear war that destroyed Bonn and Beograd. Gibson is deliberately vague about the fate of the United States, never mentioning what happens to it as a nation after the war in any of the novels. In an NPR interview he explains that this "was done in deliberate reaction to this overwhelming tendency in American science fiction to see the future as America": "And I think at one time the world believed that America was the future, but now the future's gone somewhere else, perhaps to Japan, it's probably on its way to Singapore soon but I don't think we're 'it' anymore" (Gross Interview). In any case, in the Sprawl universe, nation-states have been superceded by corporations as governing agencies, Gibson imagining a future where the Japanese management approaches that were so lauded in the post-war period when Japan experienced incredible economic growth have been universalized: in this future, employees of large corporations are the "haves" and nearly everyone else is a "have-not."

Despite being named for the Sprawl, relatively little of the *Trilogy* is actually set there, and therefore the name may seem misleading: only *Count Zero* uses the Sprawl as a primary setting, *Neuromancer* being set primarily in Japan and in orbit, and *Mona Lisa Overdrive* being set in London, Tokyo, and the Rust Belt. The Sprawl, however, serves as an emblem for what is happening in Gibson's imagined twenty-first century as a result of technology: the entire world seems to be developing a sprawling monoculture that incorporates into itself elements from most of the industrialized world.

The universe within which *The Sprawl Trilogy* is set developed out of some of Gibson's early short stories, including "Johnny Mnemonic" (1981), "Burning Chrome" (1982), and "New Rose Hotel" (1984). Molly Millions, a primary character in both *Neuromancer* and *Mona Lisa Overdrive*, is introduced in "Johnny Mnemonic" (1981), and the "run" that Bobby Quine and Automatic Jack make in "Burning Chrome" provides a basis for the plot of Gibson's first novel. All three Sprawl stories are collected in *Burning Chrome* (1986), and the first and last were made into films.

In a 2007 interview with *Wired*, Gibson reports that he had no intention of developing *Neuromancer* into a trilogy: "I tacked that 'He never saw Molly again' on the end of *Neuromancer* to indicate no sequel was to be expected" (Ellis Interview). In *Count Zero*, however, his second novel, he returns to the Sprawl universe, following up on the changes that occurred in cyberspace with the merging of two artificial intelligences, Wintermute and Neuromancer: characters from the first novel are mentioned only incidentally. *Mona Lisa Overdrive* is a more traditional sequel to *Count Zero* in the sense that it continues the story of two of its primary characters, Bobby Newmark and Angelina Mitchell: it also continues the story of what has happens to cyberspace after it becomes sentient. Molly Millions, a character from *Neuromancer*, also appears in the final volume of the Trilogy, calling herself "Sally Shears."

*Neuromancer* is widely recognized as having established cyberpunk as a genre both critically and commercially, winning the Nebula, Hugo, and Philip K. Dick Awards and being listed by *Time* magazine as one of the 100 best English-language novels since 1923, Lev Grossman describing it as "Violent, visceral, and visionary." It eventually sold seven million copies. *Count Zero* and *Mona Lisa Overdrive*, both of which were nominated for the Nebula and Hugo awards, were popular successes as well, though they received significantly less critical attention.

*See also Count Zero*; Cyberspace; Hackers; Millions, Molly; *Mona Lisa Overdrive*; *Neuromancer*; Newmark, Bobby; Politics; Tessier-Ashpool Family

• *References and further reading*

Alkon, Paul. "Deus Ex Machina in William Gibson's Cyberpunk Trilogy." *Fiction 2000: Cyberpunk and the Future of Narrative*. Ed. George Slusser and Tom Shippey. Athens: University of Georgia Press, 1992. 75–87. Print.

Gibson, William. *Count Zero*. New York: Ace 1987. Print.

_____. *Mona Lisa Overdrive*. New York: Spectra, 1997. Print.

_____. *Neuromancer*. New York: Ace, 1994. Print.

Mead, David G. "Technological Transfiguration in William Gibson's Sprawl Novels: *Neuromancer, Count Zero*, and *Mona Lisa Overdrive*." *Extrapolation: A Journal of Science Fiction and Fantasy* 32.4 (1991): 350–60. Print.

Moylan, Tom. "Global Economy/Local Texts: Utopian/Dystopian Tension in William Gibson's *Cyberpunk Trilogy*." *Minnesota Review* 43–44 (1994–1995): 182–97. Print.

Schroeder, Randy. "Neu-Criticizing William Gibson." *Extrapolation: A Journal of Science Fiction and Fantasy* 35.4 (1994): 330–41. Print.

Siivonen, Timo. "Cyborgs and Generic Oxymorons: The Body and Technology in William Gibson's Cyberspace Trilogy." *Science Fiction Studies* 23 (1996): 227–44. Print.

# The Tessier-Ashpool Family

The Tessier-Ashpools, a secretive industrial clan based in high–Earth orbit, figure largely in two of the three volumes of *The Sprawl Trilogy*, arguably being the story of the demise of the family as an institution in the face of social and economic transformations brought on by new technologies. Indeed, one could argue that the *Trilogy* is about the Tessier-Ashpools since in their efforts to survive as both a family and a corporation, they create the artificial intelligences that, upon merging, bring into existence a new order of being, one based in cyberspace rather than the physical universe.

The Tessier-Ashpools cannot be fully distinguished from Tessier-Ashpool S.A., a private corporation that results from the marriage of Marie-France Tessier, heiress to a fortune derived from advances in applied biochemistry, and John Harness Ashpool, heir to an Australian engineering company. Ashpool promptly converts 90 percent of the corporation's holdings to orbital properties and space shuttle utilities and then builds Freeside, an artificial moon that serves first as an illicit data haven and then a major resort. Tessier, in turn, commissions the construction of two artificial intelligences, Wintermute and Neuromancer, in an effort to create a Tessier-Ashpool hive mind of sorts, one in which individual members of the clan will be largely spared "the more painful aspects of self-awareness" (*Neuromancer* 217). *Neuromancer* relates the efforts of the two AIs to merge into a single entity, which, attaining full sentience, incorporates itself into the matrix.

The couple's two children, Jean and Jane, are born of and raised by surrogates until their home in Biarritz is sold to finance a cryogenic lab where ten cloned embryos of each are stored until birthed. The children then live with their increasingly reclusive parents in Villa Straylight, the family estate located in the spindle of Freeside, sometimes frozen in the lab, sometimes awake: upon becoming adults, the children and their clones take turns, together with their parents, running the corporation, keeping it under their direct control. Not surprisingly, perhaps, the scheme to retain control fails as members of the family become increasingly unstable, possibly because of their unusual existences: Ashpool murders Tessier after learning about the AIs she commissioned and he is, in turn, destroyed by 3Jane, the third clone of Jane, who tampers with the controls of his cryogenic unit, making him insane. Increasingly insane herself, 3Jane, the only family member present in Straylight when Henry Case and Molly Millions arrive, is forced by Millions to reveal the code that allows the family's two AIs to merge.

*Count Zero* addresses what remains of the Tessier-Ashpool family only indirectly, indicating that 3Jane has become "increasingly eccentric" but saying little else about her: it does, however, relate more about the results of the merging of the two Tessier-Ashpool's artificial intelligences, the resulting super-being having integrated itself into the matrix itself, only to fragment into pieces once it becomes aware of another matrix based in Alpha Centauri. Now a recluse, 3Jane apparently occupies herself with the family's past, her AI arranging family artifacts into Cornell boxes—that is, Joseph-Cornell–based artwork that combines physical objects into a sort of pastiche.

3Jane appears in *Mona Lisa Overdrive*, or at least her consciousness does, 3Jane herself having died, but not before she arranged to have a construct of herself placed in an "aleph" or "pocket universe." Completely insane now, what remains of 3Jane attempts to have Angelina Mitchell abducted, mainly because she obsessively envies her ability to enter into cyberspace directly, an ability that would have given 3Jane some form of immortality, had she been able to acquire it while alive. 3Jane also hopes to capture Millions, so that she can avenge herself upon her for forcing her two reveal that code that allowed the two AIs to merge, leading to the final dissolution of her family. Ultimately, 3Jane fails in both endeavors and loses control of the aleph as well, becoming a last, "sad and tentative" remnant of a once-great family whose time, like the time of all great families, has passed. Although her consciousness still exists in the aleph, it will continue to do so for only for a year or less, the aleph's power supply being limited.

On one level, of course, the demise of the Tessier-Ashpool family and their corporation reflects changing social and economic conditions: family corporations can no longer compete with true multinationals, which are represented by a new form of *zaibatsu*, that is, large, many-headed organizations that are not subject to any particular jurisdiction. On another level, however, the demise of the Tessier-Ashpools represents the demise of family in general, families no longer being basic units of social organization. This point seems to be underscored by the fact that the only families that appear in *The Sprawl Trilogy* are highly dysfunctional, Angelina Mitchell's father having committed suicide, as did Kumiko's mother, and Bobby Newmark's mother being a simstim addict. Apparently, it is not just great families that are a thing of the past for Gibson but families in general.

*See also Count Zero*; Dislocation; *Mona Lisa Overdrive*; *Neuromancer*; *The Sprawl Trilogy*

• *References and further reading*

Gibson, William. *Count Zero*. New York: Ace 1987. Print.
_____. *Mona Lisa Overdrive*. New York: Spectra, 1997. Print.
_____. *Neuromancer*. New York: Ace, 1994. Print.

## "Thirteen Views of a Cardboard City"

Arguably a poem based on Wallace Stevens' "Thirteen Ways of Looking at a Blackbird" (1917) rather than a story or sketch, "Thirteen Views of a Cardboard City" (1996) makes its subject a squatter's community that existed in the Tokyo's Shinjuku Railway station until it was destroyed by fire in 1998. The work is divided into thirteen sections, each of which describes in detail a fixed image of the Cardboard City. The opening sections begin with references to camera angles and perspectives, as if it is the content of photographs that are being described. As the narrative proceeds, however, the speaker seems to enter into the photos, describing them from the inside rather than the outside. Although the tone is still detached, the speaker uses his own experiences for references at times, for example describing sleeping spaces in terms of the "Norfolk & Western sleeping cars" he used as a child when traveling by train with his mother. The speaker re-establishes some of his earlier distance in the sections that follow, but in the final section the distance collapses as he describes images he found within the image—photographs of one of the men living in the Cardboard City. Entering the image again, he looks behind a tape recorder and finds, "almost concealed," a Filofax. Suddenly the sadness of the dislocated people who have built this shelter becomes real to the speaker as he realizes that the "names" and "numbers" held therein represent a "a map back out of the underground" to their owner, a way to re-enter society.

"Thirteen Views of a Cardboard City" first appeared in *New Worlds*, an anthology edited by David Garnett that attempts to revive the spirit of an earlier British magazine by that name that featured experimental "New Wave" science fiction in the 1960s and 70s. In his review of the anthology for sfsite.com, one of the more influential science fiction websites, Steven Silver comments that Gibson's piece takes his "longtime theme of isolation in a modern world a step further." He adds: "It leaves the reader disjointed and disassociated, perhaps the way in which Garnett [the editor of the anthology in which Gibson's text appeared] felt the reader should depart from this anthology." It was republished in 2007 in James Kelly's *Rewired: The Post-Cyberpunk Anthology*.

Gibson uses the Cardboard City as a setting in *All Tomorrow's Parties* (1990), the final volume of *The Bridge Trilogy*. Like the Bridge, the Cardboard City is an interstice of sorts, a gap that can serve both as both a refuge and as a point of resistance. It is from this city that protagonist Colin Laney challenges billionaire Cody Harwood's efforts to shape unfolding events to his advantage.

*See also All Tomorrow's Parties*; Laney, Colin

• *References and further reading*

Gibson, William. *All Tomorrow's Parties*. New York: Berkley, 2003. Print.
Silver, Stephen. "New Worlds." *Stephen Silver's Reviews*, SFsite.com, n.d. Web.

## Toei, Rei

Rei Toei is a computer-generated pop star featured in the last two volumes of *The Bridge Trilogy*, who is of a different order than the mainframe-based artificial intelligences of most science fiction and as such, is one of Gibson's most original, interesting characters. Although projected from a platform, her essence is independent of the platform in the same way that the content of a DVD is independent of the machine playing it. There is an important difference between her and a DVD or any other recording, however; her essence is not fixed but rather "serial.... Entirely *process*" (*Idoru* 217). As one character succinctly puts it, "she is information" (190). Although still early in her development in *Idoru*, she rapidly acquires sentience, being "an emergent system, a self continually being iterated from experiential input," as Colin Laney indicates in *All Tomorrow's Parties* (197).

Much of the plot of *Idoru* centers on her and a human rockstar Rez's plan to "marry," so that they can develop together, Rei Toei hoping to transcend the digital by becoming more human and Rez hoping to transcend the human by becoming more digital. On one level, Gibson seems to be satirizing celebrity culture, suggesting that celebrity can become something independent of the person it is ostensibly based on, that it can become self-sustaining, a media entity, as it were. On another level, however, Gibson seems to be exploring — and to some extent satirizing — theories of hyperreality and the posthuman propounded by Jean Baudrillard, Donna Haraway, Gilles Deleuze and Felix Guattari, among others; indeed, Gibson even employs some of Deleuze and Guattari's terminology, having the Idoru's creator refer to her as the product of an array of "desiring machines" (191). *Idoru*'s ending is fairy-tale like, the couple using nanotechnology to rebuild the Kowloon Walled City as a marital palace of sorts on an artificial island made out of *gomi* in the Tokyo Bay. As such it resembles the sort of celebrity marriage that might be featured in a tabloid, like the Michael Jackson–Lisa Marie Presley marriage that occurred in the mid–90s when *Idoru* was being written or the Angelina Jolie–Brad Pitt marriage of today.

In *All Tomorrow's Parties* we learn that the union of the two was a failure, presumably because as Rez becomes posthuman, Toei becomes post-digital, their two paths intersecting only briefly and then diverging. Although Rez effectively disappears from the story, going on an extended tour in the former Soviet Union, Toei remains a critical character as she aligns with Colin Laney, Berry Rydell, Silencio, members of the Walled City, and others to prevent media baron Cody Harwood from shaping the future to his benefit. It is Toei's relationship with Colin Laney that is most significant, however — and most entertaining. A master of discerning patterns in information because of experimental drugs he had been given as a child, he becomes Henry Higgins to Toei's Eliza Doolittle, Gibson borrowing from the Pygmalion story: interacting with her almost daily, he teaches her not only about information flows but about what it is to be human and, in the process, falls "in love with her" (198). As in *Pygmalion*, the love he feels for Toei is transformative: "He loved her, and in loving her understood that his most basic sense of what the word might mean had changed, supplanting every previous concept" (198): in effect, his love for Toei, an object of desire who has become much more, humanizes him, as it were. She is transformed, too: no longer just a "desiring machine," she becomes a loving machine, a Mother Teresa figure of sorts, who becomes increasingly "interested in other people," the poor and suffering in particular (202). The latter becomes apparent when, in response to Rydell's assertion that many people would think him poor, she says, "But more would think you rich": "There are, literally, more humans alive at this moment who have measurably less than you do. You have this sleeping place [a small room], you have clothing, I see you have eaten" (185). As Toei discovers what it is to be human, it seems, she learns what it is to suffer, and in the end she intervenes at a critical moment to prevent Harwood to add to that suffering by empowering himself. The manner in which she intervenes is also significant: because of her capacity for empathy, she alone is able to communicate effectively with the autistic-seeming Silencio, inducing him to track Harwood as he tries to absent himself, thereby enabling others to prevent him from shaping the future.

The novel ends with Toei becoming a corporeal being through a largely unexplained process involving the use of nanotechnology: ultimately, Toei not only becomes real but is reproduced in great numbers, a living copy of her emerging from the "nanofax" machines that have been installed in Lucky Dragon convenience stores all over the world. Ironically, in becoming a corporeal being, Toei can no longer be everything to everyone — a perfect object of desire, something underscored by street kid Boomzilla's emergence from the machine: "Light over the hatch turns green, and the hatch slides up and out crawls, unfolds sort of, this butt-naked girl, black hair, Chinese, Japanese something, she's long and thin, not much titties on her the way Boomzilla likes but she's smiling" (326). The novel — and thus *The Bridge Trilogy*— ends with an unexplored question: what will the world be like with thousands of Rei Toei's in it? The reader only knows what Laney apprehends from his study of information flows— that the old world has come to an end and a new one is beginning.

See also *All Tomorrow's Parties*; Henry, Hollis; Hyperreality; *Idoru*; Laney, Colin

• *References and further reading*

Baudrillard, Jean. *Simulacra and Simulation*. Trans. Sheila Fraser. Ann Arbor: University of Michigan Press, 1995. Print.
Farnell, Ross. "Posthuman Topologies: William Gibson's 'Architexture' in *Virtual Light* and *Idoru*." *Science Fiction Studies* 26.3 (1998): 459–60. Print.
Gibson, William. *All Tomorrow's Parties*. New York: Berkley, 2003. Print.
_____. *Idoru*. New York: Berkley, 1997. Print.
Murphy, Graham. "Post/Humanity and the Interstitial: A Glorification of Possibility in Gibson's Bridge Sequence." *Science Fiction Studies* 30 (2003): 72–90. Print.

# Uncollected Stories

*Burning Chrome* (1986) remains Gibson's only collection of short stories, Gibson having focused on novels, screenwriting, and other projects since that time. Gibson reports that "[w]riting short fiction requires a different kind of muscle" (Van Belkom Interview). He adds: "After having spent years and years writing novels, I've tried to do short stories and I just don't know how to make it all fit in to a twenty-seven page manuscript anymore." He did, however, produce a number of stories since 1986, most of them very short. Some, like "Skinner's Room" developed into larger works like *Virtual Light*, while others, like "Academy Leader" afforded him an opportunity to experiment in way that would be difficult in a longer form like the novel. His principal uncollected stories include the following: "Hippie Hat Brain Parasite" (1983), "Darwin" (1990), "Skinner's Room" (1990), "Academy Leader" (1991), "Thirteen Views of a Cardboard City" (1996), and "Dougal Discarnate" (2010). Separate entries have been prepared for each of these stories. Other uncollected fiction includes "Tokyo Collage" (*SF Eye* 1988); "Cyber-Clause" (*Washington Post Book World* 1991); and "Where the Holograms Go" (*Wild Palms Reader* 1993). Gibson's friend and collaborator, Tom Maddox also makes reference to an early story entitled "The Nazi Lawn Dwarf Murders," though, if the story exists, it appears to be unpublished.

See also "Academy Leader"; "Darwin"; "Dougal Discarnate"; "Skinner's Room"; "Thirteen Views of a Cardboard City"

• *References and further reading*

Gibson, William. "Cyber-Claus." *The Washington Post Book World*, 1 Dec. 1991. Print.
_____. "Tokyo Collage." *Science Fiction Eye* 4 (August 1988). Print.
_____. "Tokyo Suite." *Penthouse* (Japan). Trans. Hisashi Kuroma. 1988. Print.
_____. "Where the Holograms Go." *Wild Palms Reader*. Ed. Roger Trilling. New York: St. Martins, 1993. 122–23. Print.

## *Virtual Light*

As Ross Farnell notes, *Virtual Light* (1993), the first volume of Gibson's *Bridge Trilogy*, received relatively little attention from either fans or critics when compared to his earlier works, in part because the science fiction aesthetic was changing and "cyberpunk was on the decline" (459). As readers of *Virtual Light* and the other two novels in the series will easily discern, Gibson's aesthetic changed as well: although the novel shares many of the features of Gibson's earlier work, including protagonists who are marginalized by an economic system that has little place for the independent-minded, it is markedly different in tone, employing both humor and satire in ways that make it postmodern in the sense that it seems to acknowledge its own artificiality. The novel also is postmodern in the way that it represents what Lance Olsen identifies as "techno hip" — an affinity for consumerist gadgets and attitudes that mark the beginning of the "posthuman" era (Olsen 1994).

Although the novel begins with a dark vision of Mexico City that is reminiscent of the Sprawl, descriptions of wasp-like gunships, "fecal snow, billowing in from the sewage flats," and a population that must use masks and respirators to protect itself from pollution and disease, quickly give way to a much lighter representation of Los Angeles, where rentacop Berry Rydell takes an armored Land Rover designed by Ralph Lauren through a specialty carwash (1). As the car-wash scene suggests, appearances are more important than realities in twenty-first century California, which has split into two states, Northern California and Southern California. Orange County has been renamed "Nissan County," and one of the novel's protagonists, Chevette Washington, appears to have been named after a car. Even though the novel addresses serious issues such as AIDS, the privatization of community resources, and the seeming disappearance of the American middle class, Gibson's frequent use of satire and humor prevent the novel from becoming bleak. If, as John Leonard suggests in *The Nation*, "the future according to Gibson is still one big Third World," it is a future we can laugh at since Gibson himself seems to approach it with humor (583).

The novel also differs from those that precede it in that it is set in the near future rather than a distant one, another element that makes the future the novel represents seem less threatening since radical changes like those Gibson describes could hardly occur in just twelve years. In *Virtual Light*, Gibson, who has long been critical of science fiction that presents itself as prophetic, writes about a pointedly impossible future rather than a possible one. As he indicates in a 2007 interview, he made "deliberate decision" to set *The Bridge Trilogy* in a world that "could never have happened" since he is more interested in addressing social issues than predicting the future (Lim Interview).

In addition to satirizing the early 1990s, *Virtual Light* satirizes cyberpunk and what it has become, Gibson himself noting that the novel was meant to "poke fun" at his "earlier work or at least a perception of it" (Shepherd Interview). As cyberpunk becomes established as a genre, he argues, it only becomes more "generic and less interesting," adding that "the chances of a consciously 'cyberpunk' fiction" becoming interesting to him, at least, are "now pretty slight" (Blair Interview). To a large extent Gibson's criticism of post-cyberpunk fiction parallels those who criticized postpunk music, particularly "New Wave," because it seemed to have lost its subversiveness, becoming just another style or "flavor." Gibson conveys such criticism through satire, using Washington, a bike messenger, to parody characters such as Y.T., the skateboard-riding courier in Neal Stephenson's *Snow Crash* (1992). The difference between *Virtual Light* and novels like *Snow Crash*, Gibson suggests, is that his own novel is "a fake that glories in being a fake" (Blair Interview). Ironically, Stephenson's novel itself is often satirical, seemingly parodying Gibson's earlier work.

As in much of his work, in *Virtual Light* Gibson draws together seemingly unrelated narratives. The first features Rydell, a young man from Knoxville whose courage, initiative, and moral sense make it impossible for him to keep a job as a police officer or even as a security guard. He relocates to Los Angeles, where he is to be featured on a reality show, *Cops in Trouble*, but is soon dropped by the program's producers, who leave him penniless. Desperate for work, he agrees to drive a private security agent to Northern California and soon becomes involved in trying to capture Washington, who, he has been told, has not only stolen valuable property — a pair of glasses that connect directly to the user's nervous system — but killed a man. Rather than capture her, however, he ends up rescuing her from his employers, who most likely would have killed her because the glasses contain valuable information about property development plans for San Francisco. With the help of the Republic of Desire, a virtual community that resists the corporatization of both cyberspace and the physical world, Rydell and Washington escape to Southern California, only to be arrested. The novel ends with Rydell again being hired again by *Cops in Trouble*, whose producers want to exploit the *"heroic* shit" he's gotten himself into by being an "honest" cop.

The second strand features Washington, a bike messenger who lives on the Bay Bridge, which has become a shanty town of sorts, with an old man named Skinner, who was involved in its initial takeover. Washington is a liminal figure, more post-punk than punk, since she resists integration into mainstream society but seems neither angry nor resentful about her situation. She steals the glasses not for profit but because the man who possessed them had harassed her at a party. In the adventures that follow, she is largely passive, being helped first by a fellow messenger, Sammy Sal and the Rydell. In this sense, she resembles Angelina Mitchell, a character in *The Sprawl Trilogy* who also largely depends on others not only to survive but to explain the significance of what is happening to her.

## THE BRIDGE, POSTMODERNITY, AND NEOFEUDALISM

Gibson represents the Bay Bridge, which is closed to traffic following an earthquake that made it structurally unsound, as an interstitial space, that is, a marginalized place that is largely unregulated and unsurveilled. In addition to providing shelter for those like Washington who live on the margins of society, the Bridge hosts an alternative community, one that has a "queer medieval energy" (69). As Skinner, one of the Bridge's original denizens, explains to Shinya Yamazaki, a Japanese graduate student, the taking of the Bridge was neither planned nor political: "people just *came*," making it their own (101, 103). In a sense, the Bridge becomes an anarchist community, having no set laws or government. Its occupants nonetheless share an identity and take collective action, particularly when threatened from outside, something that becomes evident when two detectives try to remove Washington from the Bridge and are assaulted by a crowd.

According to Tama Leaver, the Bridge is also interstitial on a metaphorical level, existing as an alternative to the "monoculture" (122) and on a paradigmatic level as a space where modernism has been supplanted by postmodernism; to quote the novel itself, modernity, which is being supplanted by the digital, has "long since" ended on the Bridge (105). As the reference cited earlier to the Bridge's "medieval energy" suggests, for Gibson the postmodern is related to the premodern in the sense that the middle class is being reabsorbed into the lower class, resulting in a neofeudalism. Although like Jean-Françoise Lyotard and Fredric Jameson, who recognize pastiche as part of the emerging aesthetic, for Gibson it represents a form of productivity available to the underclass rather than a symptom of ethical crisis or failure in historicity. As he puts it in "Burning Chrome" (1982), "The street finds its own uses for things."

Although as an interstitial space the Bridge serves as a site for resistance, it is a temporary one: as Leaver observes, interstitial spaces are ephemeral by their very nature since once they are discovered they are either appropriated by the dominant culture or destroyed by it (123–24). By the third volume of the *Trilogy*, the Bridge has become San Francisco's "number one postcard" (79). It is largely destroyed before it becomes fully "theme-parked," however, since the powerful Cody Harwood recognizes it as a threat that he may not be able to fully contain, and therefore sets fire to it with incendiaries (80). If interstitial spaces like the Bridge can be destroyed, the impulse behind them cannot be: other interstices such as the Republic of Desire or the Walled City are continually being discovered and/or created and resistance to the dominant culture continues, albeit sometimes in new forms. Significantly, though heavily damaged, the Bridge still stands at the end of the novel due to "unorganized cooperation" of the "bridge folk," who in saving themselves, saved a symbol of their resistance (335).

## Hyperart, Thomassons, and a Commitment to the Past

Gibson introduces the concept of the Hyperart into his narrative through Shinyu Yamazaki, a graduate student in sociology from Osaka University who takes a particular interest in what Japanese artist Genpei Akasegawa termed "Thomassons," that is, useless objects found in cityscapes that resemble art, either conceptually or aesthetically, such as a stairway leading nowhere or a window sealed with plywood. As Yamazaki explains, the term "Thomassons" are named for Gary Thomasson, a "very handsome, very powerful" American baseball player who could no longer hit once he came to the Yomiyuri Giants (72): like an overpaid player who sits on the bench, Thomassons are "useless and inexplicable monuments" according to Yamazaki, objects that hold an "existential meaning" even though that meaning is hard to articulate (72, 100). He has come to Northern California to study the Bridge, which he considers the most "magnificent" Thomasson in "all the world" (70).

Not surprisingly, perhaps, Yamazaki has a difficult time doing a sociological study of what he considers to be a work of art, gradually discovering that the meaning of the Bridge is not to be found by diagramming "sewage collection arrangements" or statistical analysis (100). Realizing he will never be able to explain to his thesis advisor what he is learning — that it is not just the Bridge but the whole city, maybe even America itself that is a Thomasson, Yamazaki gives up, announcing from the top of the Bridge that he no longer cares about his original project (252). What he discovers is that unlike Japanese, who embrace the destruction caused by an earthquake as "the most astonishing of opportunities," a chance to begin anew, Americans simply repair the old after their own earthquake, something that is symbolized by a brace applied to the top of the Transamerica Pyramid to hold its spire upright (252). This point is underscored by the intrigue surrounding the urban renewal plans contained in the Virtual Light glasses: developers are having difficulty enacting plans to build a new San Francisco because they know the city's residents will resist. As Harwood's agent, Loveless, observes, there are "millions ... who would *object* to the fact that this sort of plan even exists" (275). Like the Bridge, the quake-damaged city has become a Thomasson, a useless monument to the past.

Although by definition useless, Thomassons are far from worthless, something Yamazaki comes to appreciate as he goes native, as it were, forsaking his spacious flat in a Victorian building for a space in Skinner's room on the Bridge. There is something beautiful in the Bridge, something "amorphic" but "startlingly organic" (69). There is also a certain freedom that comes with rejecting the future, a freedom from control. Certainly the Republic of Desire recognizes this, preferring an "infrastructure with a lot of holes in it," like San Francisco's, to the seamlessness of post-quake Tokyo (339). As noted earlier, interstices can serve as points of resistance since they are relatively unregulated and unsurveilled.

## PARODY AND HUMOR

Gibson's humor emerges most consistently in his over-the-top satire of things such as reality television, televangelism, and the legal system. *Cops in Trouble*, the show that hires Rydell after he shoots a man in the line of duty, replaces him with a more "balls-out telegenic" female cop, and then rehires him when he proves himself to be a "crazy, outrageous motherfucker," seems to be a hybrid of shows like *Cops* and *Inside Edition*, both of which debuted in 1989 (36, 342). Here Gibson, who seems to anticipate the emergence of both reality television and celebrity-based programming, ridicules them before they were even fully established.

Gibson lampoons the legal system as well. Rydell loses his job with the Knoxville police department, for example, because the girlfriend of the crazed drug addict he shot — a woman who was being held hostage by him along with her children — sues both Rydell and the department for depriving her of her sole means of support (20). Once the Adult Survivors of Satanism, a group the man belonged to, becomes interested in suing as well, Rydell is compelled to leave the state. The case ends only when the girlfriend gets caught robbing a muffler shop (35). Gibson also parodies televangelism through Rydell's former partner at InternSecure, Sublett, who comes from a religious sect that believes that television is "the Lord's preferred means of communicating, the screen itself a kind of perpetually burning bush" (10). As Gibson indicates in a 1993 interview, he consciously "went after Christians because I find them a singular pain in the butt, an easy target, and always deserving" (Shepherd Interview). In addition, Gibson finds humor in little things like the fact that the amount one is expected to tip seems to be continually rising, reaching 30 percent in the novel (69), and the idea that it's easier to become a licensed security guard in Southern California than a hairdresser (10). He also mocks celebrities like Michael Jackson and refers to a pornographic virtual reality program featuring a Madonna impersonator named "McDonna."

*See also All Tomorrow's Parties*; *The Bridge Trilogy*; Counterculture; Hackers; *Idoru*

• *References and further reading*

Cavallaro, Dani. *Cyberpunk and Cyberculture: Science Fiction and the Work of William Gibson*. Athlone Press, 2000. Print.
Farnell, Ross. "Posthuman Topologies: William Gibson's 'Architexture' in *Virtual Light* and *Idoru*." *Science Fiction Studies* 26.3 (1998): 459–60. Print.
Gibson, William. *All Tomorrow's Parties*. New York: Berkley, 2003. Print.
_____. *Idoru*. New York: Berkley, 1997. Print.
_____. *Virtual Light*. New York: Spectra, 1994.
Grace, Dominick M. "From *Videodrome* to *Virtual Light*: David Cronenberg and William Gibson. *Extrapolation: A Journal of Science Fiction and Fantasy* 44.3 (2003): 344–57. Print.
Jameson, Fredric. *Postmodernism, or, the Logic of Late Capitalism*. Durham: Duke University Press, 1991. Print.
Jones, Gwyneth. *Deconstructing the Starships: Science Fiction and Reality*. Liverpool: Liverpool University Press, 1999. Print.
Leaver, Tama. "Interstitial Spaces and Multiple Histories in William Gibson's *Virtual Light*, *Idoru*, and *All Tomorrow's Parties*." *Limina: A Journal of Historical and Cultural Studies* 9 (2003). Web.

Murphy, Graham. "Post/Humanity and the Interstitial: A Glorification of Possibility in Gibson's Bridge
     Sequence." *Science Fiction Studies* 30 (2003): 72–90. Print.
Stephenson, Neal. *Snow Crash*. New York: Bantam Spectra, 2000. Print.

## "The Winter Market"

First published in *Vancouver Magazine* in 1985 and collected in *Burning Chrome*, "The Winter Market" is one of Gibson's most technically accomplished short stories in that he utilizes narrative complexity to express not only the narrator's own angst but that of society at large. The story, which is set in Vancouver in the early twenty-first century, is told from the perspective of a man named Casey who edits neuroelectronic recordings for the entertainment industry. He becomes emotionally involved with Lise, a dying artist he meets at a party who, with Casey's help, is able to transcend her corporeal existence and become a virtual being. The artist, a quadriplegic who can only move with the assistance of a motorized exoskeleton, acquires the resources and connections to do this by recording her alienation and despair for others to experience: the software becomes exceedingly popular because she is able to express what so many people in this dystopian future have come to feel—"that they aren't going anywhere," that there are "[n]o dreams, no hope" (134). Over the course of the story, Casey comes to realize that for all of his good health and professional success, he, too, is limited by forces beyond his control—he, too, lives as if in a cage.

Gibson gives the story narrative complexity by relating it through a narrator who changes as he processes not only his relationship with Lise but also the implications of her transition to a bodiless existence. Engaging in what amounts to a talking cure, Casey presents the story in short sections, moving back and forth from present to past from a perspective that is not quite stable. He also expresses himself metaphorically at times, employing vehicles that are themselves metaphorical—such as *gomi*, a Japanese word that is used to denote not only physical waste like that his friend, Rubin, uses as material for his kinetic sculptures, but for people and even the human condition. His use of *gomi* is particularly suggestive to those familiar with Vancouver, since the Market that the story's title refers to is located on an island formed in part out of the city's waste: refuse, it seems, is not necessarily degenerate. Perhaps the most remarkable element of the story, however, is the way Gibson uses sound imagery to convey Casey's growing realization that he is every bit as constrained by society as Lise is by her exoskeleton. He does this by using clicking sounds to connect the exoskeleton to Rubin's kinetic sculptures, sculptures that do exactly as they are programmed to do. In the story's closing lines, it is the timely clicking of one of Rubin's creations that brings Casey to understand how effectively caged he is himself, how for him, just as for Lise and for the youths warming themselves around open fires at the all-but-abandoned Market, there are no real hopes or dreams.

"The Winter Market" is a cyberpunk story in the sense that Lise is a liminal figure who uses technology in novel ways to resist the dictates of the dominant culture. Punk sensibility is also reflected in the way Gibson uses *gomi* as a metaphor for alienation since, as Paul Delaney notes, "Punks used a garbage-based semiotic system to define themselves as 'human waste,' making adornments from objects conventionally designated as worthless or a nuisance." Given the story's bleak ending, however, the story is arguably more "grunge" than "punk," grunge being a post-punk movement centered in the Seattle area that is marked more by angst than anger.

*See also Burning Chrome*

• *References and further reading*

Delaney, Paul. "'Hardly the Center of the World': Vancouver in William Gibson's 'The Winter Market.'" *Vancouver: Representing the Postmodern City*. Ed. Paul Delaney. Vancouver: Arsenal Pulp Press, 1994. 179–92. Print.

Gibson, William. "The Winter Market." *Burning Chrome*. New York: Ace, 1986. Print.

Hicks, Heather J. "'Whatever It Is That She's Since Become': Writing Bodies of Text and Bodies of Women in James Tiptree, Jr.'s 'The Girl Who Was Plugged In' and William Gibson's 'The Winter Market.'" *Contemporary Literature* 37.1 (1996): 62–93. Print.


## The X-Files

A longtime viewer of *The X-Files*, which was initially filmed in Vancouver where he lives, Gibson co-authored two episodes for the series with Tom Maddox: "Kill Switch" (1998) and "First Person Shooter" (2000). He also wrote the Introduction to *The Art of the X-Files* (2000). Gibson, who admired the show's "sublime weirdness and humor" (Silberman), became acquainted with Chris Carter, its creator, in 1995 after visiting the set with his daughter, Claire, and then encountering Carter frequently when flying to Los Angeles (Allemang Interview). Gibson eventually proposed writing a script with friend and fellow writer Tom Maddox, who worked at nearby Evergreen College. Gibson and Maddox developed the story for "Kill Switch" over the course of more than a year and then completed it in collaboration with Carter and *X-Files* writer Frank Spotnitz, who made sure the episode, which concerns a sentient computer that tries to kill its maker, was consistent with the rest of the series (Strachan). According to Gibson, one of his and Maddox's goals was "to try and get at what Bill Gates would have become if he'd had really bad luck. The creator of the supercomputer in the show is a kind of Gates alter ego, Gates as Job" (Allemang Interview). The story also includes stereotypical cyberpunk elements, including bikers, drug dealers, a shoot-out in a diner, and a female lead character, Esther Nairn, whose look was modeled on Daryl Hannah's in *Blade Runner* (Dupont Interview). With the help of Mulder and Scully, Nairn is able to throw the kill switch, a virus designed to compromise the artificial intelligence. The episode ends with Nairn somehow uploading herself into cyberspace, just as characters do works such as "The Winter Market" and *Mona Lisa Overdrive*. The episode, which ran against CBS's Sunday night broadcast of the 1998 Winter Olympics, was a success and was rebroadcast repeatedly in subsequent years. Gibson himself reported being "delighted with everything" except for Nairn's eye makeup (Allemang Interview).

"First Person Shooter," which ran two years later, takes its name from the imaginary virtual reality game it features, a game that becomes deadly when a female non-player character, Maitreya, from a different but related program somehow projects herself into "First Person Shooter," taking it over. Maitreya, it turns out, was created as a side project by a game designer, Phoebe, who wanted to include a female character in a version of the game she created for her own personal use. Predictably, perhaps, both Mulder and then Scully enter into the game themselves to fight the female warrior. Despite her heroic efforts, Scully is unable to defeat Maitreya; she and Mulder are saved, however, by Phoebe, who, watching the game from the control room, reveals the kill code, erasing the program. Although "First Person Shooter" is memorable for its critique of the testosterone-driven gaming industry, the story offers no plausible explanation as to how a digital, non-player character can shoot one real person and behead another and, as a result, the episode appears to be less about paranormal phenomena than it is about Mulder and Scully. Like many of the episodes from the series' later seasons, "First Person Shooter" is more interesting than it is provocative or haunting.

• *References and further reading*
Gibson, William. Introduction. *The Art of the "X-Files."* Chris Carter. New York: HarperPrism, 2000. Print.
Silberman, Steve. "William Gibson to Write *X-Files* Episode." Wired.com, *Wired*, 13 Jan. 1998. Web.
Strachan, Alex. "Gibson Writes This Sunday's *X-Files*." *Vancouver Sun*, 14 Feb. 1998. Web.

## Zero History

The final volume of *The Bigend Trilogy*, *Zero History* (2010) is set in the near present addressing what Gibson terms "the 2010 zeitgeist." He comments: "If *Pattern Recognition* was about the immediate psychic aftermath of 9/11, and *Spook Country* about the deep end of the Bush administration and the invasion of Iraq, I could say that *Zero History* is about the global financial crisis as some sort of nodal event" (blog 5/31/2010). Certainly it is the financial crisis that leads one of the novel's protagonists, Hollis Henry, to agree to work for Hubertus Bigend again as she did in *Spook Country*, she having lost "about half" her money in "the crash" (52). The crisis also drives much of the novel's plot as Bigend inadvertently comes into conflict with a dangerous arms dealer, Michael Preston Gracie, over "recession-proof" military clothing contracts. *Zero History* is more than just a realist novel about how difficult the times have become, however: there is little sense of gloom in the novel, and commerce proceeds apace everywhere from coffee shops to the music industry to high finance. Instead, Gibson's primary subject seems to be the idea that resistance to the new order has become all but impossible, making *Zero History* arguably his darkest, most dystopian novel. Even Garreth Wilson and his associate, "the old man," a pair who in *Spook Country* were able to offer some form of resistance to the powers-that-be, are reduced to "scrawling graffiti on the secret machineries of history" (154). Indeed, as Wilson avers, their "perverse, fiendishly complex exploits resembling Surrealist *gestes*" now seem pointless, the time for "tricks" being "over" (261).

For the most part, the novel alternates between two narrative strands, one focusing on Hollis Henry and the other on Milgrim, both of whom are in the employ of Bigend, owner of the Blue Ant agency. Henry's assignment is to identify the designer of the Gabriel Hounds line of clothing, a "secret" brand that has developed a significant cult following. To Bigend, she is a "wild card," someone who is of value to him because she is not entirely predictable, being motivated not only by money and status but other things as well, including an ethical sense that Bigend is completely incapable of understanding (24): she brings an element of chaos into the Blue Ant organization, one that is potentially productive because it can lead to unexpected outcomes. The fact that she is willing to work for Bigend, even though she dislikes and distrusts him, is, of course, significant: the world has become a place where the will of people like Bigend and corporations like Blue Ant cannot be resisted, even by those who would like to: even strong independent characters like Wilson and Heidi Hyde ultimately serve Bigend, or at least advance his interests, Wilson organizing an operation to free Bobby Chombo, a person critical to Bigend's plans, from Gracie, and Hyde recapturing Chombo and returning him to Bigend's control. Henry ultimately discovers that the designer of the Gabriel Hounds line is, in fact, Cayce Pollard, whom Gibson introduced in *Pattern Recognition*, the first volume of *The Bigend Trilogy*. Unlike Henry, Pollard has managed to escape Bigend's control, something that suggests just how much worse things have become in the course of the decade.

Milgrim, too, provides readers with a means of measuring just how much things have changed. As someone with "zero history," a phrase indicating that he has left no appreciable trace upon the world for some years, Milgrim begins the novel as a blank slate, someone who, having been reborn following his drug addiction, has to be remade, there being little indication that he has either the will or ability to remake himself. Although hardly monstrous, he resembles Victor Frankenstein's monster, an experiment of sorts, Bigend having paid for his drug rehabilitation and then giving him increasingly important responsibilities within Blue Ant just "to see what happens" (225). Unlike Frankenstein's monster, however, Milgrim remains loyal to Bigend despite being consistently dehumanized by him. Here Gibson's message seems to diverge sharply from Mary Shelley's, Shelley making the point one might expect in a Romantic novel about dehumanization leading to dissatisfaction and then rebellion: for Gibson, dehumanization only leads to greater control. As a minor character named Voytek Biroshak observes, we are now living in the world George Orwell imagined, "Orwell's boot in [our] face *forever*" (289).

The strands centering on Henry and Milgrim draw together when Bigend insists that Milgrim work with Henry as she pursues the identity of the Gabriel Hounds designer, Bigend intuiting that it will lead to interesting results. As it turns out, he is correct in this, Milgrim having attracted the attention of both Gracie and a U.S. government agent, Winnie Tung Whitaker, while on his previous assignment for Blue Ant. Whitaker, who is after Gracie, a former U.S. army officer, for various offensives he has committed as an arms dealer and military contractor, is able to use Milgrim to convey to Bigend the danger that Gracie represents. When Gracie kidnaps Chombo, someone essential to Bigend's most important project, Bigend is willing to exchange Milgrim for him, even though he knows Milgrim will be hurt if not killed by Gracie's agents, who blame Milgrim for an earlier injury. Milgrim's association with Henry leads her love interest Garreth Wilson to intercede, something that saves Milgrim from Gracie but returns Chombo to Bigend's power. As it turns out, Chombo's return is absolutely essential to Bigend since Chombo has figured out how to determine "order flow," that is, the aggregate of all market activity — "Stocks, bonds, gold, anything" (177). Through such knowledge, Bigend can effectively control markets, giving him the type of power desired by James Bond villains and the like. The novel thus ends with Bigend having gained almost unimaginable power, power he acquires by treating people as means to an end, playing them against each other and exploiting the relationships that develop between them.

*Zero History* differs from the novels that precede it in the *Trilogy* in terms of both structure and style. Whereas *Pattern Recognition* presents its story primarily through the consciousness of a single character and *Spook Country* employs three, including the enigmatic Tito, *Zero History* is much more linear, at least structurally, being distributed evenly between two strands, one centering on Henry and the other on Milgrim. The sum of the most recent novel is more than its parts, however, Bigend gradually emerging as a primary character even though his consciousness is never represented directly. Arguably this is because Bigend's consciousness cannot be represented directly, Bigend being essentially inhuman somehow. Certainly he is characterized in such a way, Henry observing at one point that he looks at her with "something she took to be an artful emulation of actual human concern" (217).

Stylistically, too, the novel is more complex than it first appears to be, Gibson varying the texture of the novel so as to manage the reader's focus. Descriptions of the Cabinet, for example, a hotel favored by Henry's friend and former band mate, Inchmale, are almost overwhelming in detail, disorienting the reader in the same way the Club's décor disorients Henry. The nature of the décor disorients her as well, the hallways leading to her room, for example, being "hung with small watercolors, landscapes unpeopled, each one featuring a distant folly. The very same folly, she'd noticed, regardless of the scene or region depicted.... Something too thoroughly liminal about them. Best not addressed" (4). Reference to the décor continue to appear throughout the novel, Henry still dreaming about it in the very last chapter, the folly depicted in the landscapes being identified in her dream, at least, as the Burj Khalifa, a $1.5 billion skyscraper built in Dubai during the recent global financial crisis. Milgrim, too, is obsessed by the décor of the Cabinet, including the watercolors, which he discovers were made in the early twentieth century by an American expatriate, Doran Lumley, and therefore cannot possibly depict the Burj Khalifa. Since, as a quick Google search will confirm, there is no Doran Lumley, the watercolors that so disturb Henry ultimately function both as a statement about the nature of reality and a joke Gibson plays on readers, who, he notes, Google virtually everything he writes.

## ROGUE MALE

Included in the detail about the décor of the Cabinet is a reference to Geoffrey Household's thriller, *Rogue Male* (1939), a novel that details the efforts of an aristocratic Englishman to hide himself from enemy agents in England after failing in a spontaneous attempt to assassinate a European dictator while on a hunting trip in Europe, the dictator clearly being modeled on Hitler. Henry, who finds the book in a birdcage in her room, begins reading it while in the hotel and brings it with her to Paris, describing its content to Milgrim. The fact that she takes an interest in a book about an individual who risks everything in an effort to stop megalomaniac raises questions not only about the individual's role in shaping history but about ethical responsibilities to others, questions Henry herself faces while in Bigend's employ. Henry could, of course, refuse to work for Bigend, and thus avoid being complicit with a man she considers "dangerous" or she could actively try to thwart him in his efforts to determine order flow, an effort Milgrim informs her of well before the novel's climax (337). Unlike the protagonist of Household's novel, however, she takes no action at all, there being no "badger holes" in which to hide afterwards as Household's protagonist does. Henry's world, it seems, is a world without interstices, a world with neither a counterculture nor spaces from which resistance can be enacted. Even Cayce Pollard, a woman who successfully left Bigend's employ and hid her subsequent activities from him, realizes that she cannot remain out of his view forever and, as mentioned above, Garreth and the old man come to realize that their subversive activities are, in fact, simply gestures, the systems of control having become nearly perfect.

## ZERO HISTORY, HEART OF DARKNESS, AND APOCALYPSE NOW

Although *Zero History* makes no direct reference to Joseph Conrad or his work as *Spook Country* does, retired U.S. Army Special Forces officer Michael Preston Gracie seems to be based on the Kurtz character that was introduced by Conrad in *Heart of Darkness* (1898) and further developed by Francis Ford Coppola in *Apocalypse Now*. Gracie, who resigned his commission after being deployed in the Philippines, Iraq, and Afghanistan, becomes a security consultant first for corporations based in Indonesia, Malaysia, Singapore, and the Philippines, and then for the governments of those countries, instructing them in tactics, counterinsurgency strategies, interrogation, and more (222). His success in areas for which he has little if any qualification reinforces his sense of "[o]mnipotence, omniscience" (223): like Kurtz in both Conrad's novella and Coppola's film, Gracie "believes he can do anything" (270). It is not just *hubris* that leads to Gracie's demise, however: he is also self-delusional, "bullshitting" not only others but himself (222). Believing his own "Rambo routine," he does something "stupid," bringing an assault rifle to a public space in London, beginning a sequence of events that leads to his capture (222).

Gibson's depiction of Gracie as a former operative gone rogue is not the only correspondence between *Zero History, Heart of Darkness*, and *Apocalypse Now*: Winnie Tung Whitaker, too, seems to be based at least loosely on characters from the other works, she being the agent assigned to bring Gracie in. As for Conrad's Charlie Marlow and Coppola's Captain Willard, there are real questions about both her authority and her actions — questions that parallel those about Gracie. In particular, as a U.S. agent Whitaker is not licensed to conduct an investigation in the United Kingdom, and the violent showdown between Gracie and Bigend that she orchestrates certainly puts others at risk. Arguably, she goes rogue herself in the same way Marlow and Willard do, bending rules if not breaking them so as to accomplish her ends.

## FASHION AND TECHNOLOGY

Like *Pattern Recognition, Zero History* focuses very much on fashion as a technology, exploring the ways in which it is not only shaped by human needs and desires but shapes them. Fashion, Gibson suggests, is anything but innocuous, it being a primary medium of expression, a means of conveying identities, connections, loyalties, and the like. As such it is virtually "recession proof," as evidenced by the commerce centering on it in the novel even though the world is in the throes of an economic crisis. Indeed, one could argue, fashion becomes increasingly important because of the crisis, being presented in the novel as the site of fierce competition because it is one of the few industries to remain lucrative.

Military fashion comes into particular focus in the novel as Bigend and Gracie vie for contracts with the U.S. military, which, in addition to being of value in themselves, will give the owners of the designs an advantage in street fashion as well since men's clothing is largely based on military designs. As Bigend indicates to Milgrim, the connection between military and street fashion has become even closer in recent years as the military increasingly uses fashion in their recruiting efforts: in short, they need clothing that will attract people to the military. Ironically, even as the military becomes more interested in street style, youth is becoming more interested in military style, as Bigend observes: "Equipment fetishism. The costume and semiotics of achingly elite police and military units. Intense desire to possess same, of course, and in turn to be associated with that world. With its competence, its cocksure exclusivity" (213). According to him, twenty-first century men need "just the right" pants in the same way "a mod ... needed the right depth of vent on a suitcoat" (213, 214).

Gibson explores other elements of the fashion industry through Henry, whom Bigend hires to identify the designer of a "secret" brand, the Gabriel Hounds. Bigend, it turns out, is less interested in the designs themselves than in the way the brand is being transmitted through "the provocative use of negative space" (23). Bigend, who has employed such strategies before, having learned about them through Cayce Pollard's investigation of "the footage" in *Pattern Recognition*, has come to believe that the designer has "read and understood" his "playbook" and is even "extending it" (24). Unbeknownst to him, the designer is Pollard herself, Pollard employing negative space by not just keeping her brand secret but by making secrecy the brand itself in a sense. Bigend succinctly characterizes such branding as the "reinvention of exclusivity," a strategy that seems to exploit people's desire to mark themselves as being special through their clothing (216). In this sense, at least, the people who obsessively pursue secret brands like Gabriel Hounds are very much like young men who have gone "gear-queer," to borrow one of Bigend's phrases (213).

See also Bigend, Hubertus; *The Bigend Trilogy*; Dystopia; The Faust Legend; Henry, Hollis; Milgrim; *Pattern Recognition*; *Spook Country*

• *References and further reading*
Conrad, Joseph. "Heart of Darkness." *"Youth" and Two Other Stories*. New York: Doubleday, Page, 1924. 45–162. Print.
Gibson, William. *Pattern Recognition*. New York: Berkley, 2005. Print.
_____. *Spook Country*. New York: Berkley, 2009. Print.
_____. *Zero History*. New York: Putnam, 2010. Print.
Household, Geoffrey. *Rogue Male*. New York: New York Review Books Classic, 2007. Print.

# Glossary

**The Aleph**    Created by 3Jane, the aleph is a self-contained virtual universe, a private cyberspace of sorts. The aleph plays a central role in *Mona Lisa Overdrive*, Bobby Newmark having stolen the aleph physically and then entered it virtually. Newmark and others are able to remain in it even after their physical bodies die.

*Amazing Stories*    The best known of Hugo Gernsback's pre-war pulp science fiction magazines. In "The Gernsback Continuum" Gibson suggests that popular science fiction of the 1920s and 30s like that featured in Gernsback's magazines fostered a form of futurism that was limiting and ultimately reactionary.

**Apophenia**    A term defined in *Pattern Recognition* as "the spontaneous perception of connections and meaningfulness in unrelated things" (117–18). A condition associated with paranoia, it is based on the human propensity to find patterns; people with apophenia not only identify patterns in things but impose them when they cannot be justified.

**Artificial Intelligence**    Non-living entities capable of thought. *The Sprawl Trilogy* features the type of artificial intelligence that has become a staple of science fiction: that is, machines designed to emulate human thinking. *Idoru* and *All Tomorrow's Parties* explore a less conventional type of artificial intelligence through Rei Toei, a dynamic program that unexpectedly emerges as an intelligence.

**Ashbaugh, Dennis**    (b. 1946) An American visual artist whose paintings and other works frequently feature biotechnology. He collaborated with Gibson on *Agrippa (A Book of the Dead)*, Gibson providing the text and Ashbaugh the artwork.

**ASP (Apparent Sensory Perception)**    A virtual reality system featured in Gibson's firsts published short story, "Fragments of a Hologram Rose," that allows users to experience the recorded experiences of others. ASP is very similar to the "simstim" (simulation stimulati) that figures large in *Neuromancer* and other novels and stories set in Gibson's Sprawl universe.

**Avatar**    A virtual representation of an identity or identities like those used in *Second Life*. In *The Bridge Trilogy*, particularly *Idoru*, people present themselves in virtual domains through avatars, modulating shape, size, color, and sound according to their desires.

**Baron Samedi**    Lord of the Graveyards, a *loa* in the Vodou tradition. In *Count Zero*, a cyberspace entity that manifests itself as Baron Samedi slays Josef Virek, or at least his avatar, an action that corresponds with Virek's physical death.

*Bildungsroman*    A literary term from the German that denotes a coming-of-age novel that focuses on the growth and development of the protagonist. A number of Gibson's earlier novels, including Count Zero, Mona Lisa Overdrive, and Idoru can be considered *bildungsroman*.

**Billy Idol**    (b. William Broad, 1955) An English post-punk rock singer with a signature sneer who became a superstar in part because of the visually striking music videos that played frequently on MTV in early 1980s. In 1993 he attempted to relaunch his career with the release of *Cyberpunk*, a poorly received album that was based in part on the work of Gibson and other cyberpunk writers. Gibson, who had not collaborated with Idol in any way, was openly critical of the album and satirizes Idol in *Pattern Recognition* through Billy Prion, a former rockstar with a botox-induced sneer who uses his celebrity to promote a Japanese soft drink.

131

**Biochips**   Advanced computer chips that make possible incredibly powerful artificial intelligences possible. In *Count Zero* the biochips that have been grafted into Angelina Mitchell's brain make it possible for her to enter directly into cyberspace, and in *Mona Lisa Overdrive* biochips enable cyberspace to reconstitute itself as a single, sentient entity.

**Blat**   A Russian term used to denote the exploitation of connections, bribes, or other illicit means to gain advantage. The term is used in *Pattern Recognition* when describing the underworld economy that existed in Russia following the dissolution of the Soviet Union.

**Blue Ant**   An advertising and media agency that serves as a corporate extension of Hubertus Bigend, its founder and owner. The agency is unusual in the way that it utilizes unpredictable, unreliable agents to remain dynamic. The Blue Ant agency figures largely in all three volumes of *The Bigend Trilogy*, ultimately affording Bigend almost unimaginable power.

**Bohemian**   A term used in *Zero History* to describe artists who exist largely outside the strictures of traditional society. Although the term surfaces only in Gibson's most recent novel, it might be applied to even the earliest of his protagonists, including *Neuromancer*'s Henry Case, who is depicted as an "artiste" who chooses to live on the margins of society.

**Bono**   (b. Paul Hewson, 1960) Lead singer of the Irish rock band U2. Gibson and Bono became acquainted in the early 1990s, and Bono later served as a model for Rez, the Irish/Chinese lead singer of the band Lo/Rez, who figures prominently in *Idoru* and incidentally in *All Tomorrow's Parties*. Bono appears in *No Maps for These Territories* (2000), a full-length documentary on Gibson.

**The Bridge**   A term for the San Francisco–Oakland Bay Bridge. In *The Bridge Trilogy*, the Bridge has been closed to traffic because of damage caused by an earth and taken over by squatters, creating an interstice of sorts that is at once connected to but detached from mainstream society. At the end of *All Tomorrow's Parties*, Bridge Cody Harwood's agents attempt to destroy the Bridge with explosives but fail, the Bridge's denizens working together to save it.

**Burroughs, William S.**   (1914–1997) An American novelist originally associated with the Beat movement. Burroughs is best known for *Naked Lunch* and *The Nova Trilogy*. Gibson lists him as a primary influence both upon his worldview and literary technique, the latter being reflected most obviously in Gibson's use of the cut-up method Burroughs pioneered. He is mentioned by name in *Pattern Recognition*, where Wingrove Pollard is described as resembling "the younger William S. Burroughs."

**Captain Swing**   A name sometimes signed to written warnings sent to landholders in the 1830s in England by farmworkers who were being displaced by machinery. In *The Difference Engine* Captain Swing appears as a mysterious Luddite leader who attempts to overthrow the government during a riot. In an interview the co-author of the book, Bruce Sterling, indicates that the Captain Swing is based primarily on British novelist Wilkie Collins.

**Cardboard City**   A homeless community comprised of cardboard boxes that was located in the Shinjuku Railway station in Tokyo until it was destroyed by fire in 1998. Colin Laney resides in the Cardboard City in *All Tomorrow's Parties*, eventually dying there.

**Cheap Truth**   A newsletter or 'zine edited by Bruce Sterling under the name "Vincent Omniaveritas" in the mid–1980s. *Cheap Truth* openly promoted the work of a group of relatively unknown science fiction writers then known as the Movement and later termed "cyberpunk." The 'zine identified Gibson as a particularly important writer well before he had published his first novel, *Neuromancer*, writing of "Burning Chrome," for example, "THIS is the shape for science fiction in the 1980's: fast-moving, sharply extrapolated, technologically literate, and as brilliant and coherent as a laser" (*Cheap Truth #2*).

**Chiba City**   A port city of nearly a million people that is approximately 40 kilometers east of Tokyo. Chiba city is a primary setting for *Neuromancer*, largely because it contains an outlaw area known as "the Zone" where illegal activities are tolerated and new technologies tested.

**Coolhunter**   A term for people who survey the popular culture for things that are likely to become fashionable so that they can be commercially exploited. In *Pattern Recognition* Cayce Pollard is of exceptional value as a coolhunter because her "fashion allegies" enable her to detect things that are overly derivative and therefore unlikely to become fads.

**Console Cowboy**   A term roughly synonymous with "hacker" that is used frequently in *Neuromancer* and the other novels and short stories set in the Sprawl. Because navigating cyberspace is a fully-immersive activity, operators being linked directly to cyberspace through the use of simstim technology, experiences there are real and can even result in death.

**Cops in Trouble**   A reality television show that generally features police officers who are having legal trouble for things they have done in the line of duty. The show, which figures prominently in *Virtual Light*, seems to be based on the Fox Television program, *Cops*, which began airing in 1998. *Idoru*, the next volume in *The Bridge Trilogy*, also addresses reality programming through the program *Slitscan*, a hybrid of reality TV and tabloid TV.

**Cornell Boxes**   A form of artwork developed by Joseph Cornell (1903–1972) that involves assembling found objects. The objects are arranged so that they can be viewed through the glass cover of the box. In *Count Zero*, an orbiting artificial intelligence that once belonged to the Tessier-Ashpool family constructs Cornell boxes out of family ephemera.

**Count Zero Interrupt**   A programming term current in the 1980s that refers to a means of preventing endless loops by launching a new function when "count zero" is reached. Bobby Newmark adopts "Count Zero" as his hacker name in *Count Zero*.

**Cyberpunk**   A subgenre of science fiction loosely associated with the punk movement of the 1970s and 1980s. Frequently described as combining "hi-tech and low life," cyberpunk narratives are often frequently feature marginalized, dispossessed characters and gritty urban settings. *Neuromancer* and the other narratives set in the Sprawl are cited as examples of cyberpunk fiction.

**Cyberspace**   A term coined by Gibson to describe standardized spatial representations of data in *The Sprawl Trilogy*. The term itself entered the language with the publication of "Burning Chrome" and Gibson is often given credit for helping to shape what cyberspace has become. In Gibson's Sprawl narratives, however, navigating cyberspace involves the use of "simstim," a technology that involves connecting the nervous system to cyberspace so the latter can be experienced directly.

**Danbala**   The Snake, a *loa* of the Vodou tradition. *In Count Zero* Danbala is an entity that assists Jackie in bypassing security systems when she enters cyberspace.

**Dancer**   A dangerous, highly addictive stimulant that tends to make users paranoid and violent. Dancer, which is likened to crack cocaine but represented as being even more powerful, figures prominently in *All Tomorrow's Parties*, many of Chevette Washington's acquaintances being users.

**Deck**   An abbreviation of the word "cyberdeck," computer terminals equipped with simstim technology that provide access to cyberspace in *Neuromancer* and the other narratives set in the Sprawl. The term "Ono-Sendai" is sometimes substituted for "deck" in Gibson's work, Ono-Sendai being the manufacturer of the best commercially-available cyberdecks.

**Desiring Machine**   A term seemingly drawn from Gilles Deleuze and Felix Guattari to describe Rei Toei's function as both a producer and a product of desire in *Idoru*. In *Anti-Oedipus*, Deleuze and Guattari argue that desire can be understood as a machine that, networked with other machines, produces reality itself.

**Duck in the Face**   A phrase uttered by Cayce Pollard when she begins to panic. The phrase, which refers to a pilot whose windshield was shattered by a duck at two hundred and fifty knots but managed to land safely, appears throughout *Pattern Recognition*.

**Eversion**   A term for the act of turning outward or inside-out. Gibson uses the word "eversion" frequently to describe the way in which new technologies become such a part of our everyday lives that we are no longer conscious of them. *Spook Country* makes the eversion of cyberspace a primary theme, and in "Google's Earth," an 2010 article for the *New York Times*, he suggests that the real and the virtual are not just contiguous but congruent.

**Ezili Freda**   A *loa* in the Vodou tradition that corresponds to the Virgin Mary. In *Count Zero* and *Mona Lisa Overdrive*, Angelina Mitchell, a young woman who has had biochips implanted into her brain so that she can enter into cyberspace directly is identified with Ezili Freda.

**5-SB**   An experimental drug that gives users a special sensitivity to patterns. Users tend to develop obsessions with celebrities, often stalking them. In *Idoru* and *All Tomorrow's Parties*, Cody Harwood develops the ability to detect nodal points in history because of the 5-SB he was given as an orphan.

**Flatline**   Brain death induced by Black ICE (database defenses) through neural feedback. In *Neuromancer*, Dixie Flatline earned his nickname for having "flatlined" numerous times when a console cowboy. Henry Case flatlines as well when he is drawn entirely into cyberspace by Wintermute and Neuromancer.

**The Footage**   Short film clips made by Nora Volkova and posted on the Net by her sister, Stella. In *Pattern Recognition*, this Footage develops a cult following, eventually drawing the attention of Hubertus Bigend, who hires Cayce Pollard to identify its maker.

**Fuller Domes**   Also known as geodesic domes, Fuller domes are spheres or partial spheres that are designed so as to distribute stress through lattice-work employing a triangular structure. The climax of "Johnny Mnemonic" takes place in the canopy formed by Fuller domes over part of the Sprawl.

**Golden Age of Science Fiction**   The period between the 1930s and 1950s in which science fiction gained recognition as an important genre. It was preceded by the Pulp Era of the 1920s and early 1930s and followed by the New Wave period of the 1960s and 1970s. In "The Gernsback Continuum" Gibson suggests that Golden Age science fiction promoted a form of futurism that was militaristic if not fascistic.

**Gomi**   A Japanese word for junk or garbage. In *Mona Lisa Overdrive*, it is a valuable resource, 35 percent of Tokyo being built upon it. It also figures prominently in "The Winter Market," both as physical waste and as a metaphor for disposable people.

**Gothicks**   A street gang based in the Sprawl that fetisizes the Gothic. In *Count Zero* the Gothicks, along with their rivals, the Kasuals, to besiege Angelina Mitchell at Jammer's, a nightclub atop a Manhattan building.

**Hammett, Dashiell**   (1894–1961) An American writer of detective fiction best known for novels such as *The Thin Man* and *The Maltese Falcon* and the character Sam Spade. He is frequently credited for developing and popularizing the "hard-boiled" style characteristic of *noir* fiction. Gibson counts him as a primary influence upon his early work.

**Heterotopia**   A term used by Michel Foucault to describe spaces that exist outside of dominating ideologies. In *The Bridge Trilogy*, the Bridge functions as a heterotopia, as does the Walled City.

**ICE**   Acronym for Intrusion Countermeasures Electronics, defensive systems designed to protect databases from intruders. The term is used frequently in *The Sprawl Trilogy* and other works set in the Sprawl. Black ICE is a system that physically injures or kills intruders through neural feedback.

**Idoru**   Japanese word for "idol." Rei Toei, a computer-generated pop star, is known as the "*idoru*" in *Idoru* and *All Tomorrow's Parties*. Over the course of the two novels, she develops into an artificial intelligence, capable of independent thought and growth.

**Interstices**   Unregulated, unsurveilled spaces. In *The Bridge Trilogy* they are associated with gaps in the infrastructure, both physical and virtual, or places that are officially unrecognized such as the Cardboard City in *All Tomorrow's Parties*.

**Iteration**   A part of a procedure in which a series of actions are repeated in order to achieve a result. *The Difference Engine* is divided into "Iterations" rather than "Chapters" as the novel's representing consciousness, which in the end of the novel is identified as an artificial intelligence that is just becoming self-aware, iterates all of the information available to it in order to arrive at self-understanding.

**Jack Draculas**   A foreigner-hating London street gang seemingly named for Jack the Ripper and Dracula. In *Mona Lisa Overdrive*, they steal Kumiko Yanaka's purse and damage Colin, the miniaturized AI that serves as her guide and protector.

**Killfile**   A term for a subprogram that automatically discards files matching a certain description. In *Idoru*, the Walled City employs the killfile concept to create an interstice within the net.

**Kinetic Sculpture**   Three-dimensional artworks whose effects rely upon their motion. Kinetic sculptures play an important role in *Mona Lisa Overdrive* when Slick Henry's sculptures are used by the protagonists to defend themselves from paramilitaries trying to reclaim the aleph. Kinetic sculptures also appear in "The Winter Market."

**Kinotrope**   Pixelated displays that are mechanical rather than electronic. In *The Difference Engine* steam-engines are used to power displays connected to computers, which run punch cards. Kinotropists in the novel correspond to computer programmers today.

**Kowloon Walled City**   A small, densely-populated settlement near Hong Kong Island that was largely unregulated and ungoverned until it was demolished by the Hong Kong government in 1994. Kowloon Walled city both provided a name and served as a model for a hacker community featured in both *Idoru* and *All Tomorrow's Parties*.

**Kunstlerroman**   A type of *bildungsroman*, or coming-of-age novel, that focuses on the development of an artist. *Count Zero* is arguably a *kunstlerroman*, telling the story of Bobby Newmark's development into a fully-fledged hacker or "console cowboy." *Idoru* and *All Tomorrow's Parties* could also be regarded as such, the two novels telling the story of pop idol Rei Toei's development.

**Legba**   A *loa* in the Vodou tradition that serves as a gatekeeper, mediating access to other *loa*. In

*Count Zero* and *Mona Lisa Overdrive*, the cyberspace being that manifests itself as Legba serves as an intermediary between humans and the other cyberspace entities.

**Lo Teks**  A street gang based in the Nighttown section of the Sprawl that rejects many forms of high technology, fetishizing low-technology. The Lo Teks appear in "Johnny Mnemonic," the storie's climax taking place on their killing floor in the canopy of Fuller Domes above part of the Sprawl.

*Loa*  The pantheon of Vodou spirits that function as intermediaries between God and people. In *Count Zero* and *Mona Lisa Overdrive* the entities that appear in cyberspace following the union of Neuromancer and Wintermute present themselves to humans as Vodou spirits in order to make themselves comprehensible to them.

**Locative Art**  Localized, public works of art that utilize both GPS technology and holograms. In *Spook Country* they are only available to people with headsets designed to make the art visible.

**Lo/Rez**  A rock band comprised of Lo, a Chinese guitarist, and Rez, a Chinese-Irish singer. The band seems to be modeled at least in part on U2, Gibson having become acquainted with Bono and The Edge in the early 1980s. Rez, a larger-than-life superstar, figures prominently in *Idoru*, much of the plot being driven by concern about his engagement to Rei Toei, a computer-generated pop idol with no corporeal existence.

**Lucky Dragon**  An international chain of convenience stores similar to 7-11 or Circle-K. The stores, which are mentioned only incidentally in *Idoru*, play an important role in *All Tomorrow's Parties*, each franchise being equipped with nanofax machines—that is, fax machines that can transmit solid object — new technology that has the potential to bring about radical social and economic change.

**Luddites**  Those who resist new technologies. In the late eighteenth and early-nineteenth century Luddites became notorious for destroying the machinery that was displacing them as workers. The term is used frequently in *The Difference Engine*, a counterfactual novel in which computers are put into production in the nineteenth century, changing the course of history. Gibson himself was sometimes thought of as a Luddite, particularly early in his career. Gibson, however, maintains that he is ambivalent towards technology, recognizing that it can be implemented in both positive and negative ways.

**MacGuffin**  An object of desire within a narrative that becomes the focus of attention, driving the plot. Gibson make use of the device to varying degrees in many of his novels, examples being the Cornell boxes in *Count Zero*, The Virtual Light glasses in *Virtual Light*, and the Footage in *Pattern Recognition*.

**Maddox, Tom**  A science fiction writer and professor of literature, language, and communication at Evergreen State College in Washington. He has written one novel, *Halo* (1991), and a number of short stories, one of which was collected in *Mirrorshades*, the definitive cyberpunk anthology of fiction. Maddox also co-authored two episodes of *The X-Files* with Gibson, "Kill Switch'" and "First-Person Shooter."

**Matrix**  A conventionalized representation of all human knowledge. Although the term sometimes seems to be used as a synonym for cyberspace, the matrix is contained within cyberspace. Both terms are introduced in "Burning Chrome" and developed in *The Sprawl Trilogy*.

**Meat**  A term console cowboys use disdainfully for their own bodies, which they view as an encumbrance. Henry Case uses the term when talking about the needs of his physical self in *Neuromancer*.

**Meat Puppet**  A term used in *Neuromancer* for high-tech prostitutes whose minds are disconnected from their bodies while they are engaged with clients.

**Mongolian Death Worm**  A large, bright red deadly worm that is said to be native to the Gobi Desert. In *Spook Country* the worms symbolize what Hollis Henry most fears.

**Nanofax**  A device that combines fax technology and nanotechnology, making it possible to transmit exact copies of physical objects. In *All Tomorrow's Parties* Rei Toei uses the nanofax machines that were installed in Lucky Dragon convenience stores to create numerous physical copies of herself.

**Nanotechnology**  Techniques and approaches for manipulating matter on a molecular level. In *The Bridge Trilogy* nanotechnology is used to rebuild Tokyo after a major earthquake, and in *All Tomorrow's Parties*, nanotechnology is combined with fax technology so that physical objects can be transmitted.

**Neuromancer**  One of two complementary artificial intelligences created by Jean-Marie Tessier to help manage Tessier-Ashpool S.A. The plot of *Neuromancer* centers around Wintermute's efforts to unify with Neuromancer in order to become fully sentient, a unification Neuromancer resists.

**New Wave Science Fiction**  An experimental movement within science fiction associated the counterculture; it is often contrasted to "hard" science fiction, its focus often being more on the effects of technology upon individuals and society rather than technology itself.

**Nighttown** A large interstice within the Sprawl comprised of strip malls that have been taken over by squatters. The climax of "Johnny Mnemonic" takes place in the Fuller Domes above Nighttown.

**Ninsei Street** A street in the part of Chiba City's known as "the Zone" that contains bars and other places associated with nightlife. In *Neuromancer* the term "Ninsei" is frequently used to designate the area in which Henry Case ran street hustles before agreeing to work for Wintermute.

**Nissan Orange County** Orange County, California, which has been renamed "Nissan Orange County," after the Japanese automobile manufacturer in *Virtual Light*. Gibson uses to term to satirize not only how pervasive corporate sponsorship has become but to parody the centrality of the automobile to Southern Californians.

**NoCal** Northern California, California having been split into two states in *The Bridge Trilogy*.

**Nodal Points** A term used in *Idoru* for prominent points in data where structure can be discerned. In *All Tomorrow's Parties* Colin Laney and Cody Harwood are able to detect nodal points in history, enabling them not only to perceive potential futures but shape them.

**Node** A start-up, London-based magazine modeled on *Wired*. The magazine, which is featured in *Spook Country*, is never published, having been founded by Hubertus Bigend primarily so that he could assign a journalist to story that would help him locate Bobby Chombo, an expert in GPS technology who produces works of locative art. The fictional magazine inspired a website by same name that provides notes and commentary on *Spook Country* and Gibson's other works.

**Omni Magazine** An American science-oriented magazine that began publishing in 1978. Because the magazine appealed to a broader audience than publications dedicated solely to science fiction, *Omni* was able to pay writers much more than most other venues. Under fiction editor Ellen Datlow, the magazine became a showcase for cyberpunk fiction, publishing works many of the works that were later to be collected in *Mirrorshades*, the definitive collection of cyberpunk fiction edited by Bruce Sterling. Two of Gibson's early stories, "Johnny Mnemonic" and "Burning Chrome," first appeared in *Omni*, helping Gibson to establish himself professionally.

**Ono-Sendai** A maker of premier computer hardware; the name of the company is frequently used to denote the computers they manufacture.

**Order Flow** The aggregate of all stock market orders, a type of information that theoretically exists but cannot be known. Hubertus Bigend acquires a means for determining it at the end of *Zero History*.

**Otaku** A Japanese term used for those who are invested in things such as *manga*, computers, *anime*, and video games to the point of being asocial. It is frequently, though not always, used in a derogatory way. The term is used in *Idoru* to refer to Masahiko, a member of the Walled City, a hacker collective.

**Ougou Feray** A Spirit of War, a *loa* in the Vodou tradition. In *Count Zero* a cyberspace entity that specializes in "icebreaking"—that is, penetrating the defensives systems of databases—manifests itself as Ougou Feray.

**Panther Moderns** An anarchist sect of technofetishists that destabilize the social order through the use of chaos and the manipulation of the media. In *Neuromancer* they assist Molly Millions and Henry Case in their raid on Sense/Net by simulating a terrorist attack.

**Pattern Recognition** The human propensity to locate and identify if not create patterns, a process that involves converting information into knowledge. *Pattern Recognition* addresses this propensity through Cayce Pollard, who, as a "coolhunter" tries to identify patterns before they are generally recognized.

**Postmodernism** An artistic approach marked by a skepticism towards not only Truth but the very idea of representation. Postmodern literary works typically eschew verisimilitude, instead highlighting their own artificiality highlight their own artificiality through the creation of flat characters with obviously invented names, implausible plots, and violations of physical laws, among other things. Following Frederick Jameson, who in 1991 identified Gibson's works as culturally significant postmodern productions, critics have increasingly come to regard Gibson as postmodern even though Gibson identifies himself as a realist if not a naturalist.

**Pynchon, Thomas** (b. 1937) An American writer best known for novels such as *The Crying of Lot 49* and *Gravity's Rainbow*. Generally considered a postmodern writer, Gibson frequently cites him as an influence both on his thinking and writing. *Pattern Recognition*, in particular, is frequently identified as Pynchonesque because of the similarities between Cayce Pollard and Pynchon's Oedipa Maas.

**Rastafarianism** A monotheistic religion with Christian elements that developed in Jamaica in the 1930s. In popular culture Rastafarianism is often associated with marijuana use, reggae music, dreadlocks, and African nationalism. In *Neuromancer*, a novel that arguably perpetuates negative stereotypes about Rastafarians, a small number of space workers choose to remain in orbit, founding a Rastafarian colony.

**Razorgirl** A term for female street samurai who have retractable razors surgically implanted in their fingertips and their nervous systems augmented so that they react extraordinarily quickly. Molly Millions, introduced as a razorgirl in "Johnny Mnemonic," is a successful independent contractor in *Neuromancer*, someone who is valued as more than just "muscle."

**Reed, Lou** (b. 1942) An American recording artist and composer who was a part of The Velvet Underground in the late 1960s. Considered by many to be a progenitor of American punk, Gibson cites him as a major influence on his writing and thinking.

**Rize** A Japanese pharmaceutical closely related to benzodiazepines that is not legally available in the United States. In *Spook Country*, Brown provides Milgrim, a benzo addict, with Rize in order to control him.

**ROM Personality Construct** A physical recording of a mind that can be accessed through computers. Constructs utilize knowledge but cannot think and thus are not artificial intelligences. Dixie Flatline is an important character in *Neuromancer* even though he is a construct, as is the Finn in *Mona Lisa Overdrive*.

**Secret Brands** A marketing strategy that exploits people's desires for exclusivity. In effect, the lack of overt branding is what marks such brand as special, people who are "in the know" being the only ones who can identify and acquire them. Secret Branding is essential to the success of Cayce Pollard's line of clothing, known as "The Gabriel Hounds."

**Sense/Net** A multinational media corporation that produces simstim recordings. In *Neuromancer* Henry Case and Molly Millions steal an illegal ROM personality construct of Dixie Flatline, and in *Count Zero* and *Mona Lisa Overdrive*, Sense/Net figures largely as Angelina Mitchell's overly controlling employer.

**Shapely, J.D.** An HIV-positive man whose blood provided a basis for a cure for AIDS. Discovered by AIDS researchers while in jail for solicitation, he is released as a research volunteer and eventually becomes rich. In *Virtual Light* and *Idoru*, Shapely, who has since been mar-

tyred, is regarded as "the AIDS saint," at least in San Francisco.

**Shirley, John** (b. 1953) An American science fiction writer best known for *City Come A-Walkin'* (1980), a novel for which Gibson wrote an introduction. Shirley co-wrote "The Belonging Kind" with Gibson (1981).

*Shuriken* A small, star-shaped traditional Japanese weapon that can be either thrown or used in hand-to-hand combat. In English they are often known as "Ninja stars." Shuriken are an important motif in *Neuromancer*, Henry Case being fascinated by them, possibly because they are "meat" weapons that he knows he can never master.

**Simstim** An immersive form of virtual reality that directly stimulates the brain, simulating the experiences of others. In the novels and stories set in the Sprawl, simstim is a primary form of entertainment. Simstim technology is also used in navigating cyberspace, users connecting their nervous systems directly into cyberspace with their cyberdecks. Simstim figures largely in *Neuromancer*, *Count Zero*, and *Mona Lisa Overdrive*.

**Simulacrum** A likeness or inexact copy of something, sometimes executed in a different medium. In his influential essay "The Precession of Simulacra," Jean Baudrillard suggests that simulacra have now been substituted for the real, resulting in the "hyperreal." Although Gibson is certainly aware of Baudrillardian thought on simulacra and the hyperreal, he does not necessarily adhere to it, suggesting in *Pattern Recognition*, for example, that while the world is replete with simulacra, the real is still available.

**Skywalker Park** San Francisco's Golden Gate Park, which has been renamed after for Luke Skywalker. In addition to satirizing corporate sponsorship in general, the references to Skywalker Park in *Virtual Light* seem to target Star Wars creator George Lucas, whose 4,700-acre Skywalker Ranch in Marin County has provoked both controversy and ridicule from some.

*Slitscan* The name of a reality television program that has become so influential that it not only reflects reality but creates it, inventing and then destroying stars for the sake of ratings. In *Idoru* it is described as a descendent of both "reality programming and the network tabloids of the late twentieth century."

**Smith, Patti** (b. 1946) An American singer and artist best-known for *Horses*, a 1975 album associated with the American punk movement. In interviews, Gibson frequently cites her as a favorite performer and influence upon his work.

**SoCal**   A term used for Southern California, California having been split into two states in *The Bridge Trilogy*. Much of *Virtual Light* is set in SoCal, Gibson using it to satirize not only the entertainment industry but the Southern California lifestyle.

**Spook**   A slang term for both ghosts and spies that is used frequently in *The Bigend Trilogy*, particularly *Spook Country*, where both senses of the term are operative, Cold War era spies now being ghosts of a past time.

**The Sprawl**   A continuous urban area stretching from Boston to Atlanta, also known as the Boston-Atlanta Metropolitan Axis (BAMA). The Sprawl serves as a setting for much of Gibson's early fiction, including "Johnny Mnemonic" and *Neuromancer*, the term "Sprawl" itself frequently used to identify the fictive universe in which the narratives are set.

**Stanwick, Michael**   (b. 1950) An American science fiction writer best known for *Stations of the Tide* (1991), which received the Nebula Award for best novel. Two of his stories have received Hugo Awards, "The Very Pulse of the Machine" in 1999 and "Scherzo with Tyrannosaur" in 2000. Stanwick co-authored "Dogfight" (1985) with Gibson.

**Steampunk**   A subgenre of science fiction that combines steam-age technology with other, more contemporary technologies. *The Difference Engine*, which Gibson co-authored with Bruce Sterling, is a prime example of steampunk, being set in alternative nineteenth century in which the steam-powered computers designed by Charles Babbage are put into use by the British and French governments.

**Steganography**   Defined in *Pattern Recognition* as the art of "concealing information by spreading it throughout other information," steganography provides Stella Volkova with a means of discreetly tracking the dissemination of her sister's footage. The digital footage is, in effect, watermarked in a way that even the most sophisticated viewers cannot detect, and therefore that watermarking does not call attention to itself.

**Sterling, Bruce**   (b. 1954) A science fiction writer known not only for novels such as *Schismatrix* (1985) and *Islands in the Net* (1988) but as a promoter of the cyberpunk movement in his influential newsletter, *Cheap Truth*. Sterling co-authored "Red Star, Winter Orbit" (1983) and *The Difference Engine* (1990) with Gibson, the latter of which was nominated for a Nebula Award in 1991.

**The Street**   A term for the socioeconomic space

that exists outside of regulated commerce. Though dangerous, the street affords certain opportunities and freedoms that are unavailable elsewhere. The term is used frequently in *Neuromancer* and the other novels and short stories set in the Sprawl. Gibson's most famous quote, "The street finds its own uses for things," comes from the short story, "Burning Chrome."

**Sunflower Corporation**   A construction firm in *Virtual Light* that plans to redevelop San Francisco following a major earthquake by using nanotechnology to "grow" buildings. The plans are hidden in a pair of "Virtual Light" glasses that serve as a MacGuffin in the novel.

***Sybil, or The Two Nations***   An 1845 novel by future Prime Minister of Great Britain, Benjamin Disraeli; *The Difference Engine* draws many characters from Disraeli's novel, including Sybil Gerard, Charles Egremont, and Dandy Mick.

**Systema**   A martial art created by the Soviets and employed by some of their special forces. In *Spook Country* Tito, a former Cuban agent of Chinese descent combines systema, freerunning, and elements of Santería, a Caribbean religion into a highly idiosyncratic system for conducting clandestine activities in New York City.

***Thomasson***   A term used by Japanese artist Genpei Akasegawa to indicate useless, inexplicable objects that nonetheless have a certain artistic appeal. The term is derived from the name of an American Major League baseball player, Gary Thomasson, who received a $1.2 million contract with the Yomiuri Giants only to play so poorly that he was benched for the final week of the season to prevent him from setting the Japanese strikeout record. In *Virtual Light* Shinyu Yamazaki uses the term to describe the San Francisco–Oakland Bay Bridge, which has been closed to traffic since being damaged in an earthquake. Towards the end of the novel he begins to wonder whether the United States itself has become a Thomasson.

**Turing Police**   In *Neuromancer* the Turing Police are an international agency charged with preventing artificial intelligences from exceeding their built-in limitations. The agency is named for Alan Turing, a British computer scientist who in 1950 devised what is now called the Turing Test, a means for determining whether a computer is intelligent.

**U2**   An Irish rock band that has been artistically and popularly acclaimed since the early 1980s. The band employed imagery drawn from The Sprawl Trilogy and related story for its Zoo TV tour in the early 1990s. Gibson and some of the band members soon became friends, Bono and the Edge appearing in *No Maps for These Territories*, a documentary featuring Gibson.

**Vasopressin**   A pharmaceutical drug that in "Burning Chrome" is used recreationally in order to enhance memories. Automatic Jack describes it as being "the ultimate in masochistic pharmacology" when used in combination with alcohol since "the juice makes you maudlin and the Vasopressin makes you remember."

**Velvet Underground**   An influential American rock band that formed in 1965. Fronted by Lou Reed and managed briefly by Andy Warhol, the band strongly influenced alternative music and the American punk scene. Gibson frequently mentions the band and Lou Reed as influences in interview and alludes to their music in his work, naming *All Tomorrow's Parties* after a Velvet Underground song, among other things.

**Villa Straylight**   The estate of the Tessier-Ashpool family, Villa Straylight is located within Freeside, an artificial moon in high orbit that serves as a resort. The climax of *Neuromancer* takes place in the Villa as Henry Case and Molly Millions force 3Jane to reveal the password necessary for them to complete their mission. Parts of *Count Zero* also take place in the Villa, which by this time has been separated from Freeside and occupied by squatters.

**Virus-Program**   A computer program designed to penetrate databases and by neutralizing their defenses, which are known as ICE (Intrusion Countermeasures Electronics). Virus Programs feature prominently in "Burning Chrome" and *Neuromancer*.

**Volapuk**   A computer-age artificial language created by Russian speakers using keyboards that employ the Roman alphabet. In *Spook Country*, Milgrim's facility with the language makes him invaluable to Brown, a quasi-government agent engaged in domestic espionage.

**Wintermute**   An artificial intelligence that, in *Neuromancer*, seeks unification with another artificial intelligence, Neuromancer, in order to become fully sentient. Wintermute has initiative and is capable of making decisions but lacks a cohesive personality; Neuromancer provides personality. *Count Zero* and *Mona Lisa Over-*

*drive* address the consequences of the unification.

**Wired**   An American technology-oriented magazine that began publication in 1993. *Wired* commissioned Gibson to write an article on Singapore, "Disneyland with the Death Penalty," which appeared in its fourth issue. Gibson wrote a number of other articles for the magazine, and in 1991 *Wired* sent him to Tokyo to write about post–Bubble Japan. In *Spook Country* Hollis Henry accepts employment with as-yet-unpublished *Node* magazine, which presents itself as a European version of *Wired*.

**Wiz**   A powerful, addictive drug that serves as both a stimulant and a hallucinogen. It appears frequently in *The Sprawl Trilogy* and in "The Winter Market," Lise uses a similar drug called "wizz."

**Yakuza**   A Japan-based organized crime syndicate that in *The Sprawl Trilogy* has become fully multinational, having absorbed the Triads, the Mafia, and the Union Corse. The Yakuza is especially prominent in *Mona Lisa Overdrive* since one its narrative strands centers on Kumiko Yanaka, the daughter of a Yakuza leader.

**Zaibatsu**   Multinational corporations modeled on the powerful, monopolistic Japanese companies of the pre–War period that essentially governed themselves and their employees. In *The Sprawl Trilogy* and the stories set in that imaginative world, *zaibatsu* have emerged as an essential part of the social order, replacing governments in many ways.

**Zero History**   A term used to indicate that a person has left virtually no trace of herself or himself in the infosphere, having no credit history, no tax history, or public records of any kind. In *Zero History*, the term is applied to Milgrim who, because of his drug addiction, virtually disappeared from any records.

**Zion Cluster**   A makeshift space station in high earth orbit founded by workers who refused to return to Earth. A Rastafarian colony, Zion cluster figures largely in *Neuromancer*, providing Henry Case and Molly Millions with a base operations for their raid on Villa Straylight.

# Appendix A: Timeline of Technological Developments

The timeline identifies technological developments that occurred during Gibson's lifetime. Entries refer either to the year of invention, appearance, or popularization. Gibson's publications are marked in bold.

*March 17, 1948: William Gibson III born in Conway, South Carolina*
1948: Norbert Wiener coins the term "cybernetics"
1949: Soviet Union detonates atomic bomb
1950: First commercially produced computer
1951: Univac 1
1952: Hydrogen bomb
1953: Transistor radio
1954: Oral contraceptives; color television
1955: Microwave oven
1955: Remote control television
1956: Hard disk computer drives
1956: Videocassette recorders; car phones
1957: Fortran programming language
1957: Sputnik
1958: Computer modems
1958: Integrated circuits; communications satellites
1959: Microchips
1960: Commercial modems; lasers
1961: Astronauts achieve orbit
1961: Industrial robots
1962: Computer games (*Spacewar*)
1962: Breast implants
1962: Telstar 1; Light-emitting diodes (LEDs)
1963: Graphic interfaces; laser holography
1963: ASCII (standardizing information exchanges between different types of computers)
1964: Mass-produced computers (IBM 650)
1964: American Airlines employs an online transaction processing system; Musical synthesizers
1965: Compact disks

1966: Handheld calculators
1967: Mouses; Random Access Memory (RAM); LSD becomes widely available
1968: Computers with integrated circuits
1969: Moon landing; UNIX
1970: Floppy disks; Automated tellers; ARPANET links computers at distant locations
1971: Personal computers; Microprocessors; VCRs; email; Creeper computer virus discovered on ARPANET
1972: advanced hand-held calculators; Home video games (*Pong*)
1973: Ethernet
1974: Liposuction; Computer workstations (Alto); The term "Internet" coined; barcode scanners
1975: Laser printers; popular personal computers; HBO becomes national cable network; Betamax videotapes
1976: Apple I; Viking probes land on Mars; Concorde supersonic airliner
1977: **"Fragments of a Hologram Rose"**; Magnetic Resonance Imaging; Commodore PET; Apple II; Atari 2600 home video game system; VHS format videotapes
1978: VisiCalc spreadsheet; *In vitro* fertilization; Navstar Global Positioning System (GPS); electronic spam sent; *Space Invaders*
1979: Sony Walkmans; USENET
1980: CNN; *Pac-Man*; cordless phones; *Missile Command*
1981: **"Johnny Mnemonic," "The Gernsback**

Continuum," "Hinterlands; MS-DOS; Portable computers; IBM personal computers

1982: **"Burning Chrome"**; Parallel processing; Human growth hormone; Commodore 64 computer; *Time* Magazine names PC the "Machine of the Year"

1983: Home computers employ Graphic User Interface (GUI); PC clones; Microsoft Word; cell phones become commercially available

1984: *Neuromancer, "New Rose Hotel"*; CD-ROMs; Macintosh computers

1985: "The Winter Market"; Windows software; Whole Earth 'Lectronic Link (WELL)

1986: *Count Zero, Burning Chrome* (story collection); PC viruses, appears; LISTSERV

1987: Floppy Disks become standard; Prozac

1988: Digital cellular phones

1989: *Mona Lisa Overdrive*; Dial-up Internet; High-Definition television; *SimCity* released by Maxis

1990: **"Darwin"**; World Wide Web (WWW); Hubble Space Telescope

1991: *The Difference Engine*, "Academy Leader"; Linux; Sid Meier's *Civilization* PC-game; Wi-Fi

1992: **Agrippa (A Book of the Dead)**; Nicotene patch; WWW made public; Microsoft Works; Windows 3.1; text messaging

1993: *Virtual Light*; Pentium processor

1994: Yahoo founded; *Doom* released; Mosaic web browser; Tunnel beneath English Channel completed.; Java programming language

1995: *Johnny Mnemonic* (film); DVDs; JavaScript; New York Stock exchange begins paperless trading

1996: *Idoru*; Chess computer Deep Blue defeats Garry Kasparov; Ebay; Dolly the Sheep is first mammal to be cloned.; *Tomb Raider*

1997: **"Thirteen Views of a Cardboard City"**; Instant messaging; Mars Pathfinder lands; Toyota Prius hybrid vehicle

1998: **"Kill Switch"** (episode of *The X-Files*); MP3 players; Google founded; iMac; Viagra

1999: *All Tomorrow's Parties*; Melissa e-mail virus infects more than one million computers; Napster; Wi-Fi commercially available

2000: **"First-Person Shooter"** (episode of *The X-Files*); With International Space Station becoming operational, people have continuous presence in space; Y2K fears prove largely unfounded; Microsoft Windows 2000; camera phones

2001: Court order shuts down Napster; Fifty nations sign Cybercrime treaty; Microsoft settles anti-trust suit with Department of Justice; iPod; Wikipedia; Space tourism

2002: Mars Odyssey probe discovers water deposits on Mars.

2003: *Pattern Recognition*; Human Genome; iTunes; MySpace; *Second Life*

2004: Gmail; Privately funded spaceships

2005: Youtube; Sunnyvale, California offers universal wi-fi; Google maps; Xbox 360

2006: Facebook becomes widely available; Wii gaming system

2007: *Spook Country*; iPhone; Amazon's Kindle e-reader; Google Docs

2008: Hydrogen-fuel cell powered vehicle; Twitter

2009: Mobile data traffic exceeds voice traffic

2010: **Zero History**; **"Dougal Discarnate"**; CERN's Large Hadron Collider becomes fully operational; iPad

# Appendix B:
# Writing and Research Topics

## General Questions

1. Gibson has commented that he was a bystander of history, having been present at events such as Woodstock and anti–Vietnam War protests in Washington, D.C., but never "being a player or a mover and shaker in any way" (Deubin Interview). Is this sense of never being a player reflected in his fiction? Do his characters play important roles in historical events or are they just bystanders? Do Gibson's representations of the roles individuals play in the shaping of history change during the course of his career?

2. Discuss the ways in which Gibson represents families in his texts. Is family important to his characters? What role does family play in his novels? What happens to the family as an institution in his various works? In addressing these questions, consider the Tessier-Ashpool family of *The Sprawl Trilogy*, Chevette Washington Berry Rydell of *The Bridge Trilogy*, and Cayce Pollard and Hollis Henry of *The Bigend Trilogy*.

3. In an interview with Ulrich Gutmair, Gibson states, "The biggest influence on my writing has been the accidental fact that I discovered the Beats and Science Fiction more or less in the same season when I was about 14 years old." In what ways can Gibson's early work be understood as Beat science fiction? Does his early work have a Beat sensibility? Can one dis-

cern the influence of writers like Jack Kerouac, Allen Ginsberg, and Gregory Corso in his work?

4. Fredric Jameson identifies Gibson's work as postmodern, and many other critics and commentators regard Gibson's work as Pynchonesque. What types of representational strategies does Gibson employ? In what senses might they be considered postmodern? In what senses might they be considered Pynchonesque?

5. Define "punk" and then explain the ways in which Gibson's early work qualifies as such. Do the novels and stories set in the Sprawl exude a punk sensibility? What about his later work? Could *The Sprawl Trilogy* be considered either "punk" or "cyberpunk"? What about *The Bigend Trilogy*?

6. As a teenager in the late 1960s, Gibson was very much a part of the drug culture. Discuss the ways in which he represents recreational drug use in works such as *Neuromancer*, *All Tomorrow's Parties*, and *Spook Country*. Does Gibson celebrate drugs in any way? Is he critical of their use? You might consider his representation of drug use in "The Gernsback Continuum," and "Dougal Discarnate" as well.

7. In a speech he gave to the 2010 Book Expo America, Gibson asserts that the world we are living in now can only be "unpacked with the toolkit of science fiction." Is the "21st Century richer, stranger, more multiplex, than any

imaginary 21st Century could every have been," as Gibson suggests? Are we living in a world that is "akin to science fiction"? More importantly, perhaps, can contemporary fiction be understood as science fiction?

8. Discuss the role interstices play in Gibson's work, beginning with the novels and stories set in the Sprawl. Why is the intersitial so important to Gibson? Why does he find its absence "unbearable" (Doctorow Interview)? Does the interstitial still exist at the end of *Zero History*?

9. Although Gibson has lived in Canada for more than forty years, he still identifies himself as American. In what ways does Gibson's work have an American sensibility? In what ways might it be considered Canadian? Be sure to consider — and possibly compare — his earliest works and his later ones.

10. In "My Own Private Tokyo" Gibson writes, "The Japanese love 'futuristic' things precisely because they've been living in the future for such a very long time now." Discuss what Gibson means by this and then consider the way he represents Japan and the Japanese in his various works. Is the Japan of *Pattern Recognition* as "futurologically sexy" as the Japan of *The Sprawl Trilogy*? What role do Japan and the Japanese play in his later work?

## Topics and Questions for *the* Burning Chrome Collection

11. Gibson completed the screenplay for *Johnny Mnemonic* (1995) more than a decade after the originally story was published. How are the two works different and what is the significance of those differences? In what way are they similar? Does Gibson address the same sort of social issues both works? Is each a product of its time?

12. At the beginning of "Johnny Mnemonic," Johnny hides an old-fashioned shotgun in an Adidas bag when he goes to confront Ralfi, knowing the latter will be employing high-tech weaponry. He explains, "if they think you're crude, go technical; if they think you're techni-

cal, go crude." Although the strategy does not work for him in this particular instance, Molly Millions employs it with great effect, defeating a hi-tech Ninja by drawing him into a low-tech environment. Discuss this concept in the context of real-world events. Is using low-tech against hi-tech a viable resistance strategy? Why or why not? Can you think of real-world examples where low tech has been employed successfully against hi tech?

13. In "Johnny Mnemonic" and *Neuromancer*, Molly Millions is called a "razorgirl." What does this term mean? What do each of the component words suggest? Do "razorboys" or their equivalent ever appear Gibson's texts? In what ways are Molly's sex and gender significant?

14. Gibson's early work is often compared to that of Raymond Chandler, the writer of detective novels such as *The Big Sleep* and *Farewell, My Lovely*. Gibson, however, distances himself from Chander, noting that he gets a "creepy, puritanical feeling from his books." What might Gibson find so objectionable about Chandler's work? How do Gibson's works compare to his in terms of both content and style?

15. "The Gernsback Continuum" is named for Hugo Gernsback, a publisher of pulp science fiction in the 1930s and the man for whom the Hugo Award is named. Examine some of the covers of Gernsback's most famous science fiction publication, *Amazing Stories*, and see if you can identify what it is about Gernsback's futurism that Gibson found so troubling. Why might Gibson associate it with fascism in his story?

16. "The Gernsback Continuum" ends with an exchange between the narrator, who is presumably white, and "a thin black man with bad teeth and an obvious wig." Review the exchange between the two and discuss its significance in racial terms. Be sure to consider the blonde couple that so "frightened" the narrator earlier in the story and other racial and cultural references that occur in the story.

17. Compare Gibson's short story, "New Rose Hotel," to Abel Ferrera's 1998 adaptation of it for film. What was changed? What was added? Did Ferrera succeed in maintaining the cyber-

punk feel of the original story? Why do you think Gibson insisted he "had absolutely nothing to do with the making of it" after the film failed both popularly and critically? Could Gibson reasonably argue that his work has been significantly altered?

18. Analyze "Hinterlands" in the context of the Cold War. How might the story be read as commentary on the U.S.-U.S.S.R rivalry? Does the story now seem dated? Is the future Gibson represents in it still imaginable?

19. Lance Olsen describes the "burning" of Chrome, that is, the raid Bobby Quine and Automatic Jack make upon Chrome's database, as a "metaphorical rape." What does he mean by this? How does the misogyny Quine and Jack express towards Chrome relate to their attitudes towards Rikki Wildside? Be sure to consider the ending of the story, in which Jack provides Wildside with the money necessary to begin a career in simstim. Does his action reflect a change in his attitude towards women in general and Wildside in particular?

20. Much of "New Rose Hotel" is set in a coffin-like capsule that serves as a hotel room near the Narita International Airport. Discuss the significance of this peculiar setting in relation to other elements of the story. That the capsules are compared to coffins is significant, of course: what else might the capsules signify?

21. "The Winter Market" features a software artist named Lise who is able to express what so many people in the story seem to feel — "that they aren't going anywhere," that there are "[n]o dreams, no hope" (134). How might this story reflect what was happening in the United States and elsewhere in the mid–1980s when the story was written? How might the story be read as social commentary?

22. In "The Winter Market," Lise is a quadriplegic woman who can only move with the help of a motorized exoskeleton. Discuss the ways in which Gibson represents disability in the story. How do Lise's physical challenges affect her psychologically? How do they affect Casey and the others that know her?

23. The short story collection *Burning Chrome* features three stories that Gibson wrote in collaboration with others: "The Belonging Kind" (1981) with John Shirley, "Red Star, Winter Orbit" (1983) with Bruce Sterling, and "Dogfight" (1985) with Michael Stanwick. Analyze two of these stories in relation to one another, seeing if you can discern Gibson's contributions to them. Do they seem like Gibson stories? In what ways do the resemble stories Gibson wrote on his own?

24. *Burning Chrome* is comprised of ten short stories. Discuss the significance of the order in which the stories are presented. Why does the collection begin with "Johnny Mnemonic" and end with "Burning Chrome"? What is the significance of other choices Gibson makes in terms of the stories' arrangement?

## *The Sprawl Trilogy*

### *Neuromancer*

25. At the end of *Neuromancer* we learn that Henry Dorsett Case returns to the Sprawl, finding "work" and a "a girl who called herself Michael." What is the significance of such an ending? Why do you think Gibson has him reintegrate himself into society so pointedly? Why does Gibson provide a "happily ever after" ending of sorts for Case? Why not for Millions? Contrast how the story ends for him and how it ends for Molly, who continues her life on the street?

26. Although Gibson introduces the term "cyberspace" in "Burning Chrome," it is in *Neuromancer* that it becomes a subject in itself. Go through the text of the latter carefully and determine just represents cyberspace. How does it compare to what we think of as cyberspace today? To what extent was Gibson's vision of cyberspace realized? What are the most important differences?

27. Part of *Neuromancer* is set in Zion cluster, an orbiting Rastafarian colony. Discuss the ways in which Gibson represents Rastafarian beliefs and values in the novel. Does he employ stereotypes, challenge them, or both? Is his representation of Rastafarians offensive?

Discuss the significance of Gibson including such a colony in the novel.

28. In *Neuromancer*, one of the agents responsible for limiting the powers of artificial intelligences suggests that in assisting *Neuromancer*, Case has, in effect, made a pact with the devil. Is the agent correct? Does Case betray his species, and if so, what are the consequences?

29. In an interview with Tatiani Rapatzikou, Gibson identifies the *shuriken*, or throwing star, that appears several times in *Neuromancer* as the novel's "key image." Why might that be? Discuss the passages in which the *shuriken* appears, particularly the last one, in which Millions places it atop her farewell note for Case. What might it symbolize?

### Count Zero

30. Istvan Csicsery-Ronay, Jr., asserts that *Count Zero* "lacks *Neuromancer*'s intensity and drive" (63). Does this seem to be correct? How would you characterize *Count Zero*? In what ways is the narrative different from *Neuromancer* and in what ways is it the same? Consider things such as narrative points of view, characterization, plot, and description.

31. In an interview he gave together with Tom Maddox, Gibson suggests that the Cornell boxes that feature so prominently in *Count Zero* are essential to understanding the story. Research Joseph Cornell and his "boxes." Why do they figure so prominently in Gibson's novel and what is their significance? Is there a connection between the things Cornell tried to express through his artwork and what the Tessier-Ashpool AI is trying to convey through its construction of its own boxes?

32. In *Count Zero*, Angelina Mitchell is essentially a passive character, passing from her father's control to Turner's, and then to that of Sense/Net. Are things any different for her in *Mona Lisa Overdrive*? Certainly she shows some initiative early in the story in trying to escape Sense/Net's control. To what extent does she succeed in acquiring agency? How does she compare in this regard to other female characters such as Mona Lisa, Kumiko Yanaka, and Molly Millions?

### Mona Lisa Overdrive

33. Much of *Mona Lisa Overdrive* is set in the Factory, an abandoned manufacturing plant that has been taken over by squatters who together form an artists' community of sorts. Discuss the significance of the Factory as an interstice, that is, as a marginal space that is relatively unsurveilled and unregulated. Compare it to the other interstices featured in *The Sprawl Trilogy* such as Zion in *Neuromancer* and the fourteen story market in *Count Zero*. What are their social and ideological functions? Are they simply refuges or are they represented as potential sites of resistance? You may also want to compare them to interstices such as the Bridge, the Republic of Desire, and the Walled City in *The Bridge Trilogy*.

34. In the fifteen years or so that pass between the action of *Neuromancer* and the action of *Mona Lisa Overdrive*, Molly Millions, who is known as "Sally Shears" in the latter novel, has changed in many ways. How is she different and what are the significance of these differences? At the end of the novel she says, "Wanna be by my fucking self for a change" before heading out across "the Solitude," a part of the Midwest that has become a wasteland. What do her words and actions signify? Why does Gibson end her story that way?

35. In *Count Zero* and *Mona Lisa Overdrive*, the intelligences that inhabit cyberspace present themselves to humans in the form of *loa* draw from Vodou tradition. How is this phenomenon explained in the text? Are the *loa* particularly suited for such a role? How might Gibson's use of *loa* in such a manner be offensive to some people?

## The Bridge Trilogy

### Virtual Light

36. In the opening chapter of *Virtual Light*, we learn that the courier who has been entrusted with the plans for the redevelopment of San Francisco has become obsessed with a representation of a woman that a virtual-reality device provides for him. Discuss Gibson's depiction of the courier's sexual obsession and its consequences. Can the difficulties he has

with Chevette Washington be attributed at least in part to the fact that he does not know how to engage with real women?

37. Like the other volumes of *The Bridge Trilogy*, *Virtual Light* is set in a future that cannot possibly happen. Set in about 2005 — just twelve years after the novel was published — California has been divided into two states, the United States has entered into a confederation with Canada, AIDS has been cured, and Tokyo has been rebuilt through the use of nanotechnology following an earthquake. Why do you think Gibson chooses such a setting? Are such settings unusual in science fiction? How do impossible-seeming settings affect the way stories are read and understood?

38. In *Virtual Light*, Shinyu Yamazaki introduces the concept of "Thomassons" as "useless and inexplicable monuments," epitomized by Gary Thomasson, a highly-paid American baseball player who came to the Yomiyuri Giants towards the end of his career and could no longer hit. Towards the end of the novel, Yamazaki realizes that in the 21st century, America itself has become a Thomasson of sorts. Explain what he means by this. If America has become a "useless and inexplicable monument," what is it a monument to? What is Gibson suggesting about the United States?

## Idoru

39. Much of *Idoru* centers on the relationship between, Rei Toei, a computer-generated pop star, and Rez, a rock superstar. Discuss the nature of their relationship and its significance. Why do the two want to marry and what would such a marriage signify? In what ways does Toei become more real as Rez becomes less so? What commentary does Gibson offer on the nature of celebrity through his depiction of the two?

40. Analyze Gibson's representations of virtual communities in Idoru, particularly the Lo/Rez fan club and the Walled City. To what extent is Mercedes Purissima Vargas-Gutierrez, a "severely deformed" twenty-six year old, able to become someone else through the use of virtual technology? What do virtual domains offer Masahiko and other *otaku*?

41. Gibson is sometimes credited with anticipating reality television in *Virtual Light* and *Idoru* because of his representation of shows such as *Cops in Trouble* and *Slitscan*. Consider reality television as it exists today: did Gibson correctly anticipate what it has become? To what extent does reality television today create reality as well as reflect it?

42. Most of *Idoru* is set in Tokyo after it has been damaged by an earthquake and rebuilt using nanotechnology. Compare Gibson's representation of Tokyo in the novel to his representation of San Francisco in *Virtual Light*? Is Tokyo a 21st century city in a way that San Francisco is not? Is Tokyo in any way idealized? You might also want to consider Gibson's depiction of both cities in *All Tomorrow's Parties*.

## All Tomorrow's Parties

43. *All Tomorrow's Parties* centers on the idea of nodal points in history, paradigmatic shifts that, in effect, change everything. One of the novel's protagonists, Colin Laney, indicates that the last such shift occurred in 1911. To what might he — and Gibson — be referring? What sort of fundamental change occurred at about that time?

44. In *All Tomorrow's Parties*, Colin Laney, Rei Toei, the Walled City and others work together to prevent Cody Harwood from shaping to future to his benefit. Discuss the significance of their coalition in terms of oppression and resistance? Is Gibson offering some sort of political prescription?

45. Discuss the attack upon the Bridge that occurs towards the end of *All Tomorrow's Parties*? What is it about the Bridge that makes it threatening to those seeking power like Cody Harwood? How do those living on the Bridge like Fontaine act to save it? To what extent do they succeed?

46. At the end of *All Tomorrow's Parties*, Rei Toei becomes a physical being, copies of her being issued from the nanofax machines all over the world. What is the significance of her transformation from a virtual being to a physical one? To Colin Laney, it is a nodal point in history, an event that changes everything. Why

might that be case? Is it the nanofax technology that changes everything or the fact that it has been used to produce thousands of Rei Toeis in physical form? Consider both possibilities.

## The Bigend Trilogy

### Pattern Recognition

47. In *Pattern Recognition*, the narrative indicates that the protagonist's first name, "Cayce," is pronounced "Case," just like the last name of the protagonist of *Neuromancer*. Although Gibson has repeatedly indicated that there is no connection between the two characters, critics, including Fredric Jameson, believe otherwise. Could the similarity in names just be a coincidence? If it is not, then what might it signify? How else might Cayce Pollard and Henry Case be related?

48. *Pattern Recognition* presents Cayce Pollard with two potential love interests, Boone Chu, to whom she is immediately attracted, and Parkaboy, whom she knows only through an online forum dedicated to the Footage. Discuss Pollard's relationship with the two men and they way they ultimately play out. How do Pollard and Parkaboy form such a strong relationship when they have never met physically? Why are Pollard and Chu unable to establish a strong relationship even though they are attracted to one another? To what extent does Chu's inability to connect meaningfully with Pollard through the use of email inhibit their potential romance?

49. Cayce Pollard is described as being "literally allergic to fashion." Discuss the nature of her allergy and how it manifests itself. How does it affect her work as a "coolhunter"—that is, as someone who identifies coming trends—and as a consultant to advertising agencies? How does her allergy relate to her conscious attitudes towards the fashion and advertising industries and how do these attitudes change over the course of the novel? What are Gibson's implicit attitudes toward these industries?

50. *Pattern Recognition* is one of the first best selling novels to address the September 11 attacks and their aftermath directly. How are the events of 9/11 and their consequences represented in the novel? What effects do they have on Cayce Pollard personally? How does she address the loss of her father in the attack on the World Trade Center? How does her loss relate to that of the Volkova sisters, who lost their father in a bombing in Russia? What role does the Footage play in addressing such losses?

### Spook Country

51. As the former singer of a well-known post-punk rock band, Hollis Henry has a certain level of celebrity, people often reacting to her fame rather than her as an individual. Discuss how Gibson addresses the nature of celebrity through Henry. What benefits does it afford her? What negative effects does it have? Is she ever able to overcome her celebrity or does it continue to define her at the end of the novel? Can she ever be anything other than the former lead singer of the Curfew?

52. *Spook Country* ends with Hollis Henry commissioning a work of locative art: she arranges for a hologram of giant Mongolian Death Worm to be being projected onto the top of Blue Ant headquarters. What is the significance of this particular image? What do Death Worms mean to Henry, and what are they supposed to represent in this particular situation? Also, what is the significance of the act itself? Is the projection an act of resistance, a prank, or gesture?

53. Analyze *Spook Country*'s title, focusing in particular on the connotations of the word "spook." In what sense can the U.S. be said to be a nation haunted by ghosts? In what sense is it haunted by quasi-legitimate intelligence agencies that formed as a result of the so-called War on Terror? What role do Cold War "spooks" such as the old man play in the novel? In answering this last question, it may be helpful to consider the roles former Cold War spooks such as Hobbs Baranov and Winfield Pollard play in *Pattern Recognition*.

54. Discuss the significance of the "game of cat and mouse" that the old man plays with the shipping container containing U.S. currency in *Spook Country*. Why does he play games with those he disapproves of—in this case those

trying to profit from the war in Iraq — rather than confront them or challenge them directly?

## Zero History

55. Why does fashion figure so largely in *Zero History*? Can fashion be understood as technology? What are its social and ideological functions? Is fashion industry essentially conservative? Can fashion serve as a potential site of resistance? Discuss the concept of "secret brands" and Cayce Pollard's Gabriel Hounds line in particular. Why does Hubertus Bigend seem to think that secret brands are so important and why is he so interested the Gabriel Hounds brand in particular?

56. On the surface, at least, the title of *Zero History* refers to the fact that Milgrim had "zero history" while he was addicted to drugs; that is, that he left no trace of himself on the so-called infoscape. What else might the book's title signify? What sort of comment might it be making upon history itself? Does history end in a sense in the novel? Have things changed in so fundamental way that the past no longer matters?

57. During his book tour for *Zero History*, Gibson said repeatedly that the villain of the novel is not so much any person as the times themselves. What does he mean by this and how is this idea manifested in the novel? What makes the times we are living in "villainous"?

58. *Zero History* ends with Hollis Henry awakening from a nightmare in which Hubertus Bigend is figured as a bloody-mouthed ferret with wooden teeth. Why does the novel — and the *Trilogy* — end with this particular image? What has Bigend become as a result of his having acquired "order flow," that is, advance knowledge of stock market activity? Has the world itself become a nightmare? Consider other details of her dream in your response.

## Other Works

### The Difference Engine

59. Research Lady Ada Byron, a historical figure who plays an important role in *The Dif-*

ference Engine. Why is she referred to as the Lady of Engines? Discuss her role in the novel in the context of her real-life contributions to computer programming and information science. Should she be recognized as an important contributor to the computer age as Gibson and Sterling seem to suggest?

60. Gibson insists that works of his that are set in the future are really about the present. Can the same be said of *The Difference Engine*, which is set in an alternative past rather than the present or future? In what ways do Gibson and co-author Bruce Sterling use the 19th century to explore 20th-century issues? What are we to learn from this novel about our own Information Age?

61. Discuss how Benjamin Disraeli's *Sybil* serves as an intertext for *The Difference Engine*. What characters and situations do Gibson and Sterling draw from *Sybil*? What themes? Is *The Difference Engine* true to Disraeli's original novel? In what ways does it differ?

### Yorkville: Hippie Haven

62. In 1967 the Canadian Broadcasting Company featured Gibson, who was then 19, in a short documentary entitled *Yorkville: Hippie Haven*. Discuss Gibson's account of the hippie subculture in this film, which appears in the beginning, and his reflections upon love, which appear towards the end. Also, discuss the way Gibson appears himself. How does he look and how does he carry himself? Does he appear to be a part of the movement he describes?

### Agrippa (A Book of the Dead)

63. Explore both the "deluxe" and "small" editions of *Agrippa* as they are represented in the "Online Archive of *Agrippa (A Book of the Dead)*" website developed by Alan Liu and others at the University of California, Santa Barbara. In what ways are the two editions materially different and what are the significances of those differences? How do the material differences between the editions affect the meaning of the poem itself, the text of which is the same for both?

64. In *Agrippa* the term "mechanism" is used to denote the camera used to take the

photographs featured in the Agrippa photo album that belonged to Gibson's father, a photo album that is the ostensive subject of the poem. As the poem proceeds, however, the word "mechanism" is used to refer to a number of other things. Discuss the way in which the poem develops "the mechanism" as a concept and then the meaning of the poem's final stanza.

### "Hippie Hat Brain Parasite" and "Dougal Discarnate"

65. Two of Gibson's stories, "Hippie Hat Brain Parasite" (1983) and "Dougal Discarnate" (2010), feature characters who seem to be based on Gibson himself. Reading the two stories in conjunction, analyze how Gibson represents himself and those around him. How might the stories be read as commentary on recreational drug use or 1960s counterculture?

### "Google's Earth"

66. In this Op-Ed piece for the *New York Times*, Gibson asserts, "Google is made of us, a sort of coral reef of human minds and their products." He adds that we "never imagined that artificial intelligence would be like this." In what sense can Google be understood as a form of artificial intelligence? In what ways is this form of artificial different from the ones imagined in works like *Neuromancer*? *Idoru*? *The Difference Engine*? Do you find Google and things like it threatening? Why or why not?

67. In both "The Road to Oceania" and "Google's Earth," Gibson discusses how new technologies have lead to methods of surveillance and control that go far beyond anything that Jeremy Bentham — or George Orwell, for that matter — might have imagined. Describe Bentham's concept of the panopticon and then discuss the ways in which it might be applied to the world we are living in now. In what sense have we moved beyond Bentham's model, technologies like Google's search engine transforming us into not just the surveilled but the surveillant?

# Bibliography

## Primary Sources

### Novels

*Neuromancer*. New York: Ace, 1984. Print.
*Count Zero*. New York: Ace, 1986. Print.
*Mona Lisa Overdrive*. New York: Bantam-Spectra, 1989. Print.
*The Difference Engine*. With Bruce Sterling. New York: Bantam Spectra, 1991. Print.
*Virtual Light*. New York. Bantam-Spectra, 1993. Print.
*Idoru*. New York: Putnam, 1996. Print.
*All Tomorrow's Parties*. New York: Putnam, 1999. Print.
*Pattern Recognition*. New York: Putnam, 2003. Print.
*Spook Country*. New York: Putnam, 2007. Print.
*Zero History*. New York: Putnam, 2010. Print.

### Short Fiction

COLLECTED

(The following stories are listed in the order they are collected in *Burning Chrome* [New York: Ace, 1986]: original publication information is also provided.)
"Johnny Mnemonic." *Omni* (May 1981). Print.
"The Gernsback Continuum." *Universe* 11 (1981). Print.
"Fragments of a Hologram Rose." *UnEarth* 3 (Summer 1977). Print.
"The Belonging Kind." With John Shirley. *Shadows* 4 (1981). Print.
"Hinterlands." *Omni* (Oct. 1981). Print.
"Burning Chrome." *Omni* (July 1982). Print.
"Red Star, Winter Orbit." With Bruce Sterling. *Omni* (July 1983). Print.
"New Rose Hotel." *Omni* (July 1984). Print.
"The Winter Market." *Vancouver* (Nov. 1985). Print.

"Dogfight." With Michael Stanwick. *Omni* (July 1985). Print.

UNCOLLECTED STORIES AND SKETCHES

"Hippie Hat Brain Parasite." *Modern Stories* 1 (Apr. 1983). Print.
"Tokyo Collage." *Science Fiction Eye* 4 (Aug. 1988). Print.
"Tokyo Suite." *Penthouse* (Japan). Trans. Hisashi Kuroma (1988). Print.
"Doing Television." *The Face*, Mar. 1990, 81–82. Print.
"Darwin." *Spin*, Apr. 1990, 60–61. Print.
"Skinner's Room." *Visionary San Francisco*. Ed. Polledri Paolo. Munich: Prestal, 1990: 153–65. Print.
"Academy Leader." *Cyberspace: First Steps*. Ed. Michael Benedikt. Cambridge: MIT Press, 1991: 27–29. Print.
"Cyber-Claus." *The Washington Post Book World*, 1 Dec. 1991. Print.
"Where the Holograms Go." *Wild Palms Reader*. Ed. Roger Trilling. New York: St. Martin's, 1993: 122–23. Print.
"Thirteen Views of a Cardboard City." *New Worlds*. Ed. David Garnett. Clarkston, GA: White Wolf, 1997: 338–49. Print.
"Dougal Discarnate." *Darwin's Bastards*. Ed. Gartner Zsuzsi. Vancouver: Douglas & McIntyre, 2010: 231–40. Print.

### Non-Fiction

REVIEWS

Review. *Gloriana*. Michael Moorcock. *Science Fiction Review*, Mar. 1979. Print.
Review. *Dracula in Love*. John Shirley. *Science Fiction Review*, Nov. 1979. Print.
Review. *Mockingbird*. Walter Tevis. *Science Fiction Review*, May 1980. Print.

Review. *City Come A-Walkin'*. John Shirley. *Science Fiction Review*, Aug. 1980. Print.

Review. *The Flute-Player*. D.M. Thomas. *Science Fiction Review*, Spring 1981. Print.

Review. *Port of Saints*. William S. Burroughs. *Science Fiction Review*, Spring 1981. Print.

Review. *Ratner's Star*. Dom DeLillo. *Science Fiction Review*. Spring 1981. Print.

Review. *Cellars*. John Shirely. *Science Fiction Review*. Fall 1982. Print.

Review. *The Acid House*. Irvine Welsh. *Science Fiction Eye*. Spring 1996. Print.

FOREWORDS AND INTRODUCTIONS

Introduction. *Heatseeker*. John Shirley. Santa Cruz: Scream Press, 1989. Print.

Introduction. *The Lost World & The Poison Belt*. Arthur Conan Doyle. San Francisco: Chronicle Books, 1989. Print.

Foreword. "Strange Attractors." *Alien Sex*. Ed. Datlow, Ellen, New York: Dutton, 1990. Print.

"The Recombinant City: A Foreword." *Dhalgren*. Samuel R. Delany. Middletown, CT: Wesleyan University Press, 1996. Print.

Foreword. *City Come A-Walking*. John Shirley. U.S.A.: Eyeball Books, 1996. Print.

"Entering the Transit Lounge." *Transit Lounge*. Ed. Ashley Crawford and Ray Edgar, Sydney: 21C/Interface Books, 1997. Print.

Introduction. *The Artificial Kid*. Bruce Sterling. San Francisco: Hardwired, 1997. Print.

Introduction. "Naples." Avram Davidson. *The Avram Davidson Treasury*. New York: Tor Books, 1998. Print.

Introduction. *The Art of the "X-Files."* Chris Carter. New York: HarperPrism, 2000. Print.

Introduction. *The Art of the Matrix*. Larry Wachowski. New York: Titan Books, 2000. Print.

"Steely Dan's Return." *Addicted to Noise* 6.3 (1 Mar. 2000). Print.

Introduction. *Ray Gun: Out of Control*. Dean Kuipers. London: Booth-Clibborn Editions, 2000. Print.

Foreword. *Multimedia: From Wagner to Virtual Reality*. Ed. Randall Packerl. New York: Norton, 2001. Print.

Introduction. *The Matrix: The Shooting Script*. Andy Wachowski and Larry Wachowski. New York: Newmarket Press, 2002. Print.

Introduction. *American Whiskey Bar*. Michael Turner. Vancouver: Arsenal Pulp Press, 2004. Print.

"She's the Business." *Stable Strategies and Others*. Eileen Gunn. San Francisco: Tachyon Publications, 2004. Print.

Introduction. *Selarc: The Monograph*. Marquard Smith. Cambridge: MIT Press, 2005. Print.

Introduction. *Labyrinths: Selected Stories & Other Writings*. Jorge Luis Borges. New York: New Directions, 2007. Print.

Introduction. *Phantom Shanghai*. Greg Girard. Toronto: Magenta Foundation, 2007. Print.

Introduction. *The Ware Tetrology*. Rudy Rucker. New York: Prime Books, 2010. Print.

ARTICLES AND ESSAYS

"Alfred Bester, SF and Me." *Frontier Crossing: A Souvenir of the 45th World Science Fiction Convention*. Ed. Robert Jackson. Brighton, U.K., Conspiracy '87, 1987. Print.

"Rocket Radio." *Rolling Stone*, 15 June 1989: 84–86. Print.

"Disneyland with the Death Penalty." Wired.com, *Wired* 1.4 (1993): 51–114. Web.

"Remembering Johnny: Notes on a Process," Wired.com, *Wired* 1.4 (1995). Web.

"The Net Is a Waste of Time ... and That's Exactly What's Right About It." *New York Times Magazine*, 14 July 1996. Web.

"'Virtual Lit': A Discussion." *Biblion: The Bulletin of the New York Public Library* (1996): 33–51. Print.

"Jack Womack and the Horned Heart of Neuropa." *Science Fiction Eye* (Fall 1997). Print.

"My Obsession." Wired.com, *Wired* 7.1 (1999). Web.

"Dead Man Sings." *Forbes ASAP*, 30 Nov. 1998: 177. Print.

"William Gibson's Fiction of Cyber-Eternity May Become a Reality." *HQ* 63:122 (1 Mar. 1999): 122. Print.

"My Obsession." Wired.com, *Wired* 7.1 (1999). Web.

"William Gibson's Filmless Festival." Wired.com, *Wired* 7.10 (1999). Web.

"Will We Plug Chips Into Our Brains?" Time.com, *Time*, 19 June 2000. Web.

"Modern Boys and Mobile Girls." Guardian.co.uk Japan issue, *The Observer*, 1 Apr. 2001. Web.

"Future Perfect." TimeAsia.com, 30 Apr. 2001. Web.

"Metrophagy." *Whole Earth* (June 2001). Web.

"My Own Private Tokyo." Wired.com, *Wired* 9.9 (2001). Web.

"Blasted Dreams in Mr. Buk's Window." *National Post*, 20 Sept. 2001. Print.

"Shiny Balls of Mud." *Tate Magazine*, 1 Sept/Oct 2002. Web.

"Since 1948." *Source Code*, 6 Nov. 2002. Web.

"The Road to Oceania." *New York Times*, 25 June 2003. Web.

"Time Machine Cuba." *Infinite Matrix*, 8 Aug. 2004. Web.

"God's Little Toys." Wired.com, *Wired* 13.7 (2005). Web.

"U2's City of Blinding Lights." Wired.com, *Wired* 13.8 (2005). Web.

"Pining for Toronto's 'Gone World.'" *Toronto Globe and Mail*, 31 May 2007. Web.

"Sci-Fi Special: William Gibson." *New Scientist* 2682 (12 Nov. 2008). Print.

"Google's Earth." *New York Times*, 31 Aug 2010. Web.

## Screenplays

"First-Person Shooter." Co-written with Tom Maddox. *The X-Files*. Season 7, Episode 13. Original Airdate: Feb 27, 2000.

"Johnny Mnemonic." Directed by Robert Longo, TriStar Pictures. Release Date: May 26, 1995.

"Kill Switch." Co-written with Tom Maddox. *The X-Files*. Season 5, Episode 11. Original Airdate: Feb 15, 1998.

## Poetry

*Agrippa (A Book of the Dead)*. New York: Begos, 1992. (First published in artists' book designed in collaboration with Dennis Ashbaugh; the text of the poem can be found on Gibson's official website: http://www.williamgibsonbooks.com/).

## Electronic Media

### BLOG

Gibson's blog can be found on his official website: http://www.williamgibsonbooks.com/

### TWITTER

Gibson's tweets can be found at the following address: http://twitter.com/GREATDISMAL.

## Drafts and Manuscripts

The University of British Columbia Archives possess many of Gibson's early manuscripts and typescripts. A description of its holdings can be found at: <http://www.library.ubc.ca./archives/u_arch/wgibs.html#bio>

## Secondary Sources

### Interviews

Adams Interview. Tim Adams. "Space to Think." Guardian.co.uk, *The Observer*, 12 Aug. 2007. Web.

Allemang Interview. John Allemang. "William Gibson Neuromances *The X-Files*." *The Back of the Moon*, 13 February 1998. Web.

Amazon Interview. "Across the Border to *Spook Country*: an Interview with William Gibson." Amazon.com, 2007. Web.

Barker Interview. Clive Barker. "Clive Barker Interviews William Gibson." *Burning City*, 13 Dec. 1997. Web.

Blair Interview. Dike Blair. *äda'web*, Apr. 1995. Web.

Blume Interview. Harvey Blume. "Q & A with William Gibson." *The Boston Globe*, 19 Aug. 2007. Web.

Brave New World Interview. *The Brave New World Radio Program*, Crankydog.com, 2002. Web.

Canavan Interview. Gerry Canavan. "Our Full Interview with William Gibson." INDYweek.com, 16 Sept. 2010. Web.

Clarke Interview. Maximus Clark. "Maximus Clarke Talks with William Gibson About Speculative Novels of Last Wednesday." *Maud Newton*, 22 Sept. 2010. Web.

Cyberpunk Interview. "Cyberpunk: an Interview with Mr. William Gibson." *The e-zone*, n.d. Web.

Deuben Interview. Alex Deuben. "William Gibson: The Father of Cyberpunk." *California Literary Review*, 2 Oct. 2007. Web.

Du Pont Interview. Alexandra Du Pont. "Alexandra Du Pont Interviews William Freakin' Gibson!!!!" *Ain't It Cool News*, 3 Feb. 2000. Web.

Ellis Interview. Warren Ellis. "Q&A: William Gibson Discusses *Spook Country* and Interactive Fiction." Wired.com, *Wired* 15.08, (July 2007). Web.

Fischlin Interview. Daniel Fischlin, Veronica Hollinger, and Andrew Taylor. "'The Charisma Leak': A Conversation with William Gibson and Bruce Sterling." *Science Fiction Studies*, 5 Apr. 1991. Web.

Gallagher Interview. Aileen Gallagher. "William Gibson on Why He Loves Twitter, Thinks Facebook Is 'Like a Mall,' and Much More." *The Vulture Transcript*, 27 Sept. 2010. Web.

Gilmore Interview. Mikal Gilmore. "The Rise of Cyberpunk." *Rolling Stone*, 4 Dec. 1986: 77–80. Print.

Graham Interview. Fiona Graham. "Finding Faces in the Clouds." Telegraph.co.uk, *Telegraph*, 30 Apr. 2003. Web.

Grimwood Interview. John Courteney Grimwood. "An Interview with William Gibson." InfinityPlus.com, n.d. Web.

Gross Interview. Terry Gross. "Terry Gross Interviews William Gibson." *Fresh Air*, National Public Radio, Feb. 1989. Print.

Gutmair Interview. Ulrich Gutmair. "William Gibson Interview." *Void Manufacturing*, 1 Oct. 2008. Web.

Handlen Interview. Zack Handlen. "Interview: William Gibson." *A.V. Club*, 7 Sept. 2010. Web.

Harper Interview. Leanne Harper. "The Culture of Cyberspace." *Bloomsbury Review* 8.5 (1998): 16–17, 30. Print.

Holman Interview. Curt Holman. "More with 'Neuromancer' Author William Gibson." *Creative Loafing Atlanta*, 14 Sept. 2010. Print.

Johnston Interview. Antony Johnston. "William

Gibson: *All Tomorrow's Parties*: Waiting for the Man." *Spike*, n.d. Web.

Josefsson Interview. Dan Josefsson. "I Don't Even Have a Modem." *William Gibson Web Ring*, 23 Nov. 1994. Web.

Leonard Interview. Andrew Leonard. "Nodal Point." Salon.com, *Salon*, 13 Feb. 2003. Web.

Lim Interview. "Now Romancer." Salon.com, *Salon*, 11 Aug. 2007. Web.

Linnemann Interview. Mavis Linnemann. "Days of Future Past: William Gibson Overdrive." *Phawker*, 15 Aug. 2007. Web.

McCaffery Interview. Larry McCaffery. "An Interview with William Gibson." *Storming the Reality Studio: A Casebook of Cyberpunk and Postmodern Science Fiction*. Ed. Larry McCaffery. Durham: Duke University Press, 1991: 263–85. Print.

Murray Interview. Noel Murray. "William Gibson." *The AV Club*, 22 Aug. 2007. Web.

Newitz Interview. Annalee Newitz. "William Gibson Talks to i09 About Canada, Draftdodging, and Godzilla." *i09*, 2007. Web.

O'Hara Interview. Andrew O'Hara. "Re:mote Induction Interview: William Gibson." *Re:mote Induction*, Oct. 1996. Web.

Owens Interview. Jill Owens. "William Gibson Country." Powells.com, Powell's Books, 26 July 2007. Web.

Pancella Interview. Angela Pancella. "Mark Neale: Mapmaker." @U2.com, 24 Apr. 2002. Web.

Parker Interview. T. Virgil Parker. "William Gibson: Sci-Fi Icon Becomes Prophet of the Present." Williamgibsonboard.com, 2007. Web.

Poole Interview. Stephen Poole. "Tomorrow's Man." Guardian.co.uk, *The Guardian*, 3 May 2003. Web.

Rapatzikou Interview. Tatiani Rapatzikou. "Appendix: Interview with William Gibson in Vancouver, Canada." *Gothic Motifs in the Fiction of William Gibson*. New York: Rodopi, 2004: 217–230. Print.

Salon Interview. "The Salon Interview: William Gibson." Salon.com, *Salon*, n.d. Web.

Salza Interview. Giuseppe Salza. "William Gibson Interview." *Electronic Frontier Foundation*, 1994. Web.

Shepherd Interview. Mark Shepherd. *Ottawa X-Press*, 22 Sept. 1993. Web.

Sullivan Interview. James Sullivan. "Bridge to Tomorrow." SFGate.com, 19 Oct. 1999. Web.

Telegraph Interview. "William Gibson Answers Readers' Questions." Telegraph.co.uk, *Telegraph*, 30 Apr. 2003. Web.

Thill Interview. Scott Thill. "William Gibson Talks Zero History, Paranoia and the Awesome Power of Twitter." Wired.com, *Wired*, 7 Sept. 2010. Web.

Van Bakel Interview. "Remembering Johnny." Wired.com, *Wired* 3.06 (June 1995). Web.

Van Belkom Interview. Edo Van Belkom. "An Interview with William Gibson" *The Edge*, 1998. Web.

Wershler-Henry Interview. Darren Wershler-Henry. "Victoria's Personal Spook, Psychic Legbreakers, Snakes and Catfood: An Interview with William Gibson and Tom Maddox." *Virus* 23 (Fall 1989): 28–36. Print.

## Articles, Books, and Essays

Alkon, Paul. "Deus Ex Machina in William Gibson's Cyberpunk Trilogy." *Fiction 2000: Cyberpunk and the Future of Narrative*. Ed. George Slusser and Tom Shippey. Athens: University of Georgia Press, 1992. 75–87. Print.

Annesley, James. "Netscapes: Gibson, Globalisation and the Representation of New Media." *Forum for Modern Language Studies* 37.2 (2001): 218–29. Print.

Armstrong, Tim. *Modernism: A Cultural History*. New York: Polity, 2005. Print.

Austin, Andrea. "Frankie and Johnny: Shelley, Gibson, and Hollywood's Love Affair with the Cyborg." *Romanticism on the Net: An Electronic Journal Devoted to Romantic Studies* 21 (2001). Web.

Barlow, John Perry. "Being and Nothingness, Virtual Reality, and the Pioneers of Cyberspace." Electronic Frontier Foundation. 1992. Web.

Baudrillard, Jean. *Simulacra and Simulation*. Trans. Sheila Fraser. Ann Arbor: University of Michigan Press, 1995. Print.

Benedikt, Michael. *Cyberspace: First Steps*. Cambridge: MIT Press, 1991. Print.

Berressem, Hanjo. "'Of Metal Ducks, Embodied Iduros, and Autopoietic Bridges': Tales of an Intelligent Materialism in the Age of Artificial Life." *The Holodeck in the Garden: Science and Technology in Contemporary American Fiction*. Ed. Peter Freese and Charles B. Harris. London: Dalkey, 2004. 72–99. Print.

Bethke, Bruce. Foreword. "'Cyberpunk'—A Short Story by Bruce Bethke." InfinityPlus.com, n.d. Web.

Bev-Tov, Sharona. "Cyberpunk: An Afterword About an Afterlife." *The Artificial Paradise: Science Fiction and America Reality*. Ed. Sharona Bev-Tov. Ann Arbor: University of Michigan Press, 1995. 175–82. Print.

Blackford, Russell. "Mirrors of the Future City: William Gibson's *Neuromancer*." *Science Fiction: A Review of Speculative Literature* 7.1 (1985): 18–22. Print.

_____. "Reading the Ruined Cities." *Science Fiction Studies* 31.2 (2004): 264–70. Print.

Booker, M. Keith. "Technology, History, and the

Postmodern Imagination: The Cyberpunk Fiction of William Gibson." *Arizona Quarterly: A Journal of American Literature, Culture, and Theory* 50.4 (1994): 63–87. Print.

Brand, David. "The Business of Cyberpunk: Symbolic Economy and Ideology in William Gibson." *Virtual Realities and Their Discontents.* Ed. Robert Markley. Baltimore: Johns Hopkins University Press, 1996. 79–106. Print.

Bredehoft, Thomas. "The Gibson Continuum: Cyberspace and Gibson's Mervyn Kihn Stories." *Science Fiction Studies* 22.2 (1995): 252–63. Print.

Brin, David. *Through Stranger Eyes: Reviews, Introductions, Tributes & Iconoclastic Essays.* Ann Arbor, MI: Nimble Books, 2008. Print.

Brouillette, Sarah. "Corporate Publishing and Canonization: *Neuromancer* and Science-Fiction Publishing in the 1970s and early 1980s." *Book History.* Ed. Ezra Greenspan and Jonathan Rose. University Park: Pennsylvania State University Press, 2002. 187–208. Print.

Bukatman, Scott. "Gibson's Typewriter." *Flame Wars: The Discourse of Cyberculture.* Ed. Mark Dery. Durham: Duke University Press, 1994. 71–89. Print.

_____. *Terminal Identity: The Virtual Subject in Postmodern Science Fiction.* Durham: Duke University Press, 1993. Print.

Bulliet, Richard W. "From Gutenberg to William Gibson: Revolutions in Knowledge from the Renaissance into the 21st Century, II: Of Encyclopedias and the End of the World." *Biblion: The Bulletin of the New York Public Library* (Fall 1994): 49–58. Print.

Burr, Ty. "All Tomorrow's Parties." EW.com, *Entertainment Weekly,* 29 Oct. 1999. Web.

Burroughs, William. "The Cut Up Method." *The Moderns: An Anthology of New Writing.* Ed. Leroi Jones. New York: Corinth Books, 1963. Print.

_____. "The Discipline of DE." *Word Virus: The William Burroughs Reader.* New York: Grove Press, 1998. Print.

_____. *The Naked Lunch.* New York: Grove Press, 1959. Print.

Butler, Judith. *Gender Trouble: Feminism and the Subversion of Identity.* New York: Routledge, 1990. Print.

Caesar, Terry. "Turning American: Popular Culture and National Identity in the Recent American Text of Japan." *Arizona Quarterly* 58.2 (2002): 113–41. Print.

Call, Lewis. "Anarchy in the Matrix: Postmodern Anarchism in the Novels of William Gibson and Bruce Sterling." *Anarchist Studies* 7.2 (1999): 99–117. Print.

Calvert, Bronwen. "Speaking the Body: The Embodiment of 'Feminist' Cyberpunk." *Speaking Science Fiction: Dialogues and Interpretations.* Ed. Andy Sawyer and David Seed. Liverpool, England: Liverpool University Press, 2000. 96–108. Print.

Cavallaro, Dani. *Cyberpunk and Cyberculture : Science Fiction and the Work of William Gibson.* Somerset, NJ: Athlone Press, 2000. Print.

Chafe, Wallace. *Discourse, Consciousness, and Time: the Flow and Displacement of Conscious Experience in Speaking and Writing.* Chicago: University of Chicago Press, 1994. Print.

Chandler, Raymond. *The Big Sleep.* New York: Random House, 1939. Print.

Cherniavsky, Eva. "(En)gendering Cyberspace in *Neuromancer*: Postmodern Subjectivity and Virtual Motherhood." *Genders* 18 (1993): 32–46. Print.

Childers, Joseph, et al. "White Men Can't ... (De)centering Authority and Jacking into Phallic Economies in William Gibson's *Count Zero.*" *Science Fiction, Canonization, Marginalization, and the Academy.* Ed. Gary Westfahl and George Slusser. Westport, CT: Greenwood, 2002. Print.

Christie, John R.R. "Of AIs and Others: William Gibson's Transit." *Fiction 2000: Cyberpunk and the Future of Narrative.* Ed. George Slusser and Tom Shippey. Athens: University of Georgia Press, 1992. 88–108, 171–82. Print.

_____. "Science Fiction and the Postmodern: The Recent Fiction of William Gibson and John Crowley." *Essays and Studies* 43 (1990): 34–58. Print.

Chun, Wendy Hui Yong. *Control and Freedom: Power and Paranoia in the Age of Fiber Optics.* Cambridge: MIT Press, 2006. Print.

Chun-li, Hui. *The Re/Shaping of the Posthuman, Cyberspace, and the Histories in William Gibson's Bridge Series.* Saarbrücken: VDM, 2009. Print.

Clayton, Jay. "Hacking the Nineteenth Century." *Victorian Afterlife: Postmodern Culture Rewrites the Nineteenth Century.* Ed. John Kucich and Dianne F. Sadoff. Minneapolis: University of Minnesota Press, 2000. 186–210. Print.

Concannon, Kevin. "The Contemporary Space of the Border: Gloria Anzaldua's *Borderlands* and William Gibson's *Neuromancer.*" *Textual Practice* 12 (1998): 429–42. Print.

Conover, Dan. "*Spook Country* a Dark Satire." *The Post and Courier.* 26 Aug. 2007. Web.

Conte, Joseph. "The Virtual Reader: Cybernetics and Technology in William Gibson and Bruce Sterling's *The Difference Engine.*" *The Holodeck in the Garden: Science and Technology in Contemporary American Fiction.* Ed. Peter Freese and Charles B. Harris. London: Dalkey, 2004. 28–52. Print.

Conrad, Joseph. *Tales of Unrest*. New York: Doubleday, Page, 1920. 3–55. Print.

_____. *"Youth" and Two Other Stories*. New York: Doubleday, Page, 1925. 45–162. Print.

Csicsery-Ronay, Istvan, Jr. "Antimancer: Cybernetics and Art in Gibson's *Count Zero*." *Science Fiction Studies* 22 (1995): 63–86. Print.

_____. "The Sentimental Futurist: Cybernetics and Art in William Gibson's *Neuromancer*." *Critique: Studies in Contemporary Fiction* 33.3 (1992): 221–40. Print.

Curl, Ruth. "The Metaphors of Cyberpunk Ontology: Epistemology, and Science Fiction." *Fiction 2000: Cyberpunk and the Future of Narrative*. Ed. George Slusser and Tom Shippey. Athens: University of Georgia Press, 1992. 230–45. Print.

Curtain, Tyler. "'Sinister Fruitiness': *Neuromancer*, Internet Sexuality and the Turing Test." *Studies in the Novel* 28.3 (1996): 414–35. Print.

Dalton, Stephen. "Cyber Class: The Neuroromance Between U2 and William Gibson." *Achtung Stations (Part Two)*. Uncut Magazine, 26 Oct. 2004. Web.

Dargis, Manohla. "Cyber Johnny." *Sight and Sound* 5.7 (1995): 6–7. Print.

Davidson, Cynthia. "Riviera's Golem, Haraway's Cyborg: Reading *Neuromancer* as Baudrillard's Simulation of Crisis." *Science Fiction Studies* 23 (1996): 188–98. Print.

de Zwann, Victoria. "Rethinking the Slipstream: Kathy Acker Reads *Neuromancer*." *Science Fiction Studies* 24.3 (1997): 459–70. Print.

Deery, June. "The Biopolitics of Cyberspace: Piercy Hacks Gibson." *Future Females, The Next Generation: New Voices and Velocities in Feminist Science Fiction Criticism*. Ed. Marleen S. Barr. Lanham, MD: Rowman & Littlefield, 2000. 87–108. Print.

Delaney, Paul. "'Hardly the Center of the World': Vancouver in William Gibson's 'The Winter Market.'" *Vancouver: Representing the Postmodern City*. Ed. Paul Delaney. Vancouver: Arsenal Pulp Press, 1994. 179–92. Print.

Delany, Samuel R. "Is Cyberpunk a Good Thing or a Bad Thing?" *Mississippi Review* 16.2–3 (1988): 28–35. Print.

_____. "Zelazny/Varley/Gibson and Quality, Part 1." *The New York Review of Science Fiction* 48 (1992): 10–13. Print.

DeLillo, Don. *White Noise*. New York: Viking, 1984. Print.

Dirda, Michael. *"All Tomorrow's Parties."* The *Washington Post*, 17 Oct. 1999. Web.

Disch, Thomas. "Lost in Cyberspace." *New York Times*, 11 Dec. 1998. Web.

_____. "Queen Victoria's Computers." *New York Times*, 10 Mar. 1991. Web.

Doctorow, Cory. "William Gibson Interview Transcript." Craphound.com, 23 Nov. 1999. Web.

Dorsey, Candas Jane. "Beyond Cyberspace." *Books in Canada* (June/July 1988): 11–13. Print.

Dozois, Gardner. "SF in the Eighties." *Washington Post*, 30 Dec. 1984. Web.

Easterbrook, Neil. "Alternate Presents: The Ambivalent Historicism of *Pattern Recognition*." *Science Fiction Studies* 33 (2006): 483–503. Print.

Ehrman, Mark. "Hack Attack: Flaming Idol." *Los Angeles Times*, 8 Aug. 1993. Web.

Eriksen, Inge. "The Aesthetics of Cyberpunk." *Foundation: The Review of Science Fiction* 53 (1991): 36–46. Print.

Fabijancic, Tony. "Space and Power: 19th-Century Urban Practice and Gibson's Cyberworld." *Mosaic: A Journal for the Interdisciplinary Study of Literature* 32.1 (1999): 105–30. Print.

Fair, Benjamin. "Stepping Razor in Orbit: Postmodern Identity and Political Alternatives in William Gibson's *Neuromancer*." *Critique* 46.2 (2005): 92–103. Print.

Farnell, Ross. "Posthuman Topologies: William Gibson's 'Architexture' in *Virtual Light* and *Idoru*." *Science Fiction Studies* 26.3 (1998): 459–460. Print.

Fitting, Peter. "The Lessons of Cyberpunk." *Technoculture*. Ed. Constance Penley and Andrew Ross. Minneapolis: University of Minnesota Press, 1991. 295–315. Print.

Foster, Derek. "The Banana-Skin Ballet of William Gibson." *Pop Can: Popular Culture in Canada*. Ed. Lynne Van Luven and Priscilla L. Walton. Scarborough, Ontario: Allyn and Bacon, 1999. 66–72. Print.

Foucault, Michel. "Of Other Spaces." *Diacritics* 16 (1986): 22–27. Print.

Genette, Gérard. *Narrative Discourse Revisited*. Trans. Jane E. Lewin. Ithaca: Cornell University Press, 1988. Print.

Gimon, Charles A. "Heroes of Cyberspace: William Gibson." *Net Writings*. Gimonca, Mar. 1997. Web.

Glazer, Miriyam. "'What Is Within Now Seen Without': Romanticism, Neuromanticism, and the Death of the Imagination in William Gibson's Fictive World." *Journal of Popular Culture* 23.3 (1989): 155–64. Print.

Goh, Robbie B. H. "Consuming Spaces: Clive Barker, William Gibson and the Cultural Poetics of Postmodern Fantasy." *Social Semiotics* 10.1 (2000): 21–39. Print.

Gozzi, Raymond. "The Cyberspace Metaphor." *ETC.: A Review of General Semantics* 51 (1994): 218–23. Print.

Grace, Dominick M. "Disease, Virtual Life, and *Virtual Light*." *Foundation* 81 (2001): 75–82. Print.

_____. "From *Videodrome* to *Virtual Light*: David Cronenberg and William Gibson." *Extrapolation: A Journal of Science Fiction and Fantasy* 44.3 (2003): 344–57. Print.

Grant, Glenn. "Transcendence through Detournement in William Gibson's *Neuromancer*." *Science Fiction Studies* 17.1 (1990): 41–49. Print.

Grimstad, Paul C. "Algorithm — Genre — Linguisterie: 'Creative Distortion' in *Count Zero* and *Nova Express*." *Journal of Modern Literature* 27.4 (2004): 82–92. Print.

Grossman, Lev. "ALL TIME 100 Novels." Time.com, *Time*, 16 Oct. 2005. Web.

Gunkel, David J., and Ann Hetzel Gunkel. "Virtual Geographies: The New Worlds of Cyberspace." *Critical Studies in Mass Communication* 14 (1997): 123–37. Print.

Gunn, Eileen. "A Difference Dictionary." *Science Fiction Eye* (1991): 40–53. Print.

Hammett, Dashiell. *The Maltese Falcon*. New York: Alfred A. Knopf, 1930. Print.

Hardin, Michael. "Beyond Science Fiction: William Gibson's *Neuromancer* and Kathy Acker's *Empire of the Senseless*." *Notes on Contemporary Literature* 30.4 (2000): 4–6. Print.

Haraway, Donna. "A Cyborg Manifesto: Science, Technology, and Socialist-Feminism in the Late Twentieth Century." *Simians, Cyborgs and Women: The Reinvention of Nature*. Ed. Donna Jeanne Haraway. New York: Routledge, 1991. 149–81. Print.

Hayles, N. Katherine. "How Cyberspace Signifies: Taking Immortality Literally." *Immortal Engines: Life Extension and Immortality in Science Fiction and Fantasy*. Ed. George Slusser, Gary Westfahl, and Eric S. Rabkin. Athens: University of Georgia Press, 1996. 111–21. Print.

Hellekson, Karen. "Looking Forward: William Gibson and Bruce Sterling's *The Difference Engine*." *The Alternate History: Refiguring Historical Time*. Ed. Karen Hellekson. Kent, OH: Kent State University Press, 2001. 76–86. Print.

Heuser, Sabine. *Virtual Geographies: Cyberpunk at the Intersection of the Postmodern*. New York: Rodopi, 2003. Print.

Hicks, Heather J. "'Whatever It Is That She's Since Become': Writing Bodies of Text and Bodies of Women in James Tiptree Jr.'s 'The Girl Who Was Plugged In' and William Gibson's 'The Winter Market.'" *Contemporary Literature* 37.1 (1996): 62–93. Print.

Hollinger, Veronica. "Cybernetic Deconstructions: Cyberpunk and Postmodernism." *Mosaic: A Journal for the Interdisciplinary Study of Literature* 23.2 (1990): 29–44. Print.

_____. "Stories About the Future: From *Patterns of Expectation* to *Pattern Recognition*." *Science Fiction Studies* 33 (2006): 452–71. Print.

Household, Geoffrey. *Rogue Male*. New York: New York Review Books Classic, 2007. Print.

Houston, Frank. "'*All Tomorrow's Parties*' by William Gibson." Salon.com, *Salon*, 29 Oct. 1999. Web.

Huntington, John. "Newness, *Neuromancer*, and the End of Narrative." *Essays and Studies* 43 (1990): 59–75. Print.

Ilgner, R. "Soul Loss and Meat Markets: The Technology of Cyberspace and Cyborgs in Gibson's *Neuromancer*." *The Image of Technology in Literature, the Media, and Society*. Ed. Will Wright and Steve Kaplan. Pueblo, CO: Society for the Interdisciplinary Study of Social Imagery, 1994. 17–20. Print.

Itzkoff, Dave. "Spirits in the Material World," *New York Times*, 26 Aug. 2007. Web.

Jameson, Fredric. *Archaeologies of the Future: The Desire Called Utopia and Other Science Fictions*. New York: Verso, 2005. Print.

_____. *Postmodernism, or, the Logic of Late Capitalism*. Durham: Duke University Press, 1991. Print.

Johnston, John. "Computer Fictions: Narratives of the Machinic Phylum." *Journal of the Fantastic in the Arts* 8.4 (1997): 443–63. Print.

_____. "Mediality in *Vineland* and *Neuromancer*." *Reading Matters: Narratives in the New Media Ecology*. Ed. Joseph Tabbi and Michael Wutz. Ithaca, NY: Cornell University Press, 1997. 173–92. Print.

Jonas, Gerald. "The Disappearing $2,000 Book." *New York Times*, 29 Aug. 1993. Web.

_____. "Science Fiction." *New York Times Book Review*, 24 Nov. 1985. Web.

Jones, Christine Kenyon. "SF and Romantic Biofictions: Aldiss, Gibson, Sterling, Powers." *Science Fiction Studies* 71 (1997): 47–56. Print.

Jones, Gwyneth. *Deconstructing the Starships: Science Fiction and Reality*. Liverpool, England: Liverpool University Press, 1999. Print.

Jones, Steven. "Second Life, Video Games, and the Social Text. *PMLA: Publications of the Modern Language Association* 124.1 (2009): 264–72. Print.

Kamioka, Nobuo. "Cyberpunk Revisited: William Gibson's *Neuromancer* and the 'Multimedia Revolution.'" *Japanese Journal of American Studies* 9 (1998): 53–68. Print.

Ketterer, David. *Canadian Science Fiction and Fantasy*. Bloomington: Indiana University Press, 1992. 140–46. Print.

Klein, Herbert. "From Romanticism to Virtual Reality: Charles Babbage, William Gibson and the Construction of Cyberspace." *Interdisciplinary Humanities* 24.1 (2007): 36–50. Print.

Konstantinou, Lee. "The Brand as Cognitive Map in William Gibson's *Pattern Recognition*." *Bound-*

*ary 2: An International Journal of Literature and Culture* 36.2 (2009): 67–97. Print.

Laidlaw, Marc. "Virtual Surreality: Our New Romance with Plot Devices." *Flame Wars: The Discourse of Cyberculture.* Ed. Mark Dery. Durham: Duke University Press, 1994. 91–112. Print.

Lambert, Laura, et al. *Internet: A Historical Encyclopedia.* Santa Barbara, CA: MTM Publishing, 2005. Print.

Latham, Rob. "Cyberpunk = Gibson = Neuromancer." *Science Fiction Studies* 20.2 (1993): 266–72. Print.

Leaver, Tama. "Interstitial Spaces and Multiple Histories in William Gibson's *Virtual Light, Idoru,* and *All Tomorrow's Parties.*" *Limina: A Journal of Historical and Cultural Studies* 9 (2003). Web.

Leblanc, Lauraine. "Razor Girls: Genre and Gender in Cyberpunk Fiction." *Women and Language* 20 (1997): 71–76. Print.

Leonard, John. "Gravity's Rainbow." *The Nation,* 15 Nov. 1993: 580–88. Print.

Lessig, Lawrence. *Remix: Making Art and Commerce Thrive in a Hybrid Economy.* New York: Penguin, 2008. Print.

Levy, Steven. *Hackers: Heroes of the Computer Revolution.* New York: O'Reilly Media, 2010. Print.

Lindberg, Kathryne V. "Prosthetic Mnemonics and Prophylactic Politics: William Gibson Among the Subjectivity Mechanisms." *Boundary* 23.2 (1996): 47–83. Print.

Link, Alex. "Global War, Global Capital, and the Work of Art in William Gibson's *Pattern Recognition.*" *Contemporary Literature* 49.2 (2008): 209–31. Print.

Linne, William. "William Gibson Hot on the Trail of Tomorrow." SFGate.com, *SFGate,* 26 Dec. 1999. Web.

Linton, Patricia. "The 'Person' in Postmodern Fiction: Gibson, Le Guin, and Vizenor." *Studies in American Indian Literatures: The Journal of the Association for the Study of American Indian Literatures* 5.3 (1993): 3–11. Print.

Lutz, Catherine, and Jane Collins. *Reading National Geographic.* Chicago: University of Chicago Press, 1993. Print.

Lyon, David. "Cyberspace: Beyond the Information Society?" *Living with Cyberspace: Technology and Society in the 21st Century.* Ed. John Armitage and Joanne Roberts. New York: Continuum, 2002. 21–33. Print.

Maddox, Tom. "Cobra, She Said: An Interim Report on the Fiction of William Gibson." *Fantasy Review* 9.4 (1986): 46–48. Print.

_____. "Maddox on Gibson." *Virus* 23 (1989). Web.

Markley, Robert. "Boundaries: Mathematics, Alienation, and the Metaphysics of Cyberspace." *Virtual Realities and Their Discontents.* Ed. Robert Markley. Baltimore: Johns Hopkins University Press, 1996. 55–77. Print.

Markoff, John. *What the Dormouse Said: How the 60s Counterculture Shaped the Personal Computer.* New York: Viking, 2005. Print.

McCaffery, Larry. *Storming the Reality Studio: A Casebook of Cyberpunk and Postmodern Science Fiction.* Durham: Duke University Press, 1992. Print.

McHale, Brian. *Constructing Postmodernism.* London: Routledge, 1992. Print.

_____. "Difference Engines." *ANQ: A Quarterly Journal of Short Articles, Notes, and Reviews* 5.4 (1992): 220–23. Print.

Mead, David G. "Technological Transfiguration in William Gibson's Sprawl Novels: *Neuromancer, Count Zero,* and *Mona Lisa Overdrive.*" *Extrapolation: A Journal of Science Fiction and Fantasy* 32.4 (1991): 350–60. Print.

Memetic Engineer. "Caffe Nero White Plastic Cup Lid." "Zero History" Blog, 11 June 2009. Web.

Miller, Laura. "They'll Always Have Tokyo." *New York Times Book Review,* 8 Sept. 1996. Web.

Moylan, Tom. "Global Economy/Local Texts: Utopian/Dystopian Tension in William Gibson's Cyberpunk Trilogy." *Minnesota Review* 43–44 (1994–1995): 182–97. Print.

Murphy, Graham. "Post/Humanity and the Interstitial: A Glorification of Possibility in Gibson's Bridge Sequence." *Science Fiction Studies* 30 (2003): 72–90. Print.

Myers, Tony. "The Postmodern Imaginary in *William Gibson's Neuromancer.*" *MFS: Modern Fiction Studies* 47.4 (2001): 887–909. Print.

Nixon, Nicola. "Cyberpunk: Preparing the Ground for Revolution or Keeping the Boys Satisfied?" *Science Fiction Studies* 19.2 (July 1992): 219–35. Print.

Novak, Amy. "Virtual Poltergeists and Memory: The Question of Ahistoricism in William Gibson's *Neuromancer.*" *Journal of the Fantastic in the Arts* 11.4 (2001): 395–414. Print.

Olsen, Lance. "The Shadow of Spirit in William Gibson's Matrix Trilogy." *Extrapolation: A Journal of Science Fiction and Fantasy* 32.3 (1991): 278–89. Print.

_____. "*Virtual Light.*" Lanceolsen.com, 1994. Web.

_____. "Virtual Termites: A Hypotextual Technomutant Explo(it)ration of William Gibson and the Electronic Beyond(s)." *Cyberspace Textuality: Computer Technology and Literary Theory.* Ed. Marie Laure Ryan. Bloomington: Indiana University Press, 1998. 224–255. Print.

_____. *William Gibson.* Mercer, WA: Starmount House, 1992. Print.

"Online Archive of Agrippa (A Book of the

Dead)." University of California, Santa Barbara. Web.

Palmer, Christopher. "*Mona Lisa Overdrive* and the Prosthetic." *Science Fiction Studies* 31.2 (2004): 227–42. Print.

_____. "*Pattern Recognition*: 'None of What We Do Is Ever Really Private.'" *Science Fiction Studies* 33.3 (2006): 473–82. Print.

Parsons, Michael. "William Gibson Brings *Spook Country* to *Second Life*." Times Online, *Times*, 3 Aug. 2007. Web.

Peppers, Cathy. "'I've Got You Under My Skin': Cyber(Sexed) Bodies in Cyberpunk Fictions." *Bodily Discursions: Genders, Representations, Technologies*. Ed. Deborah S. Wilson and Christine Moneera Laennac. Albany: State University Press of New York, 1997. 163–85. Print.

Person, Lawrence. "Notes Toward a Postcyberpunk Manifesto." Slashdot.org, *Slashdot*, 9 Oct. 1999. Web.

Pham, Andrew, X. "Virtually a Bestselling Book: William Gibson Returns to the 21st Century in *Idoru*." *Metroactive Books* 12 Sept. 1996. Web.

Poole, Stephen. "Nearing the Nodal." Guardian.co.uk, *The Guardian*, 30 Oct. 1999. Web.

_____. "Spook Country." Guardian.co.uk, *The Guardian*, 18 Aug. 2007. Web.

Porush, David. "Cybernauts in Cyberspace: William Gibson's *Neuromancer*." *Aliens: The Anthropology of Science Fiction*. Ed. George C. Slusser and Eric Rabkin. Carbondale: Southern Illinois University Press, 1987. 168–78. Print.

Proietti, Salvatore. "Out of Bounds: The Walled City, the Virtual Frontier, and Recent U.S. Science Fiction." *America Today: Highways and Labyrinths*. Ed. Gigliola Nocera. Siracusa, Italy: Grafià, 2003. 247–54. Print.

Punday, Daniel. "The Narrative Construction of Cyberspace: Reading *Neuromancer*, Reading Cyberspace Debates." *College English* 63.2 (2000): 194–214. Print.

Punter, David. "Postmodern Geographies." *Span: Journal of the South Pacific Association for Commonwealth Literature and Language Studies* 52 (2002): 194–213. Print.

Pynchon, Thomas. *The Crying of Lot 49*. New York: Perennial, 1966. Print.

_____. *Gravity's Rainbow*. New York: Viking, 1973. Print.

Rapatzikou, Tatiani G. *Gothic Motifs in the Fiction of William Gibson*. Amsterdam: Rodopi, 2004. Print.

Rirdan, Danny. "The Works of William Gibson." *Foundation: The Review of Science Fiction* 43 (1988): 36–46. Print.

Roe, Phillip. "Textual Dreaming: Dis-Ease in the Interface." *Fiberculture Journal* 3 (2004). Web.

Ross, Andrew. "Getting Out of the Gernsback Continuum." *Critical Inquiry* 17.2 (1991): 411–33. Print.

_____. *Strange Weather: Culture, Science, and Technology in the Age of Limits*. London: Verso, 1991. Print.

Rowen, Iain. "*Neuromancer* by William Gibson." InfinityPlus.com, 2001. Web.

Ruddick, Nicholas. "Putting the Bits Together: Information Theory, *Neuromancer*, and Science Fiction." *Journal of the Fantastic in the Arts* 3.4 (1994): 84–92. Print.

Sanders, Leonard Patrick. *Postmodern Orientalism: William Gibson, Cyberpunk and Japan*. Doctoral Thesis. Massey University, 2008. Print.

Schellenberg, Stephen. "*Neuromancer*." Challenging Destiny.com, 20 Apr. 2004. Web.

Schmitt, Ronald. "Mythology and Technology: The Novels of William Gibson." *Extrapolation: A Journal of Science Fiction and Fantasy* 34.1 (1993): 64–78. Print.

Schroeder, Randy. "Determinacy, Indeterminacy, and the Romantic William Gibson." *Science Fiction Studies* 21.2 (1994): 155–63. Print.

_____. "Neu-Criticizing William Gibson." *Extrapolation: A Journal of Science Fiction and Fantasy* 35.4 (1994): 330–41. Print.

Schwenger, Peter. "*Agrippa*, or, The Apocalyptic Book." *Flame Wars: The Discourse of Cyberculture*. Ed. Mark Dery. Durham: Duke University Press, 1994. 61–70. Print.

Seidel, Kathryn Lee. "Asians and Aliens in Cyberculture Film and Fiction." *Hybridity: Journal of Cultures, Texts and Identities* 1.1 (2000): 17–29. Print.

SFAN. "What Is Cyberpunk?" Cyberpunkreview. com, 19 Feb. 2007. Web.

Shu-Shun Chan, Herbert. "Interrogation from Hyperspace: Visions of Culture in *Neuromancer* and 'War Without End.'" *Simulacrum America: The U.S.A. and the Popular Media*. Ed. Elisabeth Kraus and Carolin Auer. Rochester, NY: Camden House, 2000. 136–45. Print.

Siivonen, Timo. "Cyborgs and Generic Oxymorons: The Body and Technology in William Gibson's *Cyberspace Trilogy*." *Science Fiction Studies* 23 (1996): 227–44. Print.

Silberman, Steve, "William Gibson to Write *X-Files* Episode." Wired.com, *Wired*, 13 Jan. 1998. Web.

Silver, Stephen. "New Worlds." *Stephen Silver's Reviews*, SFsite.com, n.d. Web.

Spencer, Nicholas. "Rethinking Ambivalence: Technopolitics and the Luddites in William Gibson and Bruce Sterling's *The Difference Engine*." *Contemporary Literature* 40 (1999): 403–49. Print.

Sponsler, Claire. "Cyberpunk and the Dilemmas of Postmodern Narrative: The Example of

William Gibson." *Contemporary Literature* 33.4 (1992): 625–44. Print.

_____. "William Gibson and the Death of Cyberpunk." *Modes of the Fantastic: Selected Essays from the Twelfth International Conference on the Fantastic in the Arts.* Ed. Robert A. Latham and Robert A. Collins. Westport, CT: Greenwood; 1995. 47–55. Print.

Stephenson, Neal. *Snow Crash.* New York: Bantam Spectra, 2000. Print.

Sterling, Bruce. "Exploring a 21st Century Pop Ideology" *Cheap Truth* 5, n.d. Web.

_____. Preface. *Burning Chrome.* New York: Ace, 1986. xi–xvi. Print.

_____. Preface. *Mirrorshades: The Cyberpunk Anthology.* New York: Arbor House, 1986. Print.

Stockton, Sharon. "'The Self Regain': Cyberpunk's Retreat to the Imperium." *Contemporary Literature* 36 (1995): 588–612. Print.

Stonehill, Brian. "Pynchon's Prophecies of Cyberspace." Pynchon.Pomona.edu, Pomona College, 1994. Web.

Strachan, Alex. "Gibson Writes This Sunday's *X-Files.*" *Vancouver Sun,* 14 Feb. 1998. Web.

Sussman, Herbert. "Cyberpunk Meets Charles Babbage: *The Difference Engine* as Alternative Victorian History." *Victorian Studies: A Journal of the Humanities, Arts and Sciences* 38.1 (1994): 1–23. Print.

Suvin, Darko. "On Gibson and Cyberpunk SF." *Foundation: The Review of Science Fiction* 46 (1989): 40–51. Print.

Tatsumi, Takayuki. "Comparative Metafiction: Somewhere Between Ideology and Rhetoric." *Critique: Studies in Contemporary Fiction* 39 (1997): 2–17. Print.

_____. "The Japanese Reflection of Mirrorshades." *Storming the Reality Studio: A Casebook of Cyberpunk and Postmodern Science Fiction.* Ed. Larry McCaffery. Durham: Duke University Press, 1991. 366–73. Print.

_____. "Junk Art City: Or, William Gibson Meets Thomasson in *Virtual Light.*" *Paradoxa: Studies in World Literary Genres* 2.1 (1996): 61–72. Print.

Thomas, Scarlett. "Networking." *New York Times,* 8 Sept. 2010. Web.

Tomas, David. "Old Rituals for New Space: Rites de Passage and William Gibson's Cultural Model of Cyberspace." *Cyberspace: First Steps.* Ed. Michael Benedikt. Cambridge: MIT University Press, 1991. 31–46. Print.

_____. "The Technophilic Body: On Technicity in William Gibson's Cyborg Culture." *The Cybercultures Reader.* Ed. David Bell and Barbara M. Kennedy. New York: Routledge, 2000. 175–89. Print.

Townsend, Aubrey. "Survival in Cyberspace."

*Foundation: The Review of Science Fiction* 78 (2000): 25–33. Print.

Turkle, Sherry. *Life on the Screen: Identity in the Age of the Internet.* New York: Simon & Schuster, 1996. Print.

Turner, Fred. *From Counterculture to Cyberculture: Stewart Brand, the Whole Earth Network, and the Rise of Digital Utopianism.* Chicago: University of Chicago Press, 2008. Print.

Voller, Jack G. "Neuromanticism: Cyberspace and the Sublime." *Extrapolation: A Journal of Science Fiction and Fantasy* 34.1 (1993): 18–29. Print.

Wagner, Thomas M. "*Mona Lisa Overdrive*" SF Reviews.net, 2007. Web.

_____. "*Spook Country.*" SF Reviews.net, 2007. Web.

Wahl, Wendy. "Bodies and Technologies: *Dora, Neuromancer,* and Strategies of Resistance." *Postmodern Culture: An Electronic Journal of Interdisciplinary Criticism* 3.2 (1993): n.p. Web.

Wark, McKenzie. "Codework: From Cyberspace to Biospace, from *Neuromancer* to *Gattaca.*" *Living with Cyberspace: Technology and Society in the 21st Century.* Ed. John Armitage and Joanne Roberts. New York: Continuum, 2002. 72–82. Print.

Warren, Fred. "Book Review: *All Tomorrow's Parties.*" Frederation, n.d. Web.

Weis, Anton Rauben. "Johnny Mnemonic Adaptations." William Gibson Aleph, n.d. Web.

Wegner, Phillip E. "The Last Bomb: Historicizing History in Terry Bisson's *Fire on the Mountain* and Gibson and Sterling's *The Difference Engine.*" *Comparatist: Journal of the Southern Comparative Literature Association* 23 (1999): 141–51. Print.

_____. "Recognizing the Patterns." *New Literary History: A Journal of Theory and Interpretation* 38.1 (2007): 183–200. Print.

Weisstein, Naomi. "Power, Resistance, and Science: A Call for a Revitalized Feminist Psychology." Feministezine.com, 1992. Web.

Westfahl, Gary. "'The Gernsback Continuum': William Gibson in the Context of Science Fiction." *Fiction 2000: Cyberpunk and the Future of Narrative.* Ed. George Slusser and Tom Shippey. Athens: University of Georgia Press, 1992. 88–108. Print.

Wood, Brent. "William S. Burroughs and the Language of Cyberpunk." *Science Fiction Studies* 23 (1996): 11–26. Print.

Wytenbroek, J.R. "Cyberpunk." *Canadian Literature* 121 (1989): 162–4. Print.

Youngquist, Paul. *Cyberfiction: After the Future.* New York: Palgrave Macmillan, 2010. Print.

Yu, Timothy. "Oriental Cities, Postmodern Futures: *Naked Lunch, Blade Runner,* and *Neuromancer.*" *Melus* 33.4 (2008): 45–71. Print.

Yule, Jeffrey Vincent. *Contemplating the Diverse Beast: Analyzing Science Fiction's Marginalization.* Master's Thesis. Ohio State University, 1991. Print.

Zeidner, Lisa. "*Pattern Recognition*: The Coolhunter." *New York Times,* 19 Jan. 2003. Web.

Zuckerman, Edward. "William Gibson: Teen Geek Makes Good, Redefines Sci-Fi." People.com, *People,* 10 June 1991. Web.

# Index

Page numbers in **bold italic** refer to entry heads.